The Software License Unveiled

The Software License Unveiled

How Legislation by License Controls Software Access

DOUGLAS E. PHILLIPS

OXFORD
UNIVERSITY PRESS

OXFORD
UNIVERSITY PRESS

Oxford University Press, Inc., publishes works that further Oxford University's objective of excellence in research, scholarship, and education.

Oxford New York
Auckland Cape Town Dar es Salaam Hong Kong Karachi Kuala Lumpur Madrid Melbourne Mexico City Nairobi New Delhi Shanghai Taipei Toronto

With offices in
Argentina Austria Brazil Chile Czech Republic France Greece Guatemala Hungary Italy Japan Poland Portugal Singapore South Korea Switzerland Thailand Turkey Ukraine Vietnam

Published by Oxford University Press, Inc.
198 Madison Avenue, New York, New York 10016

Library of Congress Cataloging-in-Publication Data

Phillips, Douglas E.
The software license unveiled : how legislation by license controls software access / Douglas E. Phillips.
p. cm.
Includes bibliographical references and index.
ISBN 978-0-19-534187-4 ((hardback) : alk. paper)
1. Copyright licenses. 2. Copyright—Computer programs 3. Open source software—Law and legislation.
I. Title.
K1443.C6P49 2009
346.04'82—dc22

2008053094

---

1 2 3 4 5 6 7 8 9

Printed in the United States of America on acid-free paper

Note to Readers
This publication is designed to provide accurate and authoritative information in regard to the subject matter covered. It is based upon sources believed to be accurate and reliable and is intended to be current as of the time it was written. It is sold with the understanding that the publisher is not engaged in rendering legal, accounting, or other professional services. If legal advice or other expert assistance is required, the services of a competent professional person should be sought. Also, to confirm that the information has not been affected or changed by recent developments, traditional legal research techniques should be used, including checking primary sources where appropriate.

(Based on the Declaration of Principles jointly adopted by a Committee of the American Bar Association and a Committee of Publishers and Associations.)

To the memory of my parents,

Edmond Phillips
and
Doris Campbell Phillips

Contents

Introduction

The Sacrament of the Software License

SOFTWARE, BASED AS IT IS ON LOGIC, seems far removed from faith. But nearly everyone in the world who uses software must first practice a quasi-religious rite. Just as the churchgoer affirms a prayer or blessing by ritualistically uttering the word "amen," the computer user, when installing software, affirms a legal sacrament—known as the software license—by ritualistically clicking the word "agree." The words "amen" and "agree" are both affirmations of assent, and in both cases, there is only one permissible answer consistent with continuing to participate. You can say "amen," but if you choose not to affirm or ratify that which is stated in the liturgy, your only option is to leave the church. Likewise, you can click "agree," but if you choose not to affirm or ratify that which is stated in the license, your only option is to exit the setup program and refrain from using the product. Indeed, at church, you at least have the temporary alternative of maintaining respectful silence. With software, not even that possible compromise exists.

Of course, if you are in a church or a setup program, you most likely have already made up your mind. You may not even be paying much attention to the exact words you are being asked to affirm. Until the 1960s, the Catholic mass was in Latin, which most people did not understand. The Latin mass is now making a comeback, perhaps suggesting that some people actually prefer not to know what the words mean. The typical software license is written in a language, sometimes called "legalese," that most people find equally difficult to follow. Practicing a religious ritual does not require critical thinking about the ideas on which the ritual is based. Some might even say the two are antithetical. Similarly, assenting to a software license does not require reading the text. Perhaps for these reasons, worshippers routinely say "amen," and software users routinely click "agree," without too many questions being asked.

A software user who does read the license, like a Christian who actually reads the Bible and finds out how many innocent people get killed, may be in for a surprise. For example, consider the Apple iTunes software license.[1] It seems unlikely that anyone, other than possibly Homer Simpson, would attempt to operate a nuclear power plant with a music player program. Nevertheless, in the iTunes software license agreement, Apple warns (in capital letters) that the software "IS NOT INTENDED FOR USE IN THE OPERATION OF NUCLEAR FACILITIES." Apple also emphasizes that it does not advise using iTunes for aircraft navigation or life support.

Perplexing license terms are by no means peculiar to Apple. Adobe, to encourage global use of its portable document format, offers free downloads of Adobe Reader on the World Wide Web, with software license terms in more than thirty languages. According to the license, however, if you use the Adobe Reader software on one computer and want to make a second copy on your laptop, it must be for your exclusive use, and both copies may not be used at the same time. Google suggests on a Web page that, if you are a real estate agent, you should upgrade from the free Google Earth version to Google Earth Pro so that you can "[s]hare your Google Earth views and data representations with your clients. . . ."[2] But the software license terms for Google Earth Pro declare that "the geographical information made available for display using the Software is . . . for . . . use only by you." Any "screen outputs," it adds, are also "for your use only."

These terms are just some of the puzzling provisions that appear in licenses for common software products that millions of people use each day. As we will see in this book, according to most U.S. judicial decisions on the subject, your click of assent to such terms makes you a party to a contract. If you have ever actually read a software license before accepting it, however, you are a most unusual person. Software license defenders and critics alike agree that almost no one reads the license text before clicking through. As the examples above suggest, it sometimes seems fair to ask whether even the lawyers who draft them do. Who would try to use iTunes to control a nuclear power plant? If Adobe invites you to download Adobe Reader whenever you like at no charge, then why does it state that the software may not be used on more than one machine at the same time? What is the point of paying for the additional sharing capabilities of Google Earth Pro if, as with the free Google

---

1. Except as otherwise stated, all references to software licenses are to the most recent versions (as of this writing) found on the Web site of the software provider or other license sponsor.

2. Google Earth, http://earth.google.com/enterprise/earth_pro.html.

Earth, its output is for use by you alone? How could such terms find their way into a contract, except through unthinking orthodoxy on both sides?

Not all license terms are as inexplicable as the ones cited above. Software licenses typically address, and often purport to restrict, what the user can do with the software, including how and for what purpose he or she can use it. They can have significant consequences, even when users do not read them. For example, as we will discuss in Chapter 1, license terms that authorize the automated transmission of information from the user's computer to the software provider play a key role in making digital rights management feasible. And clauses that limit the software provider's liability for defects remove a potential incentive for investment in software reliability. Nevertheless, the provisions that apply to popular software products, despite our constantly having to agree to them, remain obscure. License terms scroll across the computer screens of millions of users, but most users pay little or no attention to what the license terms say. The licenses are, in effect, hidden in plain sight. Yet the "click-through" software license has the same legal effect as a contract that two large companies might negotiate over a period of months. And in many cases, it has an effect equivalent to that of legislation that Congress might enact over a period of years. To understand why the software license has ended up this way, and how it affects software access, we must explore this counterintuitive state of affairs.

Although software licenses are the subject of debate in the legal and software communities, the debate for the most part has not centered on the obscurity of license terms. Participants have focused, instead, on the philosophical divide between those who believe in the exploitation of software access rights as a legitimate commercial opportunity and those who do not. For the heirs of Bill Gates at Microsoft, the "proprietary" software licensing model has been the key to making the United States the global software leader—not to mention reportedly turning more than ten thousand Microsoft employees into Microsoft millionaires.[3] For Richard Stallman and the Free Software Foundation, the concept of "copyleft," embodied in the GNU General Public License—or GPL—is the key to inducing people to stop "hoarding" software and start "sharing" it. We have seen this conflict of licensing ideologies (and, some might say, ideologues) for nearly two decades in the competition between Windows and Linux for control of the server and ultimately the desktop (a competition in which Windows, at least for

3. *See* Julie Bick, *The Microsoft Millionaires Come of Age*, NEW YORK TIMES, May 29, 2005.

now, remains comfortably ahead). The release of version 3 of the GPL in 2007 intensified the conflict and sharpened tensions within the broader "open source" movement itself, which now offers a long list of alternative licensing models.

Judging solely from the debate between proprietary software, on one hand, and free and open source software, on the other, one could easily conclude that the most distinctive feature of software licensing today is the lack of consensus. In fact, though, nearly all current software licensing models, spanning the spectrum from proprietary to free, share a key feature. The GPL, no less than the typical proprietary end user license agreement—or EULA—uses a complex, privately written license document, rather than a simple set of property rights defined by public law, to regulate software access and attendant software rights. The GPL requires, among other things, that any software work even partly based on a GPL-licensed program be distributed, if at all, under the GPL. As a result, the second work must be provided free of any licensing fees—even for parts of the work that are entirely new. Whereas the sale of a printed copy of a book has legal consequences that the Copyright Act defines, software licenses allow each license author to write his or her own law. The terms may be as apparently pointless as stating that software for playing songs should not be used to pilot an airplane or as substantial as asserting that a social network site is free to do anything it wants with its users' content. Free and open source licenses pursue different kinds of goals, but also specify what the software user can and cannot do.

This book proposes that a key challenge for software licensing is to look beyond the philosophies of software access that motivate particular license forms and to consider both the legitimacy and the utility of the extent to which the private software license, rather than public law, now controls software access. Does the aggressive use of increasingly complex licenses on both sides of the philosophical divide represent a fair and efficient solution, with increased choices for users? Or, by imposing provisions that most users do not read and would find difficult to understand if they did, does it skew market outcomes toward suboptimal terms? For those who support proprietary software, is the EULA really necessary or desirable? For those who oppose the proprietary model, is an anti-EULA really the answer?

Contracts in general involve a kind of private law-making, because they create obligations for the parties that the law otherwise does not impose. The law they make applies only to the contracting parties, however, and that fact, traditionally, has limited the scope of such private law. The situation changes in the digital world. Access to licensed works can be made completely contingent on assent to standardized license terms. Acceptance of a EULA is a required step to install most proprietary software, and free and open source software is also typically subject to a non-negotiable license. The privately made law set forth in the license, for practical purposes, becomes a form of intellectual property and commercial law itself.

A substantial literature focuses on public intellectual property law and its reach, which many prominent scholars consider to be too broad. James Boyle describes contemporary intellectual property law as a sequel to the enclosure movement that, beginning in fifteenth-century England, fenced off common land and turned it into private property.[4] Enclosures, Boyle writes, "have appropriately been called a revolution of the rich against the poor."[5] He asserts that "new state-created property rights" are giving rise to a "second enclosure movement," which he calls "the enclosure of the intangible commons of the mind."[6] Siva Vaidhyanathan contends that "[c]opyright should be policy, not property," and that "[m]any recent trends and changes in copyright laws . . . are bad policy."[7] Even Richard Posner, generally considered a friend of property rights, suggests that "'depropertizing' intellectual property rights may sometimes be the soundest policy economically."[8] All intellectual works build on what has come before, and intellectual property law that restricts access to preexisting works increases the cost of creating new works. Much of the intellectual property debate focuses on such issues of public law.

But given the strength of the freedom of contract principle, and analogous principles in the case of a noncontractual license such as the GPL, the private law of the license serves as an important legal regime in its own right. And when public law is revised or reinterpreted, the law of the license can be used to nullify the changes. The famous case of the telephone white pages succinctly illustrates this effect. In 1991, the U.S. Supreme Court held in *Feist Publications, Inc. v. Rural Telephone Service Co.*[9] that the white pages of the telephone directory are so devoid of originality that they are not protected by

---

4. James Boyle, *The Public Domain: The Second Enclosure Movement and the Construction of the Public Domain,* 66 LAW & CONTEMP. PROB. 33, 33–34 (2003).

5. *Id.* at 35.

6. *Id.* at 37.

7. SIVA VAIDHYANATHAN, COPYRIGHTS AND COPYWRONGS: THE RISE OF INTELLECTUAL PROPERTY AND HOW IT THREATENS CREATIVITY 15 (2001).

8. WILLIAM M. LANDES & RICHARD A. POSNER, THE ECONOMIC STRUCTURE OF INTELLECTUAL PROPERTY LAW 14 (2003).

9. 499 U.S. 340 (1991).

copyright. This decision, as a matter of intellectual property law, placed the white pages in the public domain. Five years later, in its 1996 decision in *ProCD, Inc. v. Zeidenberg,*[10] the U.S. Court of Appeals for the Seventh Circuit held that, even if a telephone directory on compact disc was not protected by copyright, the same result—prohibition of copying—was achieved through a standard-form license that accompanied the CD. In a sense, for the ProCD product, the author of the license not only made private law but, in doing so, overruled the Supreme Court.

The software license had gained so much legal significance by 1998 that Robert Gomulkiewicz, then a senior corporate attorney at Microsoft, was able to assert, "For most software products, the license is the product; the computer program provides functionality to the user, but the license delivers the use rights."[11] A federal court decision quotes with approval licensing scholar Raymond Nimmer's statement to the same effect in expert testimony he gave on behalf of Adobe.[12] And the concept is enshrined in the prefatory note to the Uniform Computer Information Transactions Act (UCITA), which states that, in the "information economy . . . , unlike in the case of a book, the contract (license) is the product."[13] Leaving aside the assumption that books are not part of the "information economy," the idea that the software license *is* the product is perhaps the ultimate statement of its primacy.

Cases such as *ProCD,* as well as the unsuccessful effort to promote state enactment of UCITA, soon prompted criticisms of the legislative license by those who believed that the EULA went too far in restricting the rights of software users. In 1999, Lawrence Lessig observed that a "race to privatize copyright law through contract" was "already far along, fueled in particular by decisions such as Judge Frank Easterbrook's in *ProCD.* . . ."[14] That same year, Mark Lemley predicted that the proposed article 2B to the Uniform Commercial Code, which eventually became UCITA, promised "to usher in an era of 'private legislation,' in which parties who are in a position to write contracts can jointly impose uniform terms that no one can escape."[15]

---

10. 86 F.3d 1447 (7th Cir. 1996).

11. Robert W. Gomulkiewicz, *The License Is the Product: Comments on the Promise of Article 2B for Software and Information Licensing,* 13 BERKELEY TECH. L.J. 891, 896 (1998) [hereinafter Gomulkiewicz, *The License Is the Product*].

12. Adobe Sys. v. One Stop Micro, Inc., 84 F. Supp. 2d 1086, 1092 (N.D. Cal. 2000).

13. UCITA Prefatory Note, http://www.law.upenn.edu/bll/archives/ulc/ucita/ucita600c.pdf.

14. LAWRENCE LESSIG, CODE AND OTHER LAWS OF CYBERSPACE 136 (1999).

15. Mark A. Lemley, *Beyond Preemption: The Law and Policy of Intellectual Property Licensing,* 87 CALIF. L. REV. 111, 148 (1999).

But despite these early warnings, and even though UCITA was enacted in only two states, the race to privatize that Lessig described has been won—and the era of private legislation that Lemley forecast has arrived.

For Lessig, however, the problem is less one of contract and more one of code. Lessig uses "code," in this context, to refer not to the "constitutions, statutes, and other legal codes" of "real space," but to "the software and hardware" that "make cyberspace what it is" and "also regulate cyberspace as it is."[16] He contends that "contracts are not as bad as code."[17] Contracts are, after all, only law, and law only counts if the courts enforce it. Code that restricts copying enforces itself. Moreover, there are some uses of private law that Lessig supports. He states that the GPL "effects a software commons," which he asserts "has become a critical raw material fueling the digital age."[18] Lessig also cites Creative Commons, an organization he created, which promotes its own set of public licenses. According to Lessig, Creative Commons has "used private law to build an effective public commons."[19]

As such comments suggest, the GPL, the Creative Commons licenses, and many other free and open source licenses, as much as the proprietary EULA, pursue legislation by license. The primary challenge to the proprietary EULA is no longer a rejection of private legislation but an attempt to use the software license to achieve other, and in some ways even more ambitious, legislative goals. To paraphrase Lemley's comments on the EULA, it is also true for today's free and open source software licenses that private parties who are in a position to write licenses can impose uniform terms that no one—or at least no one who wants to use a particular piece of software—can escape.

The GPL and open source alternatives aim to strengthen the commons, and some scholars have suggested that using such licenses is similar to placing works in the public domain. Molly Shaffer Van Houweling states that, although works licensed under the GPL or Creative Commons licenses are not "technically" in the public domain "at least as narrowly defined," such licenses make the works "available to the public for many uses that copyright law would otherwise forbid."[20] But in key respects, licensing

16. Lawrence Lessig, Code Version 2.0 5 (2006).

17. *Id.* at 187.

18. *Id.* at 199.

19. *Id.*

20. Molly Shaffer Van Houweling, *Cultural Environmentalism @ 10: Cultural Environmentalism and the Constructed Commons,* 70 Law & Contemp. Probs. 23, 25–26 (2007). *Cf.* Maria Alessandra Rossi, *Decoding the Free/Open Source Software Puzzle, in* The Economics of Open Source Software Development 41 (Jürgen Bitzer & Philipp J.H. Schröder eds.,

works under the GPL is quite different from dedicating them to the public domain. Rather than placing works in the commons with no strings attached, the GPL wraps each work in the dense web of the GPL's own self-replicating terms. These terms, already complex, are becoming increasingly so—in version 3, the GPL's length has nearly doubled, rivaling that of many EULAs.

It is possible both to damn private law in the case of proprietary licenses and to praise it in the case of the GPL if the criticism addresses the proprietary goals of a particular type of license, rather than the basic concept of legislation by license. In a 2006 article, Elizabeth Winston concludes that intellectual property owners are using contracts to "augment" intellectual property rights and to "circumvent" restrictions on those rights.[21] Although not specifically mentioning the GPL, Winston asserts, "Some licenses promote progress, while others retard it."[22] Concerns about the purposes and effects of particular licenses are important and will be examined in the pages that follow—as Winston points out, the power of the proprietary license continues to grow. But this book also asks whether *any* kind of complex private software license, whether it augments or restricts the software provider's rights, is a desirable way to regulate software access.

Such questions are important not only for software licensing, but also for the broader ongoing debate over the proper interaction between the ancient institutions of property and contract. They bear significantly on the limits, if any, to freedom of contract—the principle that individuals should be free to enter into, and bind themselves to, any sort of agreement they wish, as long as they are competent and the object is lawful. The use of software licenses that legislate with complex terms is part of a larger long-term trend in the modern economy toward increasingly complex form agreements that take this principle to extremes. Examples are easy to find in other areas, including one that has taken on pronounced economic importance—mortgage lending. The essential terms of the 30-year fixed mortgage are relatively simple to understand. The monthly payment of principal and interest is the same for the entire term of the loan. But a Federal Trade Commission report on disclosures accompanying the more complex mortgages of later years finds that

---

2006) ("There is often some confusion concerning the question whether F/OSS belongs to the public domain.").

21. Elizabeth I. Winston, *Why Sell When You Can License? Contracting around Statutory Protection of Intellectual Property*, 14 GEO. MASON L. REV. 93, 93–94 (2006).

22. *Id.* at 95.

"many borrowers were confused by the . . . mortgage cost disclosures and did not understand key terms in the disclosure forms, such as the APR, amount financed, and discount fees."[23] In other words, the borrowers did not know how much their mortgage loans were actually going to cost.

As a result, many borrowers "had loans that were significantly more costly than they believed, or contained significant restrictions, such as prepayment penalties, of which they were unaware."[24] These problems, which have obvious effects on foreclosure risk, did not stem from a lack of consumer search. "Some of these borrowers reported that they had spent considerable time shopping and comparing loan offers, but still experienced problems or misunderstandings," and the lack of comprehension persisted even when borrowers relied on the lender's reputation.[25] Although the extent to which incomprehensible loan disclosures contributed to the so-called subprime mortgage crisis can be debated, few would suggest that such transactions—even when justified as a matter of freedom of contract—have promoted desirable economic outcomes.

There are, of course, different kinds of software and different kinds of software licenses. The focus of this book is on software that is not custom developed and on licenses that are not individually negotiated. The book considers licenses to which users assent by conduct, such as using the software, or by an automated process, such as clicking a button. The term "shrinkwrap license" refers to a EULA to which the user manifests assent by tearing open the cellophane wrapping on a box containing the software.[26] When the user instead assents by clicking an onscreen button with the word "accept" or "agree," the license is often called a "clickwrap" or "click-through" license. In free and open source licensing, different labels are used, but the licenses also typically are not individually negotiated and are accepted through conduct. Because cases and commentators use terms such as "EULA" and "shrinkwrap license" more or less interchangeably, this book

---

23. Bureau of Economics, Federal Trade Commission, Improving Consumer Mortgage Disclosures: An Empirical Assessment of Current and Prototype Disclosure Forms ES-6 (June 2007).

24. *Id.*

25. *Id.*

26. Ed Foster prefers the term "sneakwrap." *See* Ed Foster, *Arbitrary Sneakwrap Takes Some Hits*, InfoWorld, June 19, 2007, http://weblog.infoworld.com/gripeline/archives/2007/06/arbitrary_sneak.html.

does so as well, noting distinctions between such terms only when they are relevant.

Part 1 describes the proprietary software license in law and practice. Chapter 1 traces the development of the law of software licenses from early decisions, under which the legal status of the shrinkwrap license was very much an open question, through more recent case law, under which virtually all license terms have been enforced. Most case law now condones legislation by license. In the early days of the EULA, however, courts were skeptical. If a license agreement was not even presented until after the software had been paid for, courts did not accept that the license could change the terms on which the user thought the software was being provided. If a license agreement purported to deprive the user of rights that would otherwise exist under the Copyright Act or the Uniform Commercial Code, it might not be enforced. But this thinking changed with the *ProCD* decision, which has had more influence than its economic rationale warrants. Now even the most far-reaching license terms are usually given full effect.

EULA defenders have maintained that, from a legal point of view, distributing software by license is necessary for the user to avoid infringement. Otherwise, they say, the user would be making copies, as part of use, which would infringe copyright and other intellectual property rights. If this is so, however, it is the license that creates the need for itself by declaring that the user does not become the owner of a copy. When the user owns a copy, use rights flow from the Copyright Act without a license. Likewise, under the patent exhaustion doctrine, no patent license is required to use a patented item that one has bought. But most proprietary software licenses state that the copy is only licensed, not sold, and the courts generally accept this view. As a result, licenses substitute their own terms for statutory rules that would otherwise provide necessary use rights. And although selling copies would not suffice for all forms of software distribution, most legitimate objectives of proprietary software providers could also be met for mass-market software distribution without licenses or with a minimal EULA.

Chapter 2 considers the contention, also advanced by EULA defenders, that software is "intangible" and that the license, rather than the software itself, is the product. If the license is the product, it follows that the license is necessary—without it, there would be no product. But the idea that software is intangible is at odds with how software actually works, and it is the software, not the EULA, for which users pay. Software in a "raw" state, without legal protection and before any copy protection has been applied, has limited appropriability or excludability—preventing use by those who do not pay is difficult, because copying is virtually costless. In addition, consumption is, in some respects, non-rivalrous—one person's consumption of one copy does not directly interfere with, or increase the cost of, another person's consumption of another copy. Intellectual property law and digital rights management techniques can change the first attribute and, indirectly, the second. Whether or not software is freely copyable, however, it is not a "ghost in the machine." Software is a tangible product, and there is nothing about the nature of software that makes the license inevitable. The concept of software as a service does not change this result.

Chapter 3 examines the proprietary software license in practice. The typical EULA is understandable to the software provider, or at least to its lawyers, but far less so to the software user. Some of the most widely used software licenses are so dense that, according to quantitative readability tests, even college graduates are unlikely to understand what they mean. The software provider has lawyers who draft such licenses, but the user ordinarily does not retain legal counsel to review them. The resulting information asymmetry produces predictable economic effects. In a legal regime dominated by these legislative licenses, the software user—unlike the provider—is unable at acceptable cost to assess the quality of the license in relation to the user's interests. The result is that EULAs tend to be, from the user's perspective, "lemons." This phenomenon, without any sort of evil conspiracy among proprietary software providers, suffices to explain why EULA terms consistently favor the software provider. Their inscrutability removes any chance for competition among providers that could result in better terms from the user's point of view. Moreover, although proprietary software is often feature rich, the low quality of the EULA is also likely to lower the reliability of the software itself.

Part 2 reviews free and open source software licensing. Chapter 4 examines the GPL, as well as the sparse case law concerning its legal effect. It then explores how, rather than providing an alternative to legislation by license, the GPL embraces it—using a number of the same techniques as the EULA, but for different goals. The GPL is, above all, a private "copyleft act." Its avowed purpose, and demonstrated effect, is to create a legal framework in which software can *only* be distributed without licensing fees. But charging for related services, or even for the physical copies necessary to run the software, is fine, as far as the GPL is concerned. This ethical loophole means that the user pays indirectly to subsidize development, even when direct payment of licensing fees would be more efficient. Questions about the "enforceability" of the GPL are natural, but misplaced. The GPL establishes license conditions, and the user who does not follow them may be an infringer. In that sense, the GPL's conditions are enforceable against licensees. The more difficult question is whether the GPL is enforceable against licensors. As a unilateral permission unsupported by consideration, the GPL's license grant is potentially revocable at will. The resulting legal uncertainty carries a significant cost.

Chapter 5 reviews broader open source licensing, which often dispenses with the copyleft condition. Permissive open source licensing does not constrain subsequent distribution as much as the GPL. But such licensing, no less than copyleft, is developer focused. And in some but not all cases, it also involves subsidies that make the resulting software less responsive to mass-market users. The rights it provides are primarily of interest to users who understand source code and have sufficient ability and interest to change it. Not surprisingly, although the open source software that results from such licensing contains features of interest to developers, it is often weak in the area of usability. This is no accident, but the consequence of a licensing model that attends primarily to developer interests. The constituency for the open source version of the legislative license is the open source community, and—with some but not many exceptions—the resulting software tends to serve its own constituency best. When one looks at how open source software is paid for, this result is not a surprise.

Chapter 6 completes the review of free and open source licensing with a discussion of the decision by the inventor of the World Wide Web and his employer to dedicate the Web technologies to the public domain, relying entirely on public law, rather than licensing them under the GPL. The Web is a natural experiment, and its results show that the web of restrictions on proprietary activity imposed by the GPL is not necessary to promote either freedom or interoperability. On the contrary, if the Web's inventor had chosen licensing of the Web software under the GPL—as he initially planned—rather than dedication to the public domain, the Web most probably would not have become what it is today. The original Web software was included in Mosaic, the graphical browser from which everything else in Web history descends. If Mosaic had been controlled by the GPL, the Web could not have attracted the investment that has made it what it is. And the "information superhighway" today might be not the Internet, but a hodge-podge of "information byways," dominated by AOL or even the Microsoft Network.

The book's conclusion discusses where we are headed. Proprietary software licenses focus on the user, and proprietary software excels in offering new features, but proprietary licenses tend to lack flexibility in use rights and lead to underinvestment in software reliability. Free and open software licenses focus on the developer, and they satisfy the developer's interests and objectives, but often lead to underinvestment in usability. In addition, the copyleft condition of the GPL limits distribution to a particular model that can inhibit proprietary investments of the kind that gave rise to the World Wide Web itself.

Proprietary software distribution, perhaps with additions to the Copyright Act for specified use rights that licensors could optionally invoke, would function more efficiently without the complex license terms that most people do not read anyway—and for some forms of distribution, without licenses at all. Free and open source software distribution would also function more efficiently if it avoided matching the proprietary EULA in restrictive complexity and instead focused on simple permissive licensing or dedication to the public domain. Open source and proprietary licensing for the same or related software should be permitted to co-exist and even to co-apply. The alternative is to head even further down a path of constraining legislative licenses that are clear to no one and mainly meet the needs of their own authors.

PART I

The Proprietary Software License in Law and Practice

ONE

Emergence of the Legislative License

JUST BEFORE THE YEAR 2000, when others were worried about the impending "Y2K" crisis that never came, an article in *Network Computing* asked about a prospect that it viewed with even more alarm: "What if the law enforced almost any term a software publisher specified in a shrink-wrap license?"[1] The article stated that the "very real prospect of this happening" as a result of proposed model legislation had "some of the nation's largest corporations running scared."[2] Explaining that shrinkwrap licenses affect businesses as well as individual users, the article noted the concern of user groups that enforcing such licenses could lead to "a parade of horrors."[3] The question's premise was that the enforceability of shrinkwrap license terms remained in doubt. Even by 1999, however, the courts had already largely resolved that issue in favor of software providers. Today, there appears to be little that a shrinkwrap or click-through software license can say to which the law will not give effect.

In the early years of the shrinkwrap license, the validity of such licenses was indeed an open question. In 1988, the U.S. Court of Appeals for the Fifth Circuit held that federal law preempted a state law that provided for the enforcement of shrinkwrap license terms, when the terms barred the reverse engineering of software.[4] In 1991, the Third Circuit held that a "box-top license" printed on a software package did not become part of the parties' contract.[5] That same year, the Third Circuit held that software products are "goods" under Article 2 of the Uniform Commercial Code (UCC),[6] causing the

1. Christy Hudgins-Bonafield, *UCC 2B: The New Law of Shrink-Wrap,* NETWORK COMPUTING, Apr. 19, 1999, http://www.networkcomputing.com/1008/1008f1.html.

2. *Id.*

3. *Id.*

4. Vault Corp. v. Quaid Software Ltd., 847 F.2d 255, 270 (5th Cir. 1988).

5. Step-Saver Data Systems, Inc. v. Wyse Technology, 939 F.2d 91, 106 (3d Cir. 1991).

6. Advent Systems Ltd. v. Unisys Corp., 925 F.2d 670, 676 (3d Cir. 1991).

UCC's expansive provisions on warranties and its restrictions on liability limitations to apply.

At the same time, copyright law decisions reinforced the concepts of the public domain and fair use. In 1991, the Supreme Court held that an ordinary white pages telephone directory lacked sufficient originality to be protected by copyright, rejecting the "sweat of the brow" theory under which effort alone qualifies for copyright protection.[7] In 1992, the Federal Circuit and the Ninth Circuit separately held that fair use extends to reverse engineering of computer programs to learn unprotected ideas.[8] In 1994, the Ninth Circuit held that, when there are few ways to express an idea in software, "the appropriate standard for illicit copying is virtual identity."[9] These copyright decisions raised further doubts about the effect of the more stringent restrictions that many software licenses contained.

Supporters of the shrinkwrap license did not shrink from the fight. It was also in the early 1990s that work began on a new Uniform Commercial Code article for information licensing. Drafters designed a proposed Article 2B to displace, for transactions in "computer information," Article 2 of the UCC, which applies to transactions in goods. The National Conference of Commissioners on Uniform State Laws eventually separated Article 2B from the UCC and released it as the Uniform Computer Information Transactions Act. One of UCITA's central aims was to ensure that courts would give effect to the EULA—or, as UCITA calls it, the "mass-market license."[10] Much of the opposition to UCITA also focused on this aim.

Despite the efforts of the Uniform Law Commission, only two states—Maryland and Virginia—enacted versions of UCITA, both in 2000.[11] In the debate that followed, by any ordinary political measure, UCITA lost. The opposition to UCITA was so strong that four states—Iowa, North Carolina, Vermont, and West Virginia—actually passed UCITA "bomb-shelter" legislation, which provides that license clauses making UCITA the governing law are voidable by residents of those states and by businesses

---

7. Feist Publications, Inc. v. Rural Telephone Service Co., 499 U.S. 340, 379–80, 381 (1991).

8. Atari Games Corp. v. Nintendo of America, Inc., 975 F.2d 832, 843 (Fed. Cir. 1992); Sega Enterprises Ltd. v. Accolade, Inc., 977 F.2d 1510, 1514 (9th Cir. 1992).

9. Apple Computer, Inc. v. Microsoft Corp., 35 F.3d 1435, 1439 (9th Cir. 1994).

10. Uniform Computer Information Transactions Act § 102(a)(43) (Final Act 2002) [hereinafter UCITA], http://www.law.upenn.edu/bll/archives/ulc/ucita/2002final.htm.

11. Md. Code § 22-101 *et seq.*; Va. Code § 59.1-501.1 *et seq.*

headquartered there.[12] In 2003, the Uniform Law Commission decided not to expend further resources to promote UCITA in state legislatures.[13]

Nevertheless, even as Article 2B and then UCITA worked their way through the deliberative process for proposed model acts, a new set of court decisions emerged. These decisions erased nearly all the previous doubts about the extent to which shrinkwrap licenses could be enforced. The turning point came in 1996 with the Seventh Circuit's *ProCD* decision, which held not only that shrinkwrap licenses are effective to form contracts but also that such contracts can bar the copying of materials that are in the public domain.[14]

In 2003, the same year the Uniform Law Commission abandoned UCITA, the Federal Circuit held that a shrinkwrap license agreement can override the fair use defense that would otherwise protect software reverse engineering.[15] In 2005, the Eighth Circuit held that license terms can override the provision of the Digital Millennium Copyright Act (DMCA) that permits the circumvention of technical means of copy protection to achieve interoperability.[16] In 2008, a federal district court accepted the validity of license terms providing that violations of role-playing game rules caused license forfeiture.[17] The same year, a New York court upheld license terms for downloaded "adware" that allowed the software provider to make unwanted pop-up ads appear on the user's screen.[18] By 2009, a decade after UCITA's release, the primacy of the license was no longer in doubt. What the proponents of UCITA had lost in the legislatures, they had won in the courts.

Ultimately, and as a result of decisions such as these, the law of the software license has come largely to be defined by each software license itself. Because the software license is privately written, all software licenses are potentially different from one another. Analysis thus involves the uninviting task of actually reading the software licenses that users have the luxury of

12. Iowa Code § 554D.125; N.C. Gen. Stat. § 66-329; 9 V.S.A. § 2463a; W. Va. Code § 55-8-15.

13. Uniform Law Commission Press Release, *UCITA Standby Committee Is Discharged*, Aug. 1, 2003, http://www.nccusl.org/nccusl/DesktopModules/NewsDisplay.aspx?ItemID=56.

14. ProCD, Inc. v. Zeidenberg, 86 F.3d 1447, 1449 (7th Cir. 1996).

15. Bowers v. Baystate Technologies, Inc., 320 F.3d 1317, 1325–26 (Fed. Cir. 2003).

16. Davidson & Associates v. Jung, 422 F.3d 630, 639 (8th Cir. 2005).

17. MDY Indus., LLC v. Blizzard Entertainment, Inc., 2008 U.S. Dist. LEXIS 53988, *19 (D. Az. July 14, 2008).

18. People v. Direct Revenue, LLC, 2008 N.Y. Misc. LEXIS 5562, *8 (Mar. 12, 2008).

simply clicking through. These licenses must then be considered in light of judicial decisions. Fortunately, software licenses are so verbose that it is relatively easy to capture the essential information in them in fewer words than the licenses themselves use. We therefore turn to a review of key elements in typical EULAs for proprietary software. As we will see in Part 2, many (but not all) free and open source software licenses are as lengthy and complex as the proprietary EULA.

Although EULAs vary in their terms, they usually contain some version of the following propositions:

- *You may have thought you just bought something, but you didn't.* The software is licensed, not sold.
- *You are now a party to a contract with a software company.* The license is a legally binding agreement between you and the software provider.
- *If it doesn't say you can do it, you can't.* The software provider grants you permission to use the software, but you may not do anything that the license does not expressly permit. Of course, you must also refrain from doing anything it expressly prohibits. For example, you may not let more than one person use the software at a time; resell or reverse engineer it; or, if the software is designated for a particular type of end user, use it without being that type of end user.
- *If you do something it doesn't say you can do (or says you can't do), then you can't use the software at all.* Your permission to use the software is conditioned on your compliance with all the terms of the license agreement, including all the terms that restrict your use. As a result, your violation of any term causes you to forfeit all your license rights and makes you not just a contract breaker but a copyright infringer.
- *If the software company wants to do something, it can.* You grant the software provider unconditional permission to include product activation, product validation, and automatic update functions in the software. These functions can affect your access to the software, and potentially to your computer, and can transmit information about the software and your computer to the software provider.
- *If something goes wrong with the software, don't count on the software company to fix it.* You agree that the software provider makes few or no warranties to you and will have little or no liability to you for software defects. You also agree that the software provider will not be responsible even for claims against you that may result if the software infringes third-party rights.

1.1 Licensed, Not Sold

Most if not all proprietary end user software licenses contain terms that define the transaction as a license rather than a sale. For example, the current license terms for Microsoft Windows and Microsoft Office declare, "The software is licensed, not sold." Although "Mac" is much cooler than "PC" in Apple's television advertisements, Apple uses equivalent language in the Software License Agreement for its OS X operating system: "The software (including Boot ROM code), documentation and any fonts accompanying this License . . . are licensed, not sold, to you by Apple. . . ."

What does it mean that the software is licensed, not sold? And why do software licenses repeat this mantra? The answer depends, in large part, on the definition of "the software." Is it the "work of authorship" that the software embodies under the U.S. Copyright Act? Or is it a "copy" of the software, such as the copy that the user receives on distribution media or downloads over the Internet or the copy that results when the software is installed? Clauses stating that the software is not sold often also affirm that the software provider retains ownership of the intellectual property. But their greater effect comes from asserting that the licensor retains title not only to the intellectual property but also to each *copy* the user receives or makes.

This distinction arises from the concept of "works of authorship," which the Copyright Act employs to describe the subject matter of copyright protection. To be protected, original works of authorship must be "fixed in [a] tangible medium of expression . . . from which they can be perceived, reproduced, or otherwise communicated, either directly or with the aid of a machine or device."[19] This formulation may give the impression that there is an intangible "work" from which tangible expressions are somehow copied. In fact, however, the concept of a work of authorship is only an abstraction from one or more physical instances of a book, computer program, or the like. Without at least one physical instance, there is no work of authorship. And if there are multiple physical instances, or copies, then the work of authorship is simply the set of all physical instances, or copies, that are the same or nearly so.[20]

---

19. 17 U.S.C. § 102(a).

20. The picture might be clearer if we used the word "counterpart" rather than the word "copy." Using the word "copy" in its noun form to refer to a physical instance of a work of authorship makes it easier to imagine, erroneously, that the physical instance is somehow "copied" or reproduced from an intangible "work." In fact, any one physical instance,

It is possible to acquire copyright ownership with respect to a work of authorship and thus to acquire a set of legal rights that extends to all copies of the copyrighted work, subject to the limits of copyright protection. And if license terms declaring that "the software" is licensed, not sold, refer to the work of authorship that the software embodies under the Copyright Act, then stating that the software is not sold is similar to stating that, when I buy a printed copy of *The Sirens of Titan,* the estate of Kurt Vonnegut, Jr., is not transferring ownership to me of the work of authorship or the copyright in the work. But Section 202 of the Copyright Act already makes clear that "[t]ransfer of ownership of any material object, including the copy . . . in which the work is first fixed, does not of itself convey any rights in the copyrighted work embodied in the object. . . ."[21] In other words, the sale of one copy is not the sale of all copies. Therefore, from a legal point of view as well as a practical one, there is no need to mention in a license that the customer who "buys" a Microsoft Office upgrade at Best Buy for $329.99 is not thereby becoming the new owner of Microsoft's IP portfolio.

If "the software" referred to in the license means or includes a particular physical instance or *copy* of the work of authorship that the user receives or makes, however, then the statement that the software is licensed, not sold, has much more legal significance. Rather than merely affirming, as the law already provides, that the user does not become the owner of all copies of the work, the statement (if given effect) then prevents the user from becoming the owner even of a single copy. The significance of such a statement rests on two key legal concepts. The first is that loading software into the computer's memory for use is a "reproduction" of the work that would infringe the copyright if not authorized by the copyright owner or protected by a statutory exception. The second is that the statutory exception in Section 117(a)(1) of the Copyright Act, which permits the owner of a copy of a computer program to reproduce it as part of its use, does not provide such protection to the copy's licensee.

A leading authority for the proposition that use of software entails copying is *MAI Systems Corp. v. Peak Computer, Inc.*[22] Peak "maintain[ed] computer

---

or counterpart, can only be reproduced from another physical instance, or counterpart. And in the case of digital works, subsequent instances are no different from the first instance, or "original." But the noun form of "copy" is so deeply embedded in copyright law that it is difficult to avoid.

21. 17 U.S.C. § 202.

22. 991 F.2d 511 (9th Cir. 1993).

systems for its clients," including systems from MAI.[23] MAI alleged that, each time Peak ran the MAI software on a Peak client's computer, Peak infringed MAI's copyright by making an unauthorized copy of the software into the computer's random access memory (RAM). The Court of Appeals for the Ninth Circuit held that "a 'copying' for purposes of copyright law occurs when a computer program is transferred from a permanent storage device to a computer's RAM."[24] The court relied on the district court's factual finding that "the loading of copyrighted computer software from a storage medium (hard disk, floppy disk, or read only memory) into the memory of a central processing unit (CPU) causes a copy to be made."[25] That is, you reproduce a computer program every time you use it.

MAI Systems is significant because the Copyright Act does not directly regulate the "use" of copyrighted works. Rather, the exclusive rights of the copyright owner under Section 106 of the Act are limited to the rights to do or to authorize the following acts:

(1) to reproduce the copyrighted work in copies,
(2) to prepare derivative works based on the copyrighted work,
(3) to distribute copies of the work to the public by sale or other transfer of ownership, or by rental, lease, or lending,
(4) to perform the copyrighted work publicly, and
(5) to display the copyrighted work publicly.[26]

This legal framework works fine for printed books. The ordinary reader of a hard cover or paperback book does not want to reproduce the book by making a copy of it, except possibly for short excerpts which are generally protected as fair use. Nor does the ordinary reader want to prepare a derivative work based on the book, such as a foreign translation or a screenplay. Likewise, the reader typically does not want to perform or display the book

23. *Id.* at 513.

24. *Id.* at 518.

25. *Id.* After *MAI Systems,* Congress amended the Copyright Act to permit companies in Peak's position to provide maintenance or repair. *See* 17 U.S.C. § 117(c). By addressing only maintenance or repair, however, the new Section 117(c) appears to support the holding that even the temporary loading into RAM of an operating system or other software constitutes reproducing the copyrighted work in one or more copies for purposes of the Copyright Act.

26. 17 U.S.C. § 106.

in public. And the reader is unlikely to want to distribute any copies of the book, except possibly by passing on the copy that the reader bought to a friend. Copyright law prohibits none of these acts, so no license is required. But if using software necessarily involves reproducing it, by copying it into memory, then use itself effectively becomes one of the copyright owner's exclusive rights.

The *MAI Systems* holding is not the first recognition that the use of a computer program entails copying it. The software industry began in earnest after IBM's announcement in 1969 that it would "unbundle" application software from hardware.[27] In one of IBM's earliest software license agreements after this unbundling, the following term appears: "For purposes of this Agreement, use is defined as copying any portion of the license[d] program's and/or optional material's instructions or data from storage units or media into the CPU for processing."[28] The early IBM software license thus defined use as reproduction.

The Copyright Act tries to accommodate the inevitable copying that occurs in using software by making an exception to the exclusive rights of Section 106. Section 117(a)(1) provides that, despite Section 106, "it is not an infringement for the owner of a copy of a computer program to make or authorize the making of another copy or adaptation of that computer program provided . . . that such a new copy or adaptation is created as an essential step in the utilization of the computer program in conjunction with a machine and that it is used in no other manner. . . ."[29] This clause takes the use of a computer program by the owner of a program copy back out of the list of the copyright owner's exclusive rights.

The key phrase here is "the owner of a copy." The National Commission on New Technological Uses of Copyrighted Works (CONTU), which was instrumental in shaping the provisions of the Copyright Act that relate to computer programs, recommended a similar provision but would have applied it to any "rightful possessor" of a program copy.[30] Section 117(a)(1) as enacted,

---

27. *See* Martin Goetz, *Memoirs of a Software Pioneer: Part 1*, IEEE ANNALS OF THE HISTORY OF COMPUTING 43, 43 (2002).

28. IBM License Agreement for Program Products, *reprinted in* ROBERT V. HEAD, GUIDE TO PACKAGED SYSTEMS (1971).

29. 17 U.S.C. § 117(a)(1).

30. FINAL REPORT OF THE NATIONAL COMMISSION ON NEW TECHNOLOGY USES OF COPYRIGHTED WORKS 12 (July 31, 1978), http://digital-law-online.info/CONTU/PDF (Chapter 3).

however, does not protect the copying that occurs as an essential step in using the program if the user is not the owner but only the licensee of the copy. Therefore, under the *MAI Systems* doctrine, if the user is not the owner of the copy, the user still requires permission from the copyright owner to engage in the copying that is part of software use.

Many EULAs expressly state that the user does not become the owner of a copy. Symantec, on the Web page that contains all its product license agreements, declares, "Symantec products are not sold; rather, copies of Symantec products are licensed all the way through the distribution channel to the end user."[31] Adobe, in the license for Adobe Reader, states that both "[t]he Software and any authorized copies that you make are the intellectual property of and are owned by Adobe Systems Incorporated and its suppliers." Other licenses are less explicit. The Microsoft Windows license, for example, does not define "the software" and does not refer to ownership of copies. The license does state, however, that its terms apply to the "software" named in the license and, somewhat recursively, that this software "includes the media on which you received it, if any." One could infer that, if the software includes the media on which you received the software, it probably also includes the copy on the media. Elsewhere, the license refers to "proof of purchase," suggesting that the buyer became the owner of something, but Microsoft would probably say that what was "purchased" was not the copy but the license.

Proponents of the Uniform Computer Information Transactions Act contended, in reliance on the principle of *MAI Systems,* that the copying of software as part of its use makes the software license necessary to avoid infringement. Carlyle Ring, chairman of the UCITA drafting committee, and Raymond Nimmer, reporter of the drafting committee, asserted, "Often, if the license with the software publisher is unenforceable, the customer's use of the software is unauthorized and copyright infringement."[32] Without a license, according to this argument, the software user—even, apparently, after paying for the software—is a potential infringer.

If using software without a valid license makes the user a potential infringer, however, this result occurs only because the license makes *itself* necessary. The "licensed, not sold" clause, by preventing the user from becoming

---

31. Symantec Product License Agreements, http://www.symantec.com/about/profile/policies/eulas/index.jsp.

32. Carlyle C. Ring, Jr., & Raymond T. Nimmer, *Series of Papers on UCITA Issues,* http://www.nccusl.org/nccusl/uniformact_qanda/uniformacts-q-ucita.asp.

an owner of a copy of the software, prevents the user from relying on Section 117(a)(1) of the Copyright Act and its protection for copying incidental to use. Without this clause in the license, the user of software would be the owner of a copy, just as the buyer of a printed copy of a book owns that copy, and Section 117(a)(1) would mean that no license was required for use. Ultimately, the license is the cause, not the consequence, of the need for a license.

A possible response is that Section 117(a)(1) of the Copyright Act applies only to a "computer program," as defined in the Act, whereas software packages may include, in addition to executable program files, files that contain media content and other data. Section 101 of the Act defines "computer program" as "a set of statements or instructions to be used directly or indirectly in a computer in order to bring about a certain result."[33] Files that are not themselves executable programs are nevertheless copied into computer memory to permit them to be accessed. These may include such items as graphical elements displayed as part of the user interface or other data used by or with the software. If *MAI Systems* applies to such files, but Section 117(a)(1), which is limited to computer programs, does not, then one could argue that a license is also required for the owner of a copy.[34]

But even if the software package includes content that is not itself a computer program, it seems likely that the sale of a copy of a computer program as part of the package would provide an implied license to the owner of the program copy to use the other material in conjunction with the program. Indeed, defenders of the EULA have acknowledged that "the rights to reproduce and to print 'clip art' provide examples in which, arguably, end users could proceed under an implied license theory."[35] The same

---

33. 17 U.S.C. § 101.

34. *Cf.* Baystate Techs. v. Bentley Sys., 946 F. Supp. 1079, 1086 (D. Mass. 1996) ("because the data structures at issue in this case do not bring about any result on their own, they are copyright protected, if at all, only as a part of the whole computer program"). But even media content, in a digital setting, may contain at least "statements," if not "instructions." For example, the Audio Home Recording Act states that "a digital musical recording may contain statements or instructions constituting the fixed sounds and incidental material, and statements or instructions to be used directly or indirectly in order to bring about the perception, reproduction, or communication of the fixed sounds and incidental material." 17 U.S.C. § 1001(5)(B)(ii). Nor can it be necessary that the statements or instructions be sufficient to bring about a certain result without any other programs, because more than one program is often required. Application programs are computer programs but do not bring about results without operating systems.

35. Robert W. Gomulkiewicz & Mary L. Williamson, *A Brief Defense of Mass Market Software License Agreements,* 22 RUTGERS COMPUTER & TECH. L.J. 335, 350 (1996) [hereinafter Gomulkiewicz & Williamson, *Brief Defense*].

conclusion seems appropriate for other types of content that are included with programs.

Because the Copyright Act requires that transfers of copyright ownership be in writing, but excludes from the definition of such transfers a "nonexclusive license," nonexclusive licenses are not required to be in writing.[36] The Melville and David Nimmer copyright treatise explains, "By negative implication, nonexclusive licenses may therefore be granted orally, or may even be implied from conduct."[37] As the court stated in *Field v. Google, Inc.*,[38] "[a]n implied license can be found where the copyright holder engages in conduct 'from which [the] other [party] may properly infer that the owner consents to his use.'"[39] If the copyright owner sells a copy of a computer program and includes, on the same distribution media or in the same download, additional digital materials, it seems reasonable to infer that the copyright owner consents to use of those materials.

The Copyright Act is not the only intellectual property law that protects software. Some EULA defenders have gone so far as to assert that, because "[s]oftware is protected by copyright, patent, trade secret, and trademark law," the "[u]se of a single software program may require a copyright license, a patent license, a trade secret license (for source code), and a trademark license."[40] But this argument, in addition to neglecting the availability of Section 117(a)(1) of the Copyright Act to obviate a copyright license, rests on a mistaken view of the law of trademarks, trade secrets, and patents. For example, trademark infringement occurs when a person uses "in commerce" a copy or imitation of a trademark "in connection with the sale, offering for sale, distribution, or advertising of any goods or services . . ." and then only if there is a likelihood of confusion, mistake, or deception about the origin of the goods or services.[41] Merely using software does not require a trademark license from the software publisher, any more than eating a Big Mac requires a trademark license from McDonald's. Likewise, drinking a cola does not

---

36. *See* 17 U.S.C. §§ 101 ("transfer of copyright ownership" does not include nonexclusive license), 204(a) (transfer of copyright ownership is not valid unless in writing).

37. 3 MELVILLE NIMMER & DAVID NIMMER, NIMMER ON COPYRIGHT § 10.03 [A][7] (2008) (footnote omitted).

38. 412 F. Supp. 2d 1106 (D. Nev. 2006).

39. *Id.* at 1116 (quoting De Forest Radio Tel. & Tel. Co. v. United States, 273 U.S. 236, 241 (1927)).

40. Gomulkiewicz & Williamson, *Brief Defense*, at 355–56.

41. 15 U.S.C. § 1114(1).

require a trade secret license to the secret formula for Coke. Nor does using a patented product ordinarily require a patent license.

In recent decades, software patents have flourished (some would say like weeds).[42] Unlike copyright law, patent law explicitly extends to "use." Subject to statutory exceptions, "whoever without authority makes, uses, offers to sell, or sells any patented invention, within the United States, or imports into the United States any patented invention during the term of the patent therefore, infringes the patent."[43] This language—and its inclusion of "use"—could suggest that every consumer of any item that embodies any patented invention needs a patent license. Obviously, however, that is not the case. Toyota holds more than 650 patents relating to hybrid technology,[44] but driving a Prius does not require holding a license under even one of them. The only license required is a license to drive.

The reason no patent license is required to own and operate a Prius is that, as the Supreme Court pointed out in *Quanta Computer, Inc. v. LG Electronics, Inc.*,[45] "[f]or over 150 years [the] Court has applied the doctrine of patent exhaustion to limit the patent rights that survive the initial authorized sale of a patented item."[46] The essence of the doctrine is that "[t]he authorized sale of an article that substantially embodies a patent exhausts the patent holder's rights and prevents the patent holder from invoking patent law to control post-sale use of the article."[47] In *LG Electronics*, the Court held that the patent exhaustion doctrine also applies to method patents.[48] As the Federal Circuit had noted in the decision below, however, "the exhaustion doctrine does not apply to an expressly conditional sale or license."[49]

It is possible that a user of software might require a license under patents owned by third parties that apply to use of the software in question.

---

42. *See* KENNETH NICHOLS, INVENTING SOFTWARE: THE RISE OF 'COMPUTER-RELATED' PATENTS 1 (1998).

43. 35 U.S.C. § 271(a).

44. Results of search at www.uspto.gov for patents assigned to Toyota relating to "hybrid" technology.

45. 128 S. Ct. 2109 (2008).

46. *Id.* at 2113.

47. *Id.* at 2122.

48. *Id.*

49. LG Elecs., Inc. v. Bizcom Elecs., Inc., 453 F.3d 1364, 1369–70 (Fed. Cir. 2006) (quoting B. Braun Medical v. Abbott Lab., 124 F.3d 1419, 1426 (Fed. Cir. 1997)).

Such third parties, if they did not exhaust their patent rights through a sale to the software provider, might be able to assert a patent infringement claim against both the provider and the user. But the typical software license is given only by the software provider, not by third parties, and in many cases the provider does not even agree to defend or indemnify the user against potential third-party infringement claims. As with copyright, the only reason that using software may require a patent license from the software provider is that the software provider characterizes the transaction as a license rather than as the sale of a copy. With patent, as with copyright, the license requires itself.

1.2 Contract-Forming Terms

In addition to providing that the transaction is a license rather than a sale, nearly every proprietary software EULA states that the license terms are an agreement that gives rise to a binding contract. The Windows and Office licenses state, "These license terms are an agreement between Microsoft Corporation (or based on where you live, one of its affiliates) and you." Adobe admonishes in the EULA for Adobe Reader, "PLEASE READ THIS CONTRACT CAREFULLY. BY USING, COPYING OR DISTRIBUTING ALL OR ANY PORTION OF THE ADOBE SOFTWARE ('SOFTWARE') YOU ACCEPT ALL THE TERMS AND CONDITIONS OF THIS AGREEMENT. . . ."

According to John C. Dvorak, the shrinkwrap software license was invented in the late 1970s by Seymour Rubinstein, the chief executive officer of MicroPro International Corp.[50] MicroPro published WordStar—one of the first popular word processing programs for personal computers. Although Rubinstein was a pioneer of the early software industry, it seems likely that MicroPro's lawyers played a key role in devising the legal concept, which was an innovative lawyerly solution to the problem of protecting the rights of the software provider when mass-market software was still new. A WordStar software package from circa 1983 (purchased unused on eBay 25 years later) was covered by shrinkwrap, but the MicroPro Limited Use Software License Agreement for the software does not actually state that it becomes effective when the user opens the shrinkwrap. Instead, the floppy disks on which the

50. John C. Dvorak, *The Software Protection Racket,* PC MAGAZINE, Sep. 1, 1998.

software resides arrived in a package with a paper seal that contains the following notice:

> DO NOT OPEN THIS SEALED PACKAGE . . .
> until you have read the Limited Use Software License Agreement located on the inside back cover of your reference guide.
> Opening this sealed package will legally obligate you to the terms of the Limited Use Software License Agreement.

The license agreement on the inside back cover of the reference guide states,

> YOU AGREE TO THE TERMS OF THIS AGREEMENT BY THE ACT OF OPENING THE SEALED PACKAGE THAT CONTAINS THE MAGNETIC MEDIUM OR MEDIA ON WHICH THE SOFTWARE IS RECORDED. DO NOT OPEN THE SEALED PACKAGE WITHOUT FIRST READING, UNDERSTANDING, AND AGREEING TO THE TERMS AND CONDITIONS OF THIS AGREEMENT. YOU MAY RETURN THE SOFTWARE FOR A FULL REFUND BEFORE OPENING THE SEALED PACKAGE.

By this relatively simple but creative mechanism, MicroPro sought the benefits of a license agreement, without the cost of obtaining each user's written assent.

Although the law has long recognized the possibility of assent by conduct, enforceability of shrinkwrap licenses was not a foregone conclusion. In *Step-Saver Data Systems, Inc. v. Wyse Technology,*[51] The Software Link, Inc. (TSL)—provider of a software product known as Multilink Advantage—printed a Limited Use License Agreement on each package.[52] The court referred to this agreement as "the box-top license."[53] The license, which stated that the user agreed to its terms by opening the box, disclaimed all express and implied warranties, "except for a warranty that the disks contained in the box are free from defects."[54] This was not much of a warranty, considering that the disks in the box were worth a small fraction of the software's price. The license also

51. 939 F.2d 91 (3d Cir. 1991).

52. *Id.* at 93–94.

53. *Id.* at 94.

54. *Id.* at 96.

provided that the sole remedy for a defective disk was its replacement, and it affirmed that the license was the parties' exclusive agreement.[55]

Step-Saver, which brought an action for alleged defects in the software, contended that the box-top license was not part of the actual contract. According to Step-Saver, "the contract for each copy of the program was formed when TSL agreed, on the telephone, to ship the copy at the agreed price."[56] This telephone contract contained none of the warranty disclaimers or liability limitations that appeared in the box-top license. Step-Saver argued that, based on the Uniform Commercial Code,[57] the telephone contract controlled.

The court concluded that, because the terms of the box-top license did not expressly state that TSL's acceptance of Step-Saver's offer was conditional on Step-Saver's assent to the additional or different terms, the box-top terms did not give rise to a conditional acceptance.[58] Rather, they were merely a proposal for additions to the contract. The buyer and seller were merchants, but even between merchants, a proposal for additions to the contract does not become part of the contract if it would materially alter the terms. Here, the terms of the box-top license would have materially altered the terms of the contact formed by the telephone call. It followed that the box-top license terms did not become part of the contract.[59]

Five years later, in *ProCD, Inc. v. Zeidenberg*,[60] the U.S. Court of Appeals for the Seventh Circuit reached a different result on contract formation, and the *ProCD* holding soon became supported by the "weight of authority."[61] ProCD sold a version of its telephone directory product called SelectPhone™

---

55. *Id.*

56. *Id.* at 97.

57. The parties agreed that the programs were "goods" under Article 2 of the UCC. See *Id.* at 94 n.6.

58. *Id.* at 103. Section 2-207(1) of the UCC provides that a timely expression of acceptance or written confirmation "operates as an acceptance even though it states terms additional to or different from those offered or agreed upon, unless acceptance is expressly made conditional on assent to the additional or different terms." Section 2-207(2) provides that "the additional terms are to be construed as proposals for addition to the contract." Between merchants, such terms can become part of the contract, but not if "they materially alter it."

59. *Id.* at 106.

60. 86 F.3d 1447 (7th Cir. 1996).

61. Peerless Wall & Window Coverings, Inc. v. Synchronics, Inc., 85 F. Supp. 2d 519, 527 (W.D. Pa. 2000).

on compact discs. Each box announced that the software came with restrictions stated in an enclosed license.[62] The license, which also appeared on the user's screen every time the software ran, limited use of the software and listings to "non-commercial purposes."[63] The district court had noted that "[t]he Select Phone™ box mentions the agreement in one place in small print" and "does not detail the specific terms of the license."[64] But these facts did not sway the Court of Appeals, which concluded that the license terms gave rise to a binding contract.[65]

Responding to the argument that the license terms were "hidden" because they were inside the box, the Seventh Circuit asserted that the only way for vendors to "put the entire terms of a contract on the outside of a box" would be "by using microscopic type, removing other information that buyers might find more useful (such as what the software does, and on which computers it works), or both. . . ."[66] This premise assumes, without explanation, that the terms of the contract are inevitably so lengthy that microscopic type would be required to fit them. Based on this premise, the court concluded, "Notice on the outside, terms on the inside, and a right to return the software for a refund if the terms are unacceptable (a right that the license expressly extends), may be a means of doing business valuable to buyers and sellers alike."[67] Courts for the most part have followed this reasoning. In *I.Lan Systems, Inc. v. NetScout Service Level Corp.*,[68] the court stated, "*Step-Saver* once was the leading case on shrinkwrap agreements. Today that distinction goes to . . . *ProCD*. . . ."[69]

The conclusion is potentially stronger under licenses to which the user clicks assent through an onscreen button with the word "accept" or "agree." The shift from "shrinkwrap" to "clickwrap" or "click-through" licensing reflects not only the *ProCD* line of cases but also the evolution of the software user interface. Early personal computers sometimes did not even have hard disk drives, and programs such as WordStar could run from floppy disks.

---

62. *Id.* at 1450.

63. 86 F.3d at 1450.

64. ProCD, Inc. v. Zeidenberg, 908 F. Supp. 640, 645 (W.D. Wis. 1996).

65. 86 F.3d at 1450.

66. *Id.* at 1451.

67. *Id.*

68. 183 F. Supp. 2d 328 (D. Mass. 2002).

69. *Id.* at 337.

When such programs were installed on hard drives, the installation typically consisted simply of copying the program files into a user-created directory from a text-based, command-line interface. Although batch files could be used to display text, the command-line interface of early operating systems did not provide a convenient mechanism for obtaining explicit assent to license terms during installation. The opening of the shrinkwrap on the software box, or the opening of a package containing the floppy disks, was one of the few specific points at which every user engaged in predictable conduct that could be made a basis for assenting to the license terms.

As personal computers and their operating systems developed, the process for software setup became increasingly automated. Through a graphical user interface, the user now runs a separate program that manages the setup process. This setup process makes it possible to require an affirmation, such as the clicking of an onscreen button on which the word "agree" or "accept" appears, before setup completes. Explicit verbal assent to software license terms is now a mandatory step in software installation.

The open question at this point is not whether a shrinkwrap or click-through license agreement forms a contract, but rather, with whom is the contact formed? In other words, who is the "you" to whom the license refers?[70] A number of major EULAs leave this question unanswered. The Software License Terms for Microsoft Windows, like those for Microsoft Office, state that they are an agreement between Microsoft and "you," but the Windows and Office license terms do not define "you." An earlier Windows license, for Windows XP, says that "you" are "either an individual or a single entity," but does not say which one "you" are or specify how to determine it. License terms for other popular software products, including those for Apple and Adobe software, also address themselves to an undefined "you."

One might assume that "you" is the person who is running the setup program in which the license terms are displayed. But the Microsoft licenses state, "By using the software, you accept these terms. If you do not accept them, do not use the software. Instead, return it to the retailer for a refund or credit." The first two sentences—"[b]y using" and "do not use"—appear to be addressed to all potential users of the software. The third sentence—"return . . . for a refund or credit"—appears to be addressed to the person who

70. This ambiguity in the term "you" is separate from the problem of authentication that also exists when someone "signs" an electronic document by clicking assent. For example, if an online agreement is presented to a named individual, there may be issues about whether the person clicking assent really is the named individual.

paid the retailer for the software (or for a computer that came preloaded with it). But the person to whom the terms are actually presented—that is, the person running the setup program—may not be the only user and may not be the person who (or entity that) paid the retailer.

The Microsoft license terms do not require that the person running the setup program agree that all other users of the software will be required to agree to the license. For example, if one family member or company employee installs the software, the terms do not say that other family members or company employees must also agree. The terms do state that "[t]he first user of the software may make a one time transfer of the software, and this agreement, directly to a third party." Before any such transfer, "the other party must agree that this agreement applies to the transfer and use of the software." But these terms apply only to a "one time transfer," not to circumstances in which no transfer has occurred but someone other than the person running the setup program uses the software.

Microsoft presumably does not intend to prohibit all use by anyone other than the person who ran the setup program and clicked "agree." A section of the Windows license captioned "License Model" states that "[t]he software is licensed on a per copy per device basis," and a section captioned "Number of Users" states that, with certain exceptions, "only one user may use the software at a time." These terms imply that different persons may use a single installation of the software on a single computer, so long as they do so at different times. But the status of those other persons under the license is unclear.

Perhaps even more puzzling is that, although the person setting up the software must click an agree button to proceed, the license states that "you" agree to its terms by using the software. It would seem more natural to say that you agree to the terms by clicking "agree." The idea that you agree by using the software rather than by clicking "agree" may be an attempt to bind all users of the software—including "non-clickers"—to the terms. But as the Second Circuit observed in its 2002 decision in *Specht v. Netscape Communications Corp.*,[71] license terms are not binding if a reasonably prudent user would not have known or learned of them.[72] Although the "splash screens" that appear when Windows and Office are loaded contain copyright notices, they do not contain a notice stating that use of the

71. 306 F.3d 17 (2d Cir. 2002).

72. *Id.* at 20.

software is subject to a license agreement. Therefore, it is entirely possible to use Windows and Office without ever being asked to agree to anything.

Symantec, in the license agreement for Norton Antivirus 2009, states, "BY OPENING THIS PACKAGE, BREAKING THE SEAL, CLICKING THE 'I AGREE' OR 'YES' BUTTON OR OTHERWISE INDICATING ASSENT ELECTRONICALLY, OR LOADING THE SOFTWARE, YOU AGREE TO THE TERMS AND CONDITIONS OF THIS LICENSE AGREEMENT." This term casts a wide net for manifestations of assent—opening, breaking, clicking, or loading will suffice. But opening the package, breaking the seal, and clicking the button typically occur only once, when the software is first opened and installed, and the license agreement does not present itself each time the software is loaded. So again, it is not clear that merely using the software binds the user to the terms.

So far, the potential ambiguity in the identity of licensees seems to have worked to the advantage of the software licensor. When Brian Johnson sued Microsoft in the U.S. District Court for the Western District of Washington, he alleged among other things that Microsoft's Windows Genuine Advantage program—which attempts to determine whether the copy of Windows being used is legitimate—violated the EULA for Windows XP.[73] The XP license states that it "is a legal agreement between you (either an individual or a single entity) and Microsoft Corporation."

Microsoft successfully argued that individuals who used computers with Windows XP but did not own the computers did not have standing to sue under the XP EULA, because they were not parties to the EULA.[74] The court agreed with Microsoft that the individuals lacked standing because "the Windows XP EULAs at issue are contracts between a computer purchaser and either the computer manufacturer or Microsoft."[75] In other words, the "you" under the license is the purchaser of the computer with Windows XP on it. This conclusion leaves unclear how other users can be subject to the license provisions. The purchaser may or may not be the person who runs the setup program and clicks "agree," and the purchaser may or may not be the only user or even a user at all.

If "you" does extend, for at least some purposes, to a person or entity other than the individual who clicks "agree," then the agreement-forming terms

---

73. Johnson v. Microsoft Corp., 2008 U.S. Dist. LEXIS 30884, *4 (W.D. Wa. Mar. 21, 2008).

74. *Id.* at *9.

75. *Id.*

inevitably raise a question of the authority of the "clicker" to bind the other person or entity. Business users of software often enter into corporate or volume license agreements that may appear to take the retail EULA out of the picture. Nevertheless, even business users may be required to click assent to install programs or updates. In *Hugger-Mugger, L.L.C. v. Netsuite, Inc.*,[76] applying California law, the district court held that a company employee lacked actual authority to bind the company by clicking an onscreen button assenting to terms of use.[77] The court went on, however, to hold that the employee had ostensible authority, which sufficed to bind the company, based in Utah, to the terms of use, including a forum selection clause that required disputes to be litigated in Santa Clara, California.[78]

1.3 What You May and May Not Do

Most EULAs do at least grant "you" (whoever that may be) the basic permission that they make necessary. The Microsoft Windows license states that "[y]ou may install one copy of the software on the licensed device" and that "[y]ou may use the software on up to two processors on that device at one time." The Microsoft Office license provides for assignment of the license to one device, which is the "licensed device," and says that "[y]ou may install and use one copy of the software on the licensed device." These permission-granting terms generally are interwoven with terms that restrict use. For example, the same provision that permits the use of clip art in Microsoft Office states that you may distribute documents and projects that you create with the clip art only "non-commercially," although that term is not defined.

A Range of Rights

One of the asserted advantages of EULAs is that they "permit software publishers to offer the wide variety of rights that are associated with the features of today's software products."[79] It is possible for a EULA to grant rights that

76. 2005 U.S. Dist. LEXIS 33003 (D. Utah Sept. 12, 2005).

77. *Id.* at *19.

78. *Id.* at *1, *20.

79. Gomulkiewicz & Williamson, *Brief Defense*, at 338.

go beyond the ones that attach to ownership of a single copy. For example, Section 2(b) of the Microsoft Office license states, "You may install another copy on a portable device for use by the single primary user of the licensed device." Development products often contain sample code or libraries that can be distributed with the user's programs. Recent operating systems software licenses provide for ancillary activities such as remote access and device connections. Otherwise, however, rights-expanding provisions are relatively rare.

Provisions that seem to grant additional rights, on closer examination, may not. The Windows license grants limited rights to use "Font Components" and "Icons, images and sounds." It provides, "While the software is running, you may use its fonts to display and print content." But this right seems to be included already in the right to use the software. More significant, apparently, are the restrictions that immediately follow—namely, that you may "only" embed fonts as permitted by the "embedding restrictions" in them and that you may only "temporarily download them to a printer or other output device to print content." Likewise, "[w]hile the software is running, you may use but not share its icons, images, sounds, and media." Again, it is not clear how the rights to use these particular software elements while the software is running go beyond the basic right to use the software, and the quoted terms limit the use and sharing of these elements.

EULAs and First Sale

EULA defenders also assert that "EULAs often grant rights that the user would not receive as a purchaser of a copy of the software under copyright law's doctrine of first sale."[80] But the first sale doctrine is merely an exception to the copyright owner's exclusive right of public distribution, and few if any current software licenses grant distribution rights that go beyond the rights of the software customer under the first sale doctrine. On the contrary, most licenses state that even lending the software is prohibited, and they also impose conditions and limitations on the transfer of the license to third parties.

The first sale doctrine originated more than a century ago when a book publisher tried and failed to impose resale restrictions on buyers of its books.

---

80. *Id.* at 350.

In *Bobbs-Merrill Co. v. Straus*,[81] Bobbs-Merrill owned the copyright on a novel known as *The Castaway*.[82]

> Printed immediately below the copyright notice on the page in the book following the title page is inserted the following notice: 'The price of this book at retail is one dollar net. No dealer is licensed to sell it at a less price, and a sale at a less price will be treated as an infringement of the copyright.'[83]

In some respects, this notice was a precursor of the shrinkwrap license, but the book was not wrapped in cellophane (which was just being invented in 1908), and more important, the notice did not purport to transform the transaction from a sale into a license.

The defendants, doing business as R.H. Macy & Co., "sold copies of the book at retail at the uniform price of eighty-nine cents a copy" without Bobbs-Merrill's consent.[84] Bobbs-Merrill contended that its exclusive right under the then-in-effect Copyright Act to "vend" a copyrighted book gave it the right to control subsequent sales of the book.[85] The Supreme Court rejected this claim, holding that copyright law did not give the copyright owner "the right to impose, by notice, such as is disclosed in this case, a limitation at which the book shall be sold at retail by future purchasers, with whom there is no privity of contract."[86] The Court emphasized that there was "no claim in this case of contract limitation, nor license agreement controlling the subsequent sales of the book."[87] The EULA, as a license agreement, seeks to overcome such objections.

The first sale doctrine is codified in Section 109(a) of the current Copyright Act. This section provides that, when a copy of a copyrighted work has been sold, the owner of that copy "is entitled, without the authority of the copyright owner, to sell or otherwise dispose of the possession of that copy. . . ."[88]

---

81. 210 U.S. 339 (1908).

82. *Id.* at 341.

83. *Id.*

84. *Id.* at 342.

85. *Id.* at 349.

86. *Id.* at 350.

87. *Id.*

88. 17 U.S.C. § 109(a).

Section 109(d) states, however, that the "privilege" it sets forth in Section 109(a) does not, "unless authorized by the copyright owner, extend to any person who has acquired possession of the copy . . . from the copyright owner . . . without acquiring ownership of it."[89] By providing that a software copy is licensed, not sold, the EULA invokes Section 109(d) and defeats the first sale doctrine of Section 109(a), which otherwise would permit the buyer of a copy to resell it.

At one time, software providers were concerned that, by selling (rather than licensing) copies of software, they might make it possible for buyers to "rent" the software to third parties, some of whom would make and retain their own unauthorized copies. Under the Computer Software Rentals Amendment Act of 1990, however, with certain exceptions for nonprofit libraries, a "person in possession of a particular copy of a computer program (including any tape, disk, or other medium embodying such program)" may not, for commercial purposes, "dispose of, or authorize the disposal of, the possession of that . . . computer program (including any tape, disk, or other medium embodying such program) by rental, lease, or lending, or by any other act or practice in the nature of rental, lease, or lending."[90] Most EULAs actually extend this restriction to any and all dispositions for noncommercial purposes, rather than in any way expanding distribution rights.

One of the few recent cases to buck the trend of enforcing license terms is *Vernor v. Autodesk, Inc.*[91] Vernor was one of the apparently large number of people who make a living selling goods on eBay.[92] He bought "authentic" but "used" packages of Autodesk's AutoCAD software package at garage and office sales and then put them up for auction. Autodesk sent notices to eBay under the Digital Millennium Copyright Act alleging that the sale of such packages would infringe its copyright. After notices and counter-notices, eBay suspended Vernor's account "for repeat infringement."[93] He sought a declaratory judgment affirming his right to resell two AutoCAD packages that remained in his possession.

The court held that Vernor was entitled to resell the packages, because the transaction in which they were provided to the original customer was—notwithstanding the Autodesk license agreement that accompanied

89. *Id.* § 109(d).

90. 17 U.S.C. § 109(b)(1)(A).

91. 555 F. Supp. 2d 1164 (W.D. Wash. 2008).

92. *Id.* at 1165.

93. *Id.* at 1166.

it—a sale rather than a license. With a "cf." citation to a 1977 Ninth Circuit criminal case involving movie prints, *United States v. Wise*,[94] the district court declared that "[t]he label placed on a transaction is not determinative."[95] Stating that it was "[t]aking direction solely from *Wise*," the *Vernor* court concluded that "the transfer of AutoCAD packages from Autodesk to [the original customer] was a sale."[96] To reach this result, the court disregarded three more recent Ninth Circuit decisions, all of which, the court acknowledged, "arrived at contrary results" in the software context.[97] Unless the Ninth Circuit changes course, the decision in *Vernor* is likely to have limited influence.

EULAs and the Public Domain

In forbidding use or copying beyond that which is expressly permitted, EULAs rarely if ever make exceptions for elements that are not protected by copyright. Section 102(b) of the Copyright Act makes clear that it protects expression, not ideas: "In no case does copyright protection for an original work of authorship extend to any idea, procedure, process, system, method of operation, concept, principle, or discovery, regardless of the form in which it is described, explained, illustrated, or embodied in such work." Copyright also does not protect expression that "merges" with ideas, and in the software context this has included circumstances in which, even though multiple expressions are possible, efficiency requires the use of a particular expression.[98] In addition, copyright does not protect *scènes à faire*,[99] or elements "dictated by external factors," such as "(1) the mechanical specifications of the computer on which a particular program is intended to run; (2) compatibility requirements of other programs with which a program is designed to operate in conjunction; (3) computer manufacturers' design

94. 550 F.2d 1180 (9th Cir. 1977).

95. 555 F. Supp. 2d at 1169.

96. *Id.* at 1170.

97. *Id.* at 1171.

98. Computer Associates Int'l, Inc. v. Altai, Inc., 982 F.2d 693, 707–08 (2d Cir. 1992).

99. In dramatic works, "[t]he principle of scènes à faire excludes copyright protection for 'incidents, characters or settings which are as a practical matter indispensable, or at least standard, in the treatment of a given topic.' . . . For example, parties, alcohol, co-eds, and wild behavior are natural elements in a story about a college fraternity." Stromback v. New Line Cinema, 384 F.3d 283, 296 (6th Cir. 2004) (citations omitted).

standards; (4) demands of the industry being serviced; and (5) widely accepted programming practices within the computer industry."[100] Nor, of course, does it protect elements taken directly from the public domain.[101]

Like ideas, facts—as distinct from their selection and arrangement—are unprotected. In *Feist Publications, Inc. v. Rural Telephone Service Co.*,[102] the Supreme Court described as "[t]he most fundamental axiom of copyright law" that "no author may copyright his ideas or the facts he narrates."[103] Even for fact compilations, which can be protected, "[o]riginality is a constitutional requirement."[104] The Court held that "[t]he selection, coordination, and arrangement" of telephone directory white pages did not satisfy this requirement because alphabetizing the listing produced "a garden-variety white pages directory, devoid of even the slightest trace of creativity."[105] Based on this decision, white pages directories are in the public domain, at least as far as copyright law is concerned.

In *ProCD, Inc. v. Zeidenberg*,[106] the software company compiled a database of names and telephone numbers from more than three thousand telephone directories.[107] Zeidenberg purchased a copy of the database under a shrink-wrap license that limited use to "non-commercial" purposes.[108] He then made the database available, "for a price," on the Internet.[109] Zeidenberg maintained, and for purposes of the decision the court assumed, that the database was not protected by copyright.[110] Nevertheless, the court held that the license was enforceable.[111] The court, in an opinion by Judge Frank Easterbrook, discussed case law but also offered an economic analysis to support this result.

---

100. *Id.* at 709–10.

101. *Id.* at 710.

102. 499 U.S. 340 (1991).

103. *Id.* at 344–45 (quoting Harper & Row, Publishers, Inc. v. Nation Enterprises, 471 U.S. 539, 556 (1985)).

104. *Id.* at 346.

105. *Id.* at 379–80.

106. 86 F.3d 1447 (7th Cir. 1996).

107. *Id.* at 1449.

108. *Id.* at 1450.

109. *Id.*

110. *Id.* at 1449.

111. *Id.*

According to the court, the development cost of the database was more than $10 million, and costs of keeping it current were also high.[112] The database was "much more valuable to some users than to others."[113] ProCD used different licenses for different classes of users, so that it could charge them different prices. In economic terms, "ProCD decided to engage in price discrimination, selling its database to the general public for personal use at a low price (approximately $150 for the set of five discs) while selling information to the trade for a higher price."[114] (The opinion does not say how much higher.) For price discrimination to succeed, a seller must "control arbitrage," and ProCD's ability to do so depended on being able to enforce the license terms.[115]

The court opined that this arrangement made good economic sense:

> If ProCD had to recover all of its costs and make a profit by charging a single price—that is, if it could not charge more to commercial users than to the general public—it would have to raise the price substantially over $150. The ensuing reduction in sales would harm consumers who value the information at, say, $200. They get consumer surplus of $50 under the current arrangement but would cease to buy if the price rose substantially. If because of high elasticity of demand in the consumer segment of the market the only way to make a profit turned out to be a price attractive to commercial users alone, then all consumers would lose out—and so would the commercial clients, who would have to pay more for the listings because ProCD could not obtain any contribution toward costs from the consumer market.[116]

The court concluded that license terms permitting price discrimination should be enforced because, without them, consumer surplus would be reduced or lost. The court's analysis, however, is explicitly hypothetical. The comments apply "*[i]f* because of high elasticity of demand in the consumer segment of the market the only way to make a profit turned out to be a price

112. *Id.*

113. *Id.*

114. *Id.*

115. *Id.* at 1450.

116. *Id.* at 1449.

attractive to commercial users alone. . . ."[117] The court cites no evidence, within or outside the record in the case, regarding the elasticity of demand in the consumer segment of the market. With no evidence regarding costs or the price necessary to "make a profit," we do not know whether the condition is met. As a result, we do not actually know whether "all consumers would lose out."

The court's focus on consumer surplus is also notable. Judge Easterbrook, like Judge Richard Posner, has had a long association with the University of Chicago and the study of law and economics. Normative law and economics ordinarily does not focus on maximizing only consumer surplus or only producer surplus. Posner, in his treatise on economic analysis of law, identifies Kaldor-Hicks efficiency, a form of potential Pareto optimality, as the touchstone.[118] More broadly, "[w]elfare economics traditionally focuses on maximizing *aggregate* welfare measures such as the sum of producers' and consumers' surpluses."[119] Easterbrook may have thought that mentioning producer surplus—that is, profit—would make his analysis seem less attractive. But there is more involved than consumer surplus alone.

Moreover, any suggestion that price discrimination necessarily increases consumer surplus clearly is incorrect. As Louis Phlips points out, "intuition suggests that price discrimination aims at taking the entire consumer surplus away from all customers, if possible."[120] In fact, "perfect" price discrimination "would involve the charge of a different price against all the different units of commodity, in such wise that the price extracted for each was equal to the demand price for it, and *no consumers' surplus was left to the buyers. . . .*"[121] Obviously, then, there is no assurance that price discrimination will increase consumer surplus, and there is a possibility that, to the extent price discrimination succeeds, consumer surplus may decline or disappear. The price discrimination that Easterbrook said would protect consumer surplus is actually a strategy for converting consumer surplus to producer profit.

For these reasons, and given that the court's own comments acknowledge that the economic effect of license-imposed price discrimination in

---

117. *Id.* (emphasis added).

118. RICHARD A. POSNER, ECONOMIC ANALYSIS OF LAW § 1.2 at 13 (7th ed. 2007).

119. LOUIS PHLIPS, THE ECONOMICS OF PRICE DISCRIMINATION 1 (1981) (emphasis in original).

120. *Id.* at 18.

121. *Id.* at 12 (quoting ARTHUR PIGOU, THE ECONOMICS OF WELFARE 279 (1920)) (emphasis in original).

particular cases depends on such factors as (undetermined) elasticities of demand, it is difficult to see how a legal standard for license enforceability could properly depend on this economic effect. Perhaps this problem is one reason the Supreme Court in *Feist* made no attempt at a similar economic analysis. A standard for license enforceability based on consumer surplus or broader efficiency either would have to rest on a broad empirical analysis of the average or overall economic effect or would have to require the consideration of economic evidence in each case. The overall economic effect could change over time, however, and if enforceability depended on economic evidence specific to the license in question, it would be difficult to know in advance whether any particular license would be enforceable or not. Therefore, it is hard to see how the economic analysis in *ProCD* can be regarded as anything but speculative. Still, it seems to have been at least part of the *ratio decidendi.*

Although *ProCD* remains one of the most influential software licensing decisions, its economic analysis also seems not to have been borne out by subsequent developments. As Carl Shapiro and Hal Varian pointed out in a book published only three years after the *ProCD* decision,

> By now there are at least a half-dozen companies that produce CD telephone directories, and prices have fallen dramatically. You can buy CD phone directories for less than $20, and there are also several directory listings on the Internet that provide the same service for free, covering their costs through advertising.[122]

In other words, the problem for CD directory providers in the 1990s was not arbitrage, as suggested by Easterbrook. Rather, the "commoditization" of such information drove the price toward marginal cost, which was zero.[123]

EULAs and Fair Use

License terms also typically prohibit reverse engineering, even when the purpose is not to copy the licensed software but only to achieve compatibility

---

122. Carl Shapiro & Hal R. Varian, Information Rules: A Strategic Guide to the Network Economy 24 (1999).

123. *Id.* at 23–24.

with the software or a related service. In this respect, EULAs also override the Copyright Act. Under Section 107 of the Act, "the fair use of a copyrighted work, including such use by reproduction in copies . . . or by any other means specified by that section [apparently Section 106], for purposes such as criticism, comment, news reporting, teaching (including multiple copies for classroom use), scholarship, or research, is not an infringement of copyright."[124] The statute states that "the factors to be considered" in determining whether a particular use is fair use include:

(1) the purpose and character of the use, including whether such use is of a commercial nature or is for nonprofit educational purposes;
(2) the nature of the copyrighted work;
(3) the amount and substantiality of the portion used in relation to the copyrighted work as a whole; and
(4) the effect of the use upon the potential market for or value of the copyrighted work.[125]

Reverse engineering is a common research technique employed by engineers. It involves studying, and sometimes taking apart, the final product in an attempt to understand the underlying ideas or methods used to implement it. A pair of 1992 decisions—by the Federal Circuit in *Atari Games Corp. v. Nintendo of America, Inc.*[126] and by the Ninth Circuit in *Sega Enterprises Ltd. v. Accolade, Inc.*[127]—held that fair use can extend to reverse engineering of computer programs to learn those unprotected ideas.[128] In the Ninth Circuit case, Sega was a developer of videogame consoles and cartridges.[129] Accolade developed cartridges designed to be compatible with the Sega Genesis console.[130] In doing so, it "transformed the machine-readable object code contained in commercially available copies of Sega's game cartridges into human-readable source code. . . ."[131] Accolade then used this source code

---

124. 17 U.S.C. § 107.

125. *Id.*

126. 975 F.2d 832 (Fed. Cir. 1992).

127. 977 F.2d 1510 (9th Cir. 1992).

128. *Atari Games*, 975 F.2d at 843; *Sega Enterprises*, 977 F.2d at 1514.

129. 977 F.2d at 1514.

130. *Id.*

131. *Id.*

not directly in its own games, but to determine how to make its games run on the Sega Genesis.[132] The court concluded that, "when the person seeking the understanding has a legitimate reason for doing so and when no other means of access to the unprotected elements exists, such disassembly is as a matter of law a fair use of the copyrighted work."[133]

An earlier decision, relying not on fair use but on the program user's rights under Section 117 of the Copyright Act, declined to enforce a shrinkwrap license term that prohibited reverse engineering. In *Vault Corp. v. Quaid Software Ltd.*,[134] the court held that a provision in the Louisiana Software License Enforcement Act that permitted software providers to prohibit decompilation or disassembly "conflicts with the rights of computer program owners under § 117 and clearly 'touches upon an area' of federal copyright law."[135] On this basis, the court held that the provision was preempted by federal law and that, accordingly, the prohibition of decompilation or disassembly was unenforceable.[136]

The Supreme Court has held, in the patent context, that state statutory law cannot prevent reverse engineering of unpatented items. In *Bonito Boats, Inc. v. Thunder Craft Boats, Inc.*,[137] Bonito developed a hull design for a fiberglass recreational boat, and Thunder Craft copied the design by direct molding.[138] Bonito sued Thunder Craft under a Florida statute that made it unlawful to use direct molding to duplicate another person's boat hull, without permission, for the purpose of sale.[139] The Supreme Court held that, by offering "patent-like protection for ideas deemed unprotected under the present federal scheme," the Florida statute conflicted with a "strong federal policy favoring free competition in ideas which do not merit patent protection."[140] As a result, the Florida statute was preempted by the Supremacy Clause of the U.S. Constitution.[141]

---

132. *Id.*

133. *Id.*

134. 847 F.2d 255 (5th Cir. 1988).

135. *Id.* at 270.

136. *Id.*

137. 489 U.S. 141 (1989).

138. *Id.* at 144.

139. *Id.* at 144–45 (citing Fla. Stat. § 559.94(2)).

140. *Id.* at 168 (quoting Lear, Inc. v. Adkins, 395 U.S. 653, 656 (1969)).

141. *Id.*

If state statutes are preempted when they bar reverse engineering to gain access to unprotected ideas, then one might think that the state law that enforces contracts—including EULAs—is preempted when it pursues similar results. And in light of *Atari Games* and *Sega Enterprises,* one might have expected courts to reach a conclusion similar to that of *Vault* based on fair use. A decade after *Atari Games,* in *Bowers v. Baystate Technologies, Inc.,*[142] the Federal Circuit reaffirmed the holding that reverse engineering of computer programs to learn their unprotected ideas is fair use.[143] But the court held that this result could be overcome through the simple expedient of a shrink-wrap license that prohibits reverse engineering.[144] Enforcing such a license, the court stated that "[p]rivate parties are free to contractually forego the limited ability to reverse engineer a software product under the exemptions of the Copyright Act."[145]

The court stated that contracts cannot create "exclusive rights" that would conflict with the Copyright Act, because contracts are enforceable only against their parties, not against the world.[146] The court did not address the argument that, by conditioning all access to software on the clicking of assent to EULA terms, a software provider can create a set of exclusive rights that is enforceable against the world for all practical purposes.[147]

EULAs and Interoperability under DMCA

In *Davidson & Associates v. Jung,*[148] the Eighth Circuit in 2005 reached a result similar to that reached in *Bowers* regarding the interoperability exception to the anti-circumvention provisions of the Digital Millennium

---

142. 320 F.3d 1317 (Fed. Cir. 2003).

143. *Id.* at 1325.

144. *Id.* at 1325–26.

145. *Id.*

146. *Id.* at 1325.

147. If a software license purports to bar the licensee's development of any software that competes with the licensor's product, then the doctrine of copyright misuse may apply. *See* Lasercomb America, Inc. v. Reynolds, 911 F.2d 970, 979 (4th Cir. 1990) (stating that "the analysis necessary to a finding of [copyright] misuse is similar to but separate from the analysis necessary to a finding of antitrust violation"). But licenses that merely proscribe reverse engineering are enforced, as outlined above.

148. 422 F.3d 630 (8th Cir. 2005).

Copyright Act. Under DMCA, "[n]o person shall circumvent a technological measure that effectively controls access to a work protected" by copyright.[149] Notwithstanding this prohibition, however:

> [A] person who has lawfully obtained the right to use a copy of a computer program may circumvent a technological measure that effectively controls access to a particular portion of that program for the sole purpose of identifying and analyzing those elements of the program that are necessary to achieve interoperability of an independently created computer program with other programs, and that have not previously been readily available to the person engaging in the circumvention, to the extent any such acts of identification and analysis do not constitute infringement [of copyright].[150]

Davidson, doing business as Blizzard Entertainment, operated "Battle.net," an online service that "allows owners of Blizzard games to play each other on their personal computers via the Internet."[151] Frustrated with Battle.net's performance, "a group of non-profit volunteer game hobbyists, programmers, and other individuals formed a group called the 'bnetd project.'"[152] Certain of these volunteers, "[b]y necessity," engaged in reverse engineering "to ensure that bnetd.org worked with Blizzard games."[153] They maintained that any copying was protected by fair use and that any circumvention was protected by the interoperability exception.[154]

Accolade reverse engineered Sega's software to create compatible games for commercial purposes, and Zeidenberg made the ProCD database available on the Internet "for a price."[155] In contrast, the Battle.net service was free, and the nonprofit bnetd project made its code freely available through open source licensing.[156] Nevertheless, the court held that the *Davidson* defendants had surrendered any reverse engineering rights under the interoperability

149. 17 U.S.C. § 1201(a)(1)(A).

150. *Id.* at § 1201(f)(1).

151. *Id.* at 633.

152. *Id.* at 635.

153. *Id.* at 636.

154. *See id.* at 637.

155. *ProCD,* 86 F.3d at 1450.

156. *Davidson,* 422 F.3d at 633.

exception of Section 1201(f) as a result of the EULA and terms of use (TOU), to which they had clicked "I Agree."[157] Both the EULA and the TOU expressly prohibited reverse engineering, and the court rejected the defense that federal law preempted enforcement of these contract terms.[158]

1.4 Comply or Forfeit

The EULA terms that grant affirmative permissions are typically presented so that the entire grant of use permission is made conditional on the licensee's compliance with all terms. Provisions that might otherwise appear to be affirmative covenants thus become limits on the scope of the license. This is important because it permits the licensor to bring a copyright infringement action—with substantially greater remedies—for what would otherwise be, at most, a breach of contract by the licensee.[159] It also permits the licensor to bring actions for contributory copyright infringement against third parties that induce any breach of license terms.

The license at issue in the 1999 decision in *Sun Microsystems, Inc. v. Microsoft Corp.*[160] was a negotiated agreement between two large companies, but the case helps explain the permission-conditioning terms of most current mass-market licenses. Sun sued Microsoft for copyright infringement, claiming in part "that Microsoft had exceeded the scope of its license by creating an enhanced version of Java that was fully operable only on Microsoft's operating system. . . ."[161] The Ninth Circuit concluded that a key threshold issue was whether the case was "a copyright or a contract case," which it said "turns on whether the compatibility provisions help define the

---

157. *Id.* at 639.

158. *Id.*

159. *See* MDY Industries, LLC v. Blizzard Entertainment, Inc., 2008 U.S. Dist. LEXIS 53988, *11–*12 n.4 (D. Az. July 14, 2008). "Breach of contract damages generally are limited to the value of the actual loss caused by the breach. . . . Copyright damages, by contrast, include the copyright owner's actual damages and any additional profits of the infringer, or statutory damages as high as $150,000 per infringed work. . . . Courts may also impose injunctive relief, seize infringing articles, and award costs and attorneys' fees." *Id.* at *12 n.4 (citations omitted).

160. Sun Microsystems, Inc. v. Microsoft Corp., 188 F.3d 1115, 1117 (9th Cir. 1999).

161. *Id.* at 1117.

scope of the license."[162] According to the court, a copyright owner that grants a nonexclusive license generally waives the right to sue for copyright infringement and can sue only for breach of contract. But if the license is "limited in scope," and the licensee "acts outside the scope," then the licensor retains the right to sue for copyright infringement.[163] The court concluded that Sun, to pursue its infringement claim, was required to establish "that the disputed terms are limitations on the scope of the license rather than independent contractual covenants."[164]

Most EULAs today seek to gain the maximum benefit of license provisions by defining the licensee's compliance with all license terms as conditions of the license grant. For example, in the Windows and Office licenses, all the license "rights" granted are conditioned on compliance with all the terms. "IF YOU COMPLY WITH THESE LICENSE TERMS, YOU HAVE THE RIGHTS BELOW FOR EACH LICENSE YOU ACQUIRE." Likewise, Section 2 of the Adobe Reader EULA grants a nonexclusive license only "[i]f you obtained the Software from Adobe or one of its authorized licensees" and "subject to your compliance with the terms of this agreement. . . ." It follows that, if you do not comply, you do not have the license rights.

Section 5 of the Apple license for OS X Leopard achieves the same results through automatic termination:

> This License is effective until terminated. Your rights under this License will terminate automatically without notice from Apple if you fail to comply with any term(s) of this License. Upon the termination of this License, you shall cease all use of the Apple Software and destroy all copies, full or partial, of the Apple Software.

In contrast, the WordStar license from the early 1980s stated, "If any of the terms and conditions of this Agreement are broken, MicroPro has the right to terminate the Agreement and demand that you return the Software to MicroPro. At that time, you must also certify in writing that you have not retained any copies of the Software." This clause did not condition the license grant on compliance with the license terms, and therefore did not make all

162. *Id.* at 1121.

163. *Id.* (citations omitted).

164. *Id.* at 1122.

those terms scope limits rather than covenants. Absent action by MicroPro, the Agreement remained in effect.

The significance of making all use rights conditional came to the fore in *MDY Industries, LLC v. Blizzard Entertainment, Inc.*,[165] a case involving the popular multiplayer online game World of Warcraft (WoW). At the time of the district court decision, WoW was "the largest and most successful multiplayer online game in the world," with some ten million active players, generating annual revenue of more than $1.5 billion.[166] The court explained,

> WoW players control characters within a virtual universe, exploring the landscape, fighting monsters, performing quests, building skills, and interacting with other players and computer-generated characters. As players succeed, they acquire in-game assets, experience, and power. Players can advance from level 1 to level 60 with the basic game, and through level 70 with an expansion module.[167]

MDY marketed a computer program known as WowGlider (hereinafter "Glider"), which was a "bot" that would automatically play WoW while the actual WoW player was doing something else.[168] Glider made it possible for its user to acquire assets and advance to higher levels without actually playing the game.[169] At the time of the litigation, MDY had sold some one hundred thousand copies[170]—meaning, in practical terms, that the level 60 paladin you thought you were playing against might actually be an algorithm.

Unlike the bnetd project in *Davidson Associates, Inc. v. Jung*, which was an alternative to Blizzard's Battle.net service, the Glider software at issue in *MDY Industries* did not replace Blizzard's WoW game. Nor was it alleged that

---

165. 2008 U.S. Dist. LEXIS 53988 (D. Az. July 14, 2008).

166. *Id.* at *3. The intensity of some users' interest in the game is evidenced by a *pro se* motion to intervene filed in the *Blizzard* case by Jonathan Riches. *See* MDY Indus., LLC v. Blizzard Entm't, Inc., 2008 U.S. Dist. LEXIS 97696 *1 (D. Ariz. Nov. 21, 2008). The court explained, "Mr. Riches asserts that WoW has 'caused his mind to live in a virtual universe' and lose 'touch with reality.' . . . He claims that this caused him, among other things to "to 'choose [WoW] over working a legit job.'" *Id.* at *2. The court denied the motion to intervene. *Id.*

167. *Id.* at *2.

168. *Id.* at *3–*4.

169. *See id.* at *4.

170. *Id.*

MDY copied or reverse engineered WoW to develop Glider. But the end user license agreement and terms of use to which WoW users were required to assent specifically prohibited playing the game with bots.[171] Blizzard alleged that, when a WoW player used Glider, the player exceeded the scope of the WoW license and by doing so infringed Blizzard's copyright in WoW.[172] According to Blizzard, MDY was liable for, among other things, contributory copyright infringement, because it materially contributed to direct infringement by Glider users.[173]

The district court examined the case under the principle of *Sun Microsystems* and concluded that the prohibition in the TOU on the use of bots did not merely amount to a contractual covenant by the licensee but was actually a condition of the license.[174] As a result, WoW players who used Glider forfeited their WoW licenses from Blizzard and became direct copyright infringers,[175] exposing MDY to liability for contributory infringement.[176] In reaching this conclusion, the court emphasized that the grant of the limited WoW license was "expressly made '[s]ubject to your agreement to and continuing compliance with this License Agreement.'"[177]

The proprietary EULA is greatly strengthened by making the rights granted conditional on the user's compliance with all the terms of the Agreement, even when those terms might otherwise be considered covenants rather than conditions. Although the licensor's objective in *MDY Industries* was to limit a third party, there was a direct effect on users, because the licensor was able to limit access by users to what third parties might otherwise provide. In *MDY Industries,* the limit may have been one that most (human) game players would applaud, but this fact was not part of the decision.

1.5 Enabling DRM

Technical anticopying measures, also known as digital rights management or DRM techniques, have become prevalent. Lawrence Lessig considers

---

171. *Id.* at *18–*19.

172. *Id.* at *8.

173. *Id.*

174. *Id.* at *17.

175. *Id.* at *19.

176. *Id.* at *32.

177. *Id.* at *14.

DRM to be a potentially greater threat to freedom than legal constraints, because DRM is not as porous.[178] Some might ask whether the EULA has much continuing significance, now that many software providers rely on DRM to enforce restrictions on copying and use. The answer is that the EULA plays an essential role in making DRM, as it is normally applied to software, legally possible. It does so by authorizing what could otherwise be illegal intrusions on the rights and privacy of the user.

Today's EULAs often contain multiple provisions relating to DRM. The Microsoft Windows license terms, for example, contain lengthy sections on mandatory activation and validation. They also contain terms that authorize the transmission of information to Microsoft in connection with automatic updates and the removal of software believed to be malicious. In addition, the Windows license contains a bold-type statement near the beginning that "using the software also operates as your consent to the transmission of certain computer information during activation, validation and for Internet-based services."

Such terms are important because, without them, the licensor would be exposed to claims that the DRM-related automated transmission of information or alteration of user systems violates federal and state law, such as privacy statutes, the common law of trespass to chattels, and even computer crime laws. For example, the federal Computer Fraud and Abuse Act, in Section (a)(2)(C), provides criminal penalties for anyone who "intentionally accesses a computer without authorization or exceeds authorized access, and thereby obtains . . . information from any protected computer if the conduct involved an interstate or foreign communication. . . ."[179] If "the offense was committed for purposes of commercial advantage or private financial gain," it can result in a fine, imprisonment up to five years, or both.[180] The statute also provides for civil actions by persons who suffer damage or loss from a violation.[181]

The Computer Fraud and Abuse Act is not limited to cases involving "hackers" or "crackers." For example, it has been invoked in a civil dispute between a domain registrar and a hosting company.[182] And in late 2008, a

---

178. *See* LAWRENCE LESSIG, CODE VERSION 2.0 187 (2006).

179. 18 U.S.C. § 1030(a)(2)(C).

180. *Id.* § 1030(b)(2)(B)(i).

181. *Id.* § 1030(g).

182. Register.com v. Verio, Inc., 356 F.3d 393, 439 (2d Cir. 2004) (domain registrar accused hosting company of CFAA violations from using whois information in an unauthorized manner).

woman was convicted of misdemeanor violations of the Act for violating the terms of use governing the MySpace social site.[183] Lori Drew had allegedly sent hurtful messages to Megan Meier under a false identity, which the terms of use prohibited, and Meier subsequently committed suicide.[184] Whether or not the convictions stand, the case demonstrates that the Computer Fraud and Abuse Act potentially reaches well beyond acts traditionally considered computer fraud and abuse.

One reason for the extensive application of the Act is that the term "protected computer" includes any computer "which is used in interstate or foreign commerce or communication. . . ."[185] Almost any use of a computer on the Internet involves "interstate or foreign . . . communication," if not commerce. Moreover, the provision is triggered even if there is authorization to access the computer, but the access exceeds that which is authorized. The term "exceeds authorized access" means "to access a computer with authorization and to use such access to obtain or alter information in the computer that the accesser is not entitled so to obtain or alter. . . ."[186] When terms of use require compliance as a condition of access, violation of the terms makes access unauthorized or in excess of that authorized—even if the violator has never read the use terms.

Software providers are not immune from the Computer Fraud and Abuse Act. DRM techniques typically involve "accessing" the user's computer to "obtain information." For example, product activation and validation routines generate encrypted information about a particular machine's configuration. This identifier enables the provider to verify both that the product being installed is not an unauthorized copy and that the product is not activated more than once (or more than some other permitted number of times).

Windows Genuine Advantage, a Microsoft validation tool, tries to determine whether a "non-genuine" copy of Windows is installed on a machine. If it concludes that the copy is not genuine, it places the software in "reduced functionality mode." Given that the software in question is the operating system, this can substantially limit the user's access to his or her own computer. A 2007 article reports that "one in five computers running Windows have failed so-called Windows Genuine Advantage tests according

---

183. Jennifer Steinhauer, *Verdict in MySpace Suicide Case,* NEW YORK TIMES, Nov. 26, 2008.

184. 18 U.S.C. § 1030(g).

185. *Id.* § 1030(e)(2)(B).

186. *Id.* § 1030(e)(6).

to data from Microsoft."[187] Specifically, "[m]ore than 22 percent of over 500 million systems that were subjected to the browser-based validation scheme were identified as invalid copies of Windows."[188] This represents more than one hundred million failed attempts to validate Windows. The high number of failed attempts to validate Windows suggests that software piracy is indeed a serious problem. Microsoft asserts that the "false positive" rate—failed validations by legitimate licensees—is "under 1 percent."[189] But 1 percent of five hundred million is also a large number.

But whether or not product activation and validation techniques actually interfere with legitimate use of properly licensed software or with the use of one's own computer, these techniques do involve intentionally accessing the user's computer and obtaining information from it in what is likely to be an interstate or foreign communication. It therefore becomes essential for the provider of software that obtains the information to include appropriate authorization in the EULA to be able to use these common DRM techniques. DRM may provide low-cost enforcement of digital rights or restrictions, but without the permissions granted by the user in the EULA, the software provider could face unacceptable liability risks in applying it.

1.6 Licensor Exculpation

EULAs typically contain three interrelated types of exculpatory provisions. First, they disclaim most warranties, including implied warranties that would otherwise apply under Article 2 of the Uniform Commercial Code or, in the two states that have enacted UCITA, under its Part 4. Second, they limit the monetary value of any damages, usually to the price paid for a copy of the software, and they exclude consequential damages. Third, they include an integration clause, providing that any representations that are not part of the EULA's terms are not part of the parties' agreement, so that marketing claims about the software do not give rise to licensor obligations.[190]

---

187. Ken Fisher, *Windows Genuine Advantage Falsely Accuses Millions,* Ars Technica, Jan. 24, 2007, http://arstechnica.com/news.ars/post/20070124-8690.html.

188. *Id.*

189. *Id.*

190. Some licenses go even further, permitting the software provider to change the software as it sees fit. For example, the license for Norton Antivirus 2009 states that, to "optimize" the software, "Symantec may, at its discretion and without notice, add, modify or remove features from the Software at any time."

The practice, especially common in early EULAs, of warranting only the physical media presents an ironic counterpoint to the argument of EULA defenders, discussed in Chapter 2, that the license is necessary because the primary value of software resides not in the media, but in the "intangible" information. When it comes to EULA warranties, the user often receives no assurance that anything *but* the media will have any value at all. And in some cases, even replacement of the media may subject the user to an additional charge.

In early decisions, courts did not always enforce the exculpatory terms in software licenses. For example, in *Sierra Diesel Injection Service, Inc. v. Burroughs Corp.*,[191] the Ninth Circuit held, despite an integration clause, that a vendor's form contract documents did not constitute the entire agreement of the parties.[192] A statement in a letter that the system would "put your inventory, receivables and invoicing under complete control" was also part of the bargain in fact.[193] In *L.S. Heath & Son., Inc. v. AT&T Information Systems, Inc.*,[194] the Seventh Circuit concluded that the parties' contract included representations in a proposal document, despite an integration clause in the Master Agreement.[195]

Courts in software cases have also applied Section 2-719(2) of the UCC, which provides that contractual limitations on remedy for breach will not apply when "circumstances cause an exclusive or limited remedy to fail of its essential purpose. . . ." For example, in another early case, *RRX Industries, Inc. v. Lab-Con, Inc.*,[196] the contract limited damages to the amount paid for the software.[197] Because the software provider neither delivered a system that worked as represented nor fixed the bugs in the software, however, the limited remedies failed of their essential purpose, and the court held that neither the limitation on the damages amount nor an exclusion of consequential damages could be enforced.[198]

More recent decisions, following the general trend toward giving effect to EULA terms, have enforced the liability limitations in click-through EULAs.

---

191. 890 F.2d 108 (9th Cir. 1989).

192. *Id.* at 112–13.

193. *Id.* at 110.

194. 9 F.3d 561 (7th Cir. 1993).

195. *Id.* at 569.

196. 772 F.2d 543 (9th Cir. 1985).

197. *Id.* at 547.

198. *Id.*

In *Moore v. Microsoft Corp.,*[199] the plaintiff alleged, among other things, violations of the New York General Business Law and deceptive trade practices.[200] The court held that the Microsoft EULA was "a validly binding contract" that barred the claims.[201] The court stated,

> The terms of the EULA were prominently displayed on the program user's computer screen before the software could be installed. Moreover, the program's user was required to indicate assent to the EULA by clicking on the 'I agree' icon before proceeding with the download of the software. Thus, the defendant offered a contract that the plaintiff accepted by using the software after having an opportunity to read the license at leisure. As a result, the plaintiff's claims are barred by the clear disclaimers, waivers of liability, and limitations of remedies contained in the EULA (*see ProCD, Inc. v Zeidenberg, 86 F3d 1447; Specht v Netscape Communications Corp., 150 F Supp 2d 585*).[202]

The court added that, because "there was no warranty given by the defendant that the software product was error free," and because "the EULA specifically conformed to the requirements of the General Business Law and disclaimed all warranties, either express or implied," it followed that "the plaintiff's claim alleging statutory violations must fail. . . ."[203]

In some states, consumer protection law limits the effect of warranty disclaimers and liability limitations, and cases of outright fraud can be reached through tort law. But EULAs generally limit liability to the maximum extent permitted by such laws. As a result, they sharply reduce the software provider's exposure to liability for software defects and failures.

1.7 Dispute Resolution

Closely related to licensor exculpation clauses are provisions that require users, in the event of a dispute, to sue in the software provider's home

199. 741 N.Y.S.2d 91 (N.Y. App. Div. 2002).

200. *Id.* at 92.

201. *Id.*

202. *Id.*

203. *Id.*

jurisdiction or not to sue at all but to pursue arbitration. Arbitration clauses not only prevent the user from suing personally in court but also effectively block class actions. Parties to arbitration generally must bear the costs of the arbitration. Moreover, for many software products, the recoverable damages suffered by any one user may not be enough to persuade plaintiff's lawyers to take the case on a contingent fee basis unless it is a class action. As a result, choice-of-forum and arbitration clauses can effectively deprive users of remedies even when the EULA or another law might otherwise permit them.

The Federal Arbitration Act strongly favors the enforcement of arbitration clauses.[204] And for the most part, courts enforce these clauses in EULAs and similar agreements. In *Hill v. Gateway 2000, Inc.*,[205] the Seventh Circuit held that Gateway could enforce an arbitration clause against customers who sought to bring a class action lawsuit over alleged defects in Gateway products.[206] The court's opinion by Judge Frank Easterbrook, who authored *ProCD* the year before, frames the question in *Hill* as follows:

> A customer picks up the phone, orders a computer, and gives a credit card number. Presently a box arrives, containing the computer and a list of terms, said to govern unless the customer returns the computer within 30 days. Are these terms effective as the parties' contract, or is the contract term-free because the order-taker did not read any terms over the phone and elicit the customer's assent?[207]

The question, thus formulated, essentially answers itself. For good measure, in addition to describing legal considerations requiring that the arbitration clause be enforced, Easterbrook identifies the following "practical considerations":

> Cashiers cannot be expected to read legal documents to customers before ringing up sales. If the staff at the other end of the phone for direct-sales

204. 9 U.S.C. § 2 (an arbitration clause "shall be valid, irrevocable, and enforceable, save upon such grounds as exist at law or in equity for the revocation of any contract"). *See* Prima Paint Corp. v. Flood & Conklin Mfg. Co., 388 U.S. 395, 406–07 (1967) (even a claim of fraud in the inducement must be arbitrated if the arbitration clause itself was not induced by fraud).

205. 105 F.3d 1147 (7th Cir. 1997).

206. *Id.* at 1150–51.

207. *Id.* at 1148.

> operations such as Gateway's had to read the four-page statement of terms before taking the buyer's credit card number, the droning voice would anesthetize rather than enlighten many potential buyers. Others would hang up in a rage over the waste of their time. And oral recitation would not avoid customers' assertions (whether true or feigned) that the clerk did not read term X to them, or that they did not remember or understand it. Writing provides benefits for both sides of commercial transactions. Customers as a group are better off when vendors skip costly and ineffectual steps such as telephonic recitation, and use instead a simple approve-or-return device. Competent adults are bound by such documents, read or unread.[208]

Easterbrook assumes that the statement of terms is inevitably so long and complex that it could not be simply summarized over the phone. *ProCD* states a similar assumption—that the EULA would have to be printed in microscopic type to fit on the outside of a software box. There is no acknowledgment of even the possibility that keeping the EULA or other terms short and sweet would change this result.

On a few occasions, courts have declined to enforce arbitration clauses in online agreements, but they have done so under general principles that competently drafted EULAs are usually able to overcome. For example, in 2002, the Second Circuit held in *Specht v. Netscape Communications Corp.*[209] that users were not bound by an arbitration clause in a software license on a Web page when the users were not required to click assent and "could not have learned of the existence of [the license] terms unless, prior to executing the download, they had scrolled down the webpage to a screen located below the download button."[210] There was no manifestation of assent, because "a reasonably prudent Internet user in circumstances such as these would not have known or learned of the existence of the license terms" before downloading the software in question.[211] *Specht* is easily overcome by requiring the user to click "agree" before downloading the software or before using it.

---

208. *Id.* at 1149.

209. 306 F.3d 17 (2d Cir. 2002).

210. *Id.* at 20.

211. *Id.*

In another 2002 case, the Northern District of California denied PayPal's motions to compel arbitration of claims in an alleged class action.[212] The court held that an arbitration clause in PayPal's user agreement was unconscionable under California law.[213] Among other things, the user agreement required the user to arbitrate, but provided that, "in the event of a dispute, PayPal 'at its sole discretion' may restrict accounts, withhold funds, undertake its own investigation of a customer's financial records, close accounts, and procure ownership of all funds in dispute unless and until the customer is 'later determined to be entitled to the funds in dispute.'"[214] In addition, PayPal alone would make "the final decision with respect to a dispute," and PayPal reserved the right to change the terms of use without prior notice.[215]

In a 2007 case involving the terms of service for Second Life, an online virtual world, the Eastern District of Pennsylvania reached a similar result on a similar arbitration clause.[216] But as the court in that case also noted, the relevant standard under California law is only that "the arbitration remedy must contain a 'modicum of bilaterality.'"[217] Other recent decisions have followed *Hill*,[218] and it appears that most EULA arbitration clauses—especially when they do not involve control of a customer's funds—will continue to be enforced if they are reasonably mutual.[219]

1.8 Adware and Spyware

Nearly every computer user is familiar with "spyware," which can be defined as "programs that monitor user activities, and transmit user information to

212. Comb v. PayPal, Inc., 218 F. Supp. 2d 1165, 1166 (N.D. Cal. 2002).

213. *Id.*

214. *Id.* at 1173–74.

215. *Id.* at 1174.

216. Bragg v. Linden Research, Inc., 487 F. Supp. 2d 593, 608 (E.D. Pa. 2007) (Second Life terms of service contained "many of the same elements that made the PayPal user agreement substantively unconscionable for lack of mutuality").

217. *Id.* at 607 (quoting Armendariz v. Foundation Health Psychcare Servs., 6 P.3d 669, 692 (Cal. 2000)).

218. *E.g.*, Schultz v. AT&T Wireless Servs., 376 F. Supp. 2d 685, 692 (N.D. W.Va. 2005); Stenzel v. Dell, Inc., 870 A.2d 133, 137 (Maine 2005).

219. Courts have long shown "a reluctance to permit the right of access to courts to be waived inadvertently" through arbitration clauses. Restatement (Second) Contracts § 23 Comment e. This tendency suggests that any limitations on the enforcement of such clauses that do exist are not specific to EULAs.

remote servers and/or show targeted advertisements."[220] Spyware includes programs that "run continuously and show advertisements specifically responding to the web sites that users visit," as well as "keystroke recorders, screen capture programs, and numerous additional software systems that surreptitiously monitor and/or transmit users' activities."[221] Spyware has given rise to a number of lawsuits on various theories.

In *Sotelo v. DirectRevenue, LLC*,[222] the district court refused to dismiss an asserted class action against an alleged spyware provider, despite the existence of a EULA that authorized the provider to serve pop-up ads on the user's computer.[223] The court emphasized that the "plaintiff claim[ed] that he was not given notice of the EULA's existence prior to installation. . . ."[224] The "triable issue of fact" was whether the plaintiff had "agreed to the EULA," not whether such an agreement would be enforced.[225]

The court summarized at length the plaintiff's description of the harm that spyware causes:

> Plaintiff alleges that Spyware wreaks havoc on a computer and its user. Spyware destroys other software programs, and Spyware and the unsolicited advertisements that clog the screen cause computers to slow down, deplete Internet bandwidth and the computer's memory, and use pixels and screen-space on monitors. Productivity is decreased because hours are wasted attempting to remove Spyware from computers, closing recurring and frequent advertisements, and waiting for slowed machines. Users are forced to keep their slowed computers running longer, which uses more electricity, decreases the useful life of [a] computer, and forces the user to incur increased Internet access charges. It costs approximately $30 per year to purchase software to effectively remove Spyware and unwanted advertisements, and to guard against future infections.[226]

---

220. Benjamin Edelman, *"Spyware": Research, Testing, Legislation, and Suits*, http://www.benedelman.org/spyware/.

221. *Id.*

222. 384 F. Supp. 2d 1219 (N.D. Ill. 2005).

223. *Id.* at 1223.

224. *Id.* at 1228.

225. *Id.*

226. *Id.* at 1224–25.

Despite these many negative consequences, the court's definition of the triable issue of fact indicated that, if the plaintiff did have notice of the EULA, the court would uphold the terms granting the spyware provider permission to inflict these costs.

Indeed, in *People v. Direct Revenue LLC*,[227] the court held that a EULA was sufficient to authorize the alleged spyware.[228] The Attorney General of New York had sought injunctive and monetary relief "for allegedly deceptive and illegal practices relating to the installation of pop-up advertising software on consumers' computers."[229] An investigator conducted seven transactions with Direct Revenue. The court stated:

> In each of the seven cases, the investigator was presented with a computer hyperlink which specifically referred to Direct Revenue's end-user license agreement (EULA). A dialog box labeled "Security Warning" appeared each time, offering the user the option of accepting the terms of the EULA by clicking "Yes" or declining it by clicking "No." The accompanying message explained that by clicking on "Yes," the user acknowledged that he or she had read the EULA and agreed to be bound by its terms.[230]

On this basis, the court dismissed the Attorney General's petition. The court concluded that there could be no "deceptive conduct or false advertising" in the transactions with Direct Revenue, "insofar as all of the completed installations were authorized by the AG investigators in accordance with the terms of the EULA."[231]

1.9 And That's Not All

The kinds of terms discussed above are just some of the many provisions that EULAs contain. For example, although publishing a book review does

227. 2008 N.Y. Misc. LEXIS 5562 (Mar. 12, 2008).

228. *Id.* at *8.

229. *Id.* at *1. The court noted that, although the Attorney General's petition characterized the software as "spyware," the parties had agreed "that the software merely generates pop-up ads geared to a consumer's Internet usage." *Id.* at *2.

230. *Id.* at *4.

231. *Id.* at *8.

not require the permission of the book's author or other copyright owner, the software license terms for Microsoft SQL Server provide, "You must obtain Microsoft's prior written approval to disclose to a third party the results of any benchmark test of the software."[232] These terms, as well as the Windows license terms, state that you may conduct "internal benchmark testing" of .NET Framework components, but you may disclose the results of such testing only if you comply with conditions set forth at a specified Web address. Moreover, if you do disclose the results and you happen to be a competitor, "Microsoft shall have the right to disclose the results of benchmark tests it conducts of your products that compete with the applicable .NET Component, provided it complies with the same conditions. . . ."[233]

Watts Humphrey, a key IBM executive in the late 1960s, describes the "asset protection" strategy that IBM used for software when it was unbundled from hardware.[234] According to Humphrey, IBM considered trade secret protection "impractical," not because it would be lost by selling copies, but because, "once secrecy was breached, the trade secret would be lost."[235] IBM also believed that, "because many people would necessarily be involved with every software release, . . . the required level of secrecy would be impractical."[236] According to Humphrey, IBM chose a "copyright-licensing strategy" because software patentability was uncertain and copyright was all that was left.[237] But IBM "viewed copyright as a weak form of protection," and so "[t]o improve the level of protection, [IBM] coupled the copyright with a license and counted on the license to provide the real protection."[238]

---

232. This language appears in the license terms for both the Developer and the Enterprise versions of Microsoft SQL Server 2008.

233. Microsoft is not alone in imposing such restrictions. For example, the EULA for ThreatSentry security software provides, "You may not disclose the results of any benchmark tests of the SOFTWARE PRODUCT to any third party without prior written approval from Privacyware." On the other hand, "Privacyware may use any technical information provided to Privacyware in connection with any SOFTWARE PRODUCT support and maintenance services provided by Privacyware, including [but apparently not limited to] for product development and support."

234. Watts S. Humphrey, *Software Unbundling: A Personal Perspective,* IEEE Annals of the History of Computing 59, 60 (2002).

235. *Id.*

236. *Id.*

237. *Id.*

238. *Id.*

It is important to remember that, until 1989, copyright protection in the United States required affirmative acts by the author.[239] Publication of works without copyright notice and without registration resulted in placing the works in the public domain. As a result, copyright could relatively easily be lost through administrative inaction. Moreover, it was not until 1980 that Congress removed any doubt about the protection of computer programs under the Copyright Act.[240] With this confirmation, and with the Computer Software Rentals Amendment Act of 1990, there was less reason to believe, as IBM had in the early days, that copyright alone might be too "weak."

A new justification for the EULA was required. The proprietary EULA came to be defended as giving users the rights they need to avoid becoming copyright infringers—or even patent and trademark infringers and trade secret misappropriators—simply by using the software for which they have paid. But as discussed in this chapter, if users require licenses to use software, then it is the licenses themselves that create that need. They do so by providing that the user's copy of the software is licensed and not sold, so that the user is not the owner of a copy with the use rights that follow under Section 117(a)(1).

The Copyright Act provides a framework in which software can be protected by copyright but also can be commercially distributed in much the same way as books, without an express license. Section 117(a)(1) allows the owner of a copy of a computer program to make the copies necessary for use and backup. Section 109(b), as amended, narrows the first sale doctrine for computer programs to remove the risk of abuse from software rental. The use of end user software licenses is a choice, not a necessity.

Because the courts have overcome initial doubts about whether mass-market software licenses form binding contracts, the choice to use these licenses has altered the rules that would otherwise apply in numerous important respects. The unconditional right under Section 117(a)(1) of the owner of a copy to use the software is replaced by a right that can be qualified in any number of ways and that is entirely conditional on compliance with any and all terms in the license, so that violation of even one term can forfeit the entire license.

The right to copy public domain elements is overridden. The right to engage in fair use is overridden. The right to circumvent technological

---

239. Berne Convention Implementation Act of 1988, Pub. L. No. 100-568.

240. Computer Software Copyright Act of 1980, Pub. L. No. 96-517.

measures for interoperability is overridden. Rights against a software provider accessing one's own computer are overridden. Warranties that would otherwise apply and remedies that would otherwise be available under commercial law are overridden. Adware is permitted. Publishing test results on software is restricted. Moreover, the terms that effect these changes are so complex that merely understanding their full legal significance carries nontrivial costs.

Early decisions that protected access to public domain elements and the fair use privilege have given way to decisions, following the legal doctrine of freedom of contract and the economic doctrine of *ProCD,* that give the private authors of software licenses broad power to write the rules that govern software access and use. It remains to be seen whether this trend advances either the legal values or the economic objectives its advocates assert.

TWO

The Product Is the Product

A FAVORITE MAXIM OF EULA defenders is that, for software, "the license is the product."[1] If this statement is correct, then it follows that software products cannot exist without licenses. The proposition that the license is the product flows, in turn, from the claim that software products are "intangible." Raymond Nimmer, the principal drafter of the Uniform Computer Information Transactions Act, declares that the U.S. economy is experiencing "radical changes in the source of value and in how that value is commercially distributed."[2] Nimmer states,

> [T]he reality centers on a single fact: intangible assets dominate the economy and entail much different policy and transactional characteristics than transactions in the old economy. The transition is from a hard-goods economy toward an economy of information, services, and other intangibles. As a focus for transactions and legal policy, intangible subject matter invokes different policy and commercial frameworks than that applicable to goods or real estate.[3]

Nimmer proceeds from the premise that software products are "intangible" to the assertion that licenses, rather than sales of copies, are the appropriate means for distributing software.[4]

The view of software products as "intangible" reflects a tendency in the legal literature to attribute to software an almost mystical form. One recent law

---

1. Gomulkiewicz, *The License Is the Product*, at 896.
2. Raymond T. Nimmer, *Licensing in the Contemporary Information Economy* (2001), http://law.wustl.edu/journal/8/p99Nimmerbookpages.pdf.
3. *Id.*
4. *Id.* "Licensing invites and enables greater flexibility in allocating rights than a sale of goods. . . . The important commercial field of computer information licensing should not be force fit into the body of law for the unrelated subject of the sale of goods." *Id.*

student note colorfully remarks, "Software is a gossamer ship on an ethereal ocean."[5] Michael Rustad contrasts "intangibles" such as software with "goods such as VCRs, toasters, and televisions," which "are tendered to consumer/buyers in stores such as WalMart, K-Mart, and Target."[6] Rustad states, "To paraphrase Gertrude Stein, with intangibles there is no there there!"[7]

Such talk takes too literally Arthur C. Clarke's third law of prediction, which posits that "[a]ny sufficiently advanced technology is indistinguishable from magic."[8] If software is an "intangible" that has no physical existence, it only can be defined by a license or some other legal instrument, which in that case may qualify as the product. But WalMart and other stores that sell toasters and televisions also sell software products, such as Microsoft Windows and Microsoft Office. Consumers seem to believe that they are receiving something of substance for their money, and it is not the EULA.

Raymond Nimmer has devoted many years to efforts aimed at improving the commercial law that applies to licensing transactions, including mass-market software licenses. In drafting UCITA, Nimmer sought to do for the "information economy" what Karl Llewellyn, principal drafter of Article 2 of the Uniform Commercial Code, did for the sale of goods. Just as Llewellyn wanted to "unhorse" the law of sales, Nimmer wanted to replace a commercial code for old-fashioned "hard goods" with one for transactions in "information." Nimmer acknowledges that "[t]he idea that 'information' can be the subject matter of a commercial exchange is not new," but maintains that "the extent to which such transactions permeate the marketplace is new."[9] He asserts,

> The dominant types of contracts for intangible property are licenses, or other limited grants, in which the transferor retains the right to control

---

5. Seldon J. Childers, *Note: Don't Stop the Music: No Strict Products Liability for Embedded Software,* 19 U. FLA. J.L. & PUB. POL'Y 125, 141–42 (2008).

6. Michael L. Rustad, *The Uniform Commercial Code Proposed Article 2B Symposium: Commercial Law Infrastructure for the Age of Information,* 16 J. MARSHALL J. COMPUTER & INFO. L. 255, 302 (1997).

7. *Id.* The avant garde icon reportedly uttered her famous line when she searched for her childhood home in Oakland, California, and could not find it. Tenderbuttons: Gertrude Stein Online, http://www.tenderbuttons.com/gsonline/alice.html.

8. ARTHUR C. CLARKE, PROFILES OF THE FUTURE 21 n.1 (1973 ed.).

9. Raymond T. Nimmer, *Images and Contract Law: What Law Applies to Transactions in Information,* 36 HOUS. L. REV. 1, 4 (1999).

> not only the information, but also the uses of the information given to the transferee. This is a far different model than a sale of goods, which gives the buyer full rights in the subject matter (i.e., the item sold).[10]

According to Nimmer, the reason commercial issues relating to information industries entail "a vastly different enterprise than does manufacturing and distributing hard goods" is that "[t]he subject matter is intangible. . . ."[11]

As Nimmer mentions, Llewellyn described goods as "wares."[12] Nimmer maintains that "information" is different, but does not remark on the fact that software, indisputably, is also a ware. As noted in Chapter 1, the concept of "works of authorship" abstracts from actual physical instances or copies. But a software "work" is intangible precisely, and only, because it is an abstraction. Software, as a product, is not intangible at all, any more than a physical instance of a gasoline-electric hybrid engine is intangible because there are intangible patent claims that describe an invention the engine embodies. The tangible character of software products is significant not only for Nimmer's vision of a uniform law for transactions in "computer information," but also for the question whether the legislative license is somehow inevitable.

2.1 What Is Intangible Property?

The word "tangible" derives from the late Latin *tangibilis,* which means, literally, "capable of being touched."[13] For purposes of property law, and thus for transactions affecting property rights, "tangibility" of property does not necessarily mean that one can touch the property with a finger. Rather, according to *Black's Law Dictionary,* it means that the property "has physical

10. *Id.*

11. *Id.*

12. *Id.*

13. Webster's Third New International Dictionary, Unabridged (2002), http://unabridged.merriam-webster.com. One meaning of "tangible," in ordinary language, is "capable of being touched: able to be perceived as materially existent especially by the sense of touch." *Id.* Tangible can also describe things that cannot be physically touched—*e.g.*, "tangible benefits," "tangible goals." *Id.*

form and characteristics."[14] In contrast, "intangible property" is "[p]roperty that lacks a physical existence."[15]

The Oxford Dictionary of Law cites as examples of intangible property "choses in action" and intangible rights in land.[16] A "chose" (or "thing") in action is "a right (e.g. a right to recover a debt) that can be enforced by legal action."[17] As James E. Penner has explained, "[i]ntellectual property rights are akin to choses in action because they are abstract legal rights, with no direct connection to any thing. . . ."[18] Both choses in action (such as corporate stocks and bonds) and intellectual property rights (such as copyrights and patents) are intangible property. They are legal constructs described in words. If the law had no force, such property would have no value. The result is no different whether one refers to all instances or only a particular instance of such property.

Choses in action and intellectual property rights may be associated with physical tokens, and intellectual property rights may apply to physical things. For example, a stock certificate evidences the ownership of stock, and U.S. Letters Patent evidence the issuance of a patent by the Patent Office. In some cases, such as bearer securities, the rightholder's possession of the physical token may be necessary to enforce the right. Even in such cases, however, the physical token's value derives from the intangible property for which it stands, not from any other use that one can make of the token. Just as the intangible rights would have no value if the law had no force, the physical tokens associated with such rights would be, in most cases, worthless.[19]

On the high seas or a desert isle, beyond the reach of the law, a stock certificate has no value, apart from any value related to the possibility that it will be returned to a jurisdiction in which its attributed value once again applies (or perhaps, in the case of the desert isle, as a souvenir of what life was like before the shipwreck). In contrast, tangible property has value that goes beyond its purely legal attributes. The stock certificate is useless on the desert isle, but a

---

14. BLACK'S LAW DICTIONARY (8th ed. 2004).

15. *Id.* Similarly, according to the *Oxford Dictionary of Law*, tangible property is "[p]roperty that has a physical existence," whereas intangible property is "[p]roperty that has no physical existence." OXFORD DICTIONARY OF LAW (2006).

16. *Id.*

17. *Id.*

18. JAMES E. PENNER, THE IDEA OF PROPERTY IN LAW 119 (1997).

19. Some such tokens may acquire secondary value as things. For example, rare coins have value as collectibles. But such value attaches to the physical token, not to the abstract legal rights it represents.

banana has at least as much value there as elsewhere—and a powerful two-way radio probably has more value in the middle of the ocean than it does in most other places. The subject matter of tangible property rights, in other words, has intrinsic value apart from any value that the law alone attributes to it. The law defines the rights, but not the item to which they apply.

One can sell an item of tangible property with minimal contract terms. The terms are not the product, because they do not define the property. In the case of intangible property, on the other hand, the subject matter of the property right is a legal construct. The terms define the property because the property does not exist apart from the terms. If one wants to transfer a right to payment, the "thing" being transferred is not a material thing at all, but a type of "jural" or legal relation.[20] The definition of the payment right is the definition of the product. One could indeed say that, in the case of true intangible property, a legal instrument that defines the property is the product. But software is not that kind of property.

2.2 What Is Software?

"Software" began as a wry neologism. Thomas Haigh has pointed out that, during the 1950s, "*hardware* was already well known as a colloquial term for computer equipment."[21] Although computers always had to be programmed, it was "only around 1960" that "a well-informed data-processing manager [would] have nodded knowledgably if *software* came up in conversation."[22] Moreover, "[w]hen *software* did achieve currency, it was as hardware's complement, describing everything else the computer manufacturer provided."[23]

Today, the word "software" may be broadly defined to extend to "the entire set of programs, procedures, and related documentation associated with a system," but it includes, and typically centers on, computer programs.[24] Section 101 of the U.S. Copyright Act defines "computer program" as "a set of

---

20. Wesley Newcomb Hohfeld, Fundamental Legal Conceptions as Applied in Judicial Reasoning 36 (2000) (first published 1919).

21. Thomas Haigh, *Software in the 1960s as Concept, Service, and Product,* IEEE Annals of the History of Computing 5, 5 (2002).

22. *Id.*

23. *Id.*

24. Webster's Third New International Dictionary, Unabridged (2002), http://unabridged.merriam-webster.com.

statements or instructions to be used directly or indirectly in a computer in order to bring about a certain result."[25] The Copyright Act also treats computer programs as "literary works," which the Act defines as certain kinds of works that are "expressed in words, numbers, or other verbal or numerical symbols or indicia, regardless of the nature of the material objects, such as books, periodicals, manuscripts, phonorecords, film, tapes, disks, or cards, in which they are embodied."[26]

The Copyright Act definition of "computer program" includes three key elements: (1) a program is a "set of statements or instructions," (2) the statements or instructions are "to be used directly or indirectly in a computer," and (3) the nature or purpose of the use is "to bring about a certain result." All three elements must be present for the term to apply. A cookbook provides sets of instructions, and people use the instructions to bring about a certain result, but (unless the cookbook is for a computer that cooks) the instructions are not "to be used directly or indirectly in a computer." As a result, a cookbook (ordinarily) is not a computer program.

Deciding whether something is to be used in a computer (and therefore potentially qualifies as a computer program) requires defining "computer." As dictionary definitions reflect, "computer" can refer to "a person who calculates," which was its meaning before computing machines arrived.[27] Today, however, "computer" commonly refers to "a programmable electronic device that can store, retrieve, and process data."[28] The so-called von Neumann architecture of most modern general purpose computers includes (1) memory, (2) processor, (3) input, and (4) output.[29] In a typical current computer, the central processing unit, or CPU, includes an arithmetic/logic unit, which performs operations using Boolean logic, and a control unit, which steps the CPU through each program. Data lines or "buses" transfer data between the various components. The CPU can be implemented on a single integrated circuit as a microprocessor.

Although we may think of "hardware" and "software" as opposites, the distinction between the computer and the computer program is far less clear

25. 17 U.S.C. § 101.

26. *Id.*

27. Webster's Third New International Dictionary, Unabridged (2002), http://unabridged.merriam-webster.com.

28. *Id.*

29. Paul E. Ceruzzi, A History of Modern Computing 178 (1998).

than it seems. The typical computer's processor implements Boolean logic in an electronic circuit. For example, in the addition of two binary digits, A and B, the presence or absence of an input voltage above a given threshold represents the value of each binary digit, or bit—the presence of the voltage may stand for 1 and the absence of the voltage for 0 (or vice versa). The input voltages pass through an XOR (exclusive-or) gate and an AND gate. The output of the XOR gate is the sum bit, and the output of the AND gate is the carry bit. If A or B equals 1, but A and B do not both equal 1, then the sum bit equals 1; otherwise, the sum bit is 0. If A and B both equal 1, then the carry bit equals 1; otherwise, the carry bit is 0. Each 1 in the result corresponds to the presence of a requisite voltage at the output of the relevant gate, and each 0 corresponds to the absence of the voltage.

In principle, any algorithm that can be implemented on a computer can be implemented entirely in hardware, by constructing a series of logic gates that leads to the result. The earliest computers were "hard wired" for particular algorithms or "programmed" by plugging in and unplugging wires to change the circuit configuration.[30] For an algorithm that requires the repeated adding of binary digits, one could construct a machine that repeats the series of logic gates described above (or the more complete series of gates that would actually be required for a binary adder) as many times as there are bits to be added. In such a case, the hardware and the software would be, essentially, one and the same.

But the power of the general purpose computer comes from the ability of a user to "instruct" the processor to perform custom sequences of basic or often-used operations by loading a set of binary instructions into the computer's memory. The control unit ties the activity of the arithmetic/logic unit to the cycles of a clock so that very large numbers of operations can be performed very fast in a sequence dictated by the instructions. The instructions, collectively, are the program. A series of binary additions is performed not by building a new binary adder for every iteration but by repeatedly using a single binary adder under the program's control.

To instruct the processor, the program must be represented in a physical form that, when acted on by an appropriate device, produces an appropriate series of voltages in the processor. Each instruction includes an operation

---

30. Alexander Randall V, *Q&A: A Lost Interview with ENIAC Co-Inventor J. Presper Eckert*, COMPUTERWORLD, Feb. 14, 2006, http://www.computerworld.com/hardwaretopics/hardware/story/0,10801,108568,00.html.

code, or opcode, which specifies an operation to be performed, and (optionally) one or more operands. As another oversimplified example, if the binary opcode 00 specifies addition of the contents of two registers and placement of the result in a third register, and if registers A, B, and C are represented by the binary codes 00, 01, and 10, respectively, then to add the contents of A and B and store the result at C, a possible machine instruction would be 00000110. Any program, however compiled or interpreted, to add the two registers on a machine with this instruction set, must physically deliver this machine instruction so as to produce corresponding voltages within the processor.[31]

It should be obvious that a physical representation of a stored program capable of producing the appropriate series of voltages in the processor is neither magic nor a legal abstraction. The physically represented program is no less tangible than the processor on which it runs. That the representation of the program that is copied into memory for processing may have been reproduced from a remote copy through an Internet data transmission, rather than having been reproduced from a local copy on a magnetic or optical medium, makes no difference. Software can also be stored as "firmware" on read only or flash memories, in which case its tangible character is more apparent. But even on disk, and even when transmitted over distances by electronic means, software has a physical existence. Unlike a stock certificate, a copy of a computer program can have as much value on a desert isle—provided that one has a computer and an electric generator or plenty of spare batteries—as it has at home.

In the patent context, the Court of Appeals for the Federal Circuit has recognized the tangible character and effect of software even when it runs on a general purpose computer. The court has explained that programming a general purpose computer "creates a new machine, because a general purpose computer in effect becomes a special purpose computer once it is

31. Through the use of microcode, some processors run in "emulation" mode. The microcode engine translates machine code written for a given "instruction set architecture" into machine commands for the particular processor on which it is actually running. By this means, which was invented by Maurice Wilkes of Cambridge in the early 1950s and commercially introduced by IBM in its System/360 series in the 1960s, multiple processor designs across a computer product line or through successive generations of a processor—such as the Intel Pentium—can be compatible with a single instruction set architecture, and thus be capable of running programs written for that architecture. Even in the case of a processor running in emulation mode, however, the instructions ultimately are executed by producing a series of voltage changes in the processor's circuitry. *See* JON STOKES, INSIDE THE MACHINE: AN ILLUSTRATED INTRODUCTION TO MICROPROCESSORS AND COMPUTER ARCHITECTURE 69–73 (2007); PAUL E. CERUZZI, A HISTORY OF MODERN COMPUTING 148–49 (1998).

programmed to perform particular functions pursuant to instructions from program software."[32] As a result, an invention that can be implemented on a general-purpose computer nevertheless can give rise to "a specific machine to produce a useful, concrete, and tangible result."[33]

One reason that software may seem "intangible," despite its physical manifestation and effects, is that much of the history of computing has involved a progression toward increasingly higher levels of abstraction in computer programming. As a result of this process, the actual machine code on which the processor acts is largely unseen and forgotten. Lawrence Lessig states, "Object code is the code that the computer reads. If you display it on your machine, it will appear as gibberish."[34] Lessig highlights the source code of a software project as the "code that allows a programmer to . . . see what makes it tick."[35] But although machine code may appear meaningless to most observers, the code that the computer "reads" is not "gibberish" at all. In fact, it is ultimately the only code that matters, and it is the code that best demonstrates software's tangible nature.

When computers began to have memory that permitted the use of stored programs, the first small step toward distancing the user from the processor was the development of assembly language. In the example above, assembly language would substitute a "mnemonic," such as "add," for the opcode, and other alphanumeric symbols, such as "A," "B," and "C," for the codes associated with registers. Because lines of assembly code usually correspond one-to-one with lines of machine code, the assembler—which converts assembly code to machine code—performs a largely one-to-one conversion. Nevertheless, assembly code looks slightly less like voltages and slightly more like words. Macro assemblers, which let the user define a single symbol to represent a block of instructions or a value, led to further abstraction.

The next major step up in level of abstraction was the introduction of the compiler, which is a program (or set of programs) that (together with a linker, when statically linked libraries are used) converts code written in "higher-level" programming languages into machine code. Compilers dispense with

---

32. In re Alappat, 33 F.3d 1526, 1545 (Fed. Cir. 1994), abrogated in part by In re Bilski, 545 F.3d 943, 959 (Fed. Cir. 2008).

33. *Id.* at 1544. In *Bilski*, the court later discarded the "useful, concrete, and tangible result" test for patentability, *see* 545 F.3d at 959, but the reasoning of *Alappat* remains applicable to the software tangibility question.

34. Lawrence Lessig, *The Limits in Open Code: Regulatory Standards and the Future of the Net*, 14 Berkeley Tech. L.J. 759, 764 (1999).

35. *Id.*

the one-to-one correspondence between the higher-level source code and the object or target code. The programmer specifies logical processes without having to specify, or even fully to understand, how the processor actually will carry them out. The interpreter simplifies programming in a similar way. The user writes a program in the source code of the interpreted language and then, to run the program, actually runs the interpreter, which translates the program line by line into machine code and executes it. An early and still-popular interpreted language is BASIC, Beginner's All-Purpose Symbolic Instruction Code, created in the early 1960s at Dartmouth. Some interpreted languages, such as Java, involve converting source code to an intermediate representation (in Java called "byte code"), which is then interpreted by virtual machine software specific to each processor's actual physical architecture.

More recently, software tool providers have emphasized visual programming environments in which an increasing part of constructing a program can be performed without any programming, in the traditional sense, at all. For example, Microsoft Access permits the user to build databases and front-end applications through a point-and-click interface. Functional definitions are stored and a run-time engine interprets them to create the data, forms, and reports that make up the application software. By dragging objects onto forms and setting properties in drop-down windows, the user can achieve substantial functionality without writing any code in the traditional sense. If the tool user wants to add custom code, he or she can do so with the relatively simple Visual Basic for Applications language.

At one time, every computer "user" was also a "programmer." Today, the vast majority of users are not programmers at all. The very concept of computer users who are not also programmers reflects the ultimate abstraction of computer use. The current user interface is almost all metaphor. We start our computers to face a "desktop." We store files in "folders." When we are ready to delete them, we send them to the "trash" or the "recycle bin," depending on our operating system preference.[36] We engage in "cloud computing." It is easy to ignore the tangible physical correlates of these metaphors, but that makes them no less tangible.

---

36. *Cf.* Pamela Samuelson, Randall Davis, Mitchell D. Kapor, & J.H. Reichman, *A Manifesto Concerning the Legal Protection of Computer Programs*, 94 Colum. L. Rev. 2308, 2324–26 (1994) (describing the use of "conceptual metaphors" by programs).

2.3 Rivalry and Excludability

UCITA refers to software as "computer information." Characterizing software as "information" contributes to the confusion about whether software is tangible. As Mark Lemley explains, "[i]nformation is what economists call a pure 'public good,' which means both that its consumption is nonrivalrous—my use of an idea does not impose any direct cost on you—and that it is not something from which others can easily be excluded."[37] In this respect, information is similar to national defense. When one person benefits from national defense, the person's neighbor benefits from it no less, but there is no way to defend only those citizens who contribute to the cost. The problem of excludability encourages some individuals to be free riders. As a result, the market does not supply an optimal amount of national defense through voluntary exchange. The government must pay for defense through taxes (or, as has become more common in recent years, through massive debt).

Kenneth Dam, in an article about intellectual property protection for software, writes that "[t]he fundamental justification for creating property rights in the results of innovation is to deal with the appropriability problem," which he defines as "the inability of the innovator to appropriate the benefits of his own R&D investments. . . ."[38] Dam explains,

> This problem arises from the simple circumstance that in the absence of an intellectual property right, the innovator would not be able to recoup his research and development (R&D) costs in competition with those who, thanks to copying, were able to sell the product without incurring those costs; therefore, the rate of R&D would be less than it would be with an intellectual property right, and specifically, from an economic point [of] view, that rate would be less than optimal.[39]

As Lemley points out, it is not necessary that producers capture all the social surplus from what they create. "In a market economy, we care only that producers make enough return to cover their costs, including a

37. Mark A. Lemley, *Property, Intellectual Property, and Free Riding*, 83 Tex. L. Rev. 1031, 1046 (2005).

38. Kenneth W. Dam, *Some Economic Considerations in the Intellectual Property Protection of Software*, 24 J. Legal Stud. 321, 333 (1995).

39. *Id.*

reasonable profit. So long as that cost is covered, the fact that consumers value the good for more than the price, or that others also benefit from the goods produced, is not considered a problem."[40]

Even if "pure" information in some sense exists and is non-excludable, however, tangible information products can indeed be at least somewhat excludable. When information is delivered in a newspaper or magazine, someone may pick up a discarded, perhaps out-of-date and incomplete publication without paying, but those who do not pay can be excluded from access at the newsstand, when the product is fresh and undamaged. With digital information products, excludability is also possible. Tyler Cowen observes that software "successively becomes more or less" a public good "in response to changes in the relative ingenuity of its buyers and sellers."[41] It is less of a public good, because it is excludable, when technological means to prevent piracy succeed over user attempts to defeat such means. Digital rights management (DRM) techniques, when effective, make digital information products, including software, as excludable as any other. Without DRM, intellectual property law provides a basis for excludability, although enforcement costs are higher and enforcement may be less effective.

Likewise, even if pure information is nonrivalrous, because one person's consumption of the information does not diminish the information that remains for another person to consume and therefore imposes no direct cost on the other person, it does not follow that tangible information products, such as software, have this characteristic. One way to test the proposition that information products are nonrivalrous is to go for a ride on the subway, sit next to someone who is reading a newspaper, and read the person's newspaper over his or her shoulder. This experiment will show that information products are in fact rivalrous, at least in the sense that the consumption of any one copy of information by one person can indeed compete with consumption of that copy by another. Likewise, if consumption of a movie is otherwise non-rivalrous, it becomes rivalrous when the theater becomes overcrowded or the person sitting behind you starts taking phone calls.

Having someone read your newspaper over your shoulder or trying to watch a movie in a packed theater are cases in which more than one person is trying to consume the same *copy* of a tangible information product at the

---

40. Lemley, *supra* note 37, at 1046.

41. Tyler Cowen, *Public Goods and Externalities: Old and New Perspectives, in* PUBLIC GOODS & MARKET FAILURES: A CRITICAL EXAMINATION 1, 6 (1988).

same time. In a sense, both are congestion effects. What makes information products potentially nonrivalrous is that inherent copying costs tend to be low, and the consumption of one copy by one person usually does not directly affect the consumption of another copy by another person. With digital information products, such as software, the cost of producing an additional copy is essentially zero. If users can also freely copy the information product, the product may be *effectively* nonrivalrous.

The characterization of software as a product characterized by nonrivalrous consumption must be qualified by the fact that even the consumption of a different copy can be in some sense rivalrous. This potential rivalry is illustrated by trade secrets, which by definition derive their value from the fact that they consist of information that is not known to others.[42] Use of a trade secret by a competitor may effectively destroy the trade secret, *qua* trade secret, leaving no trade secret for its owner to "consume." This effect occurs even though the competitor uses a different copy of the secret. And even when information is not a trade secret, someone who pays to obtain it expecting a competitive advantage as a result may see that advantage disappear if others can freely access it. But if software is widely distributed to the public, and if sharing is otherwise possible, then the user is likely to be able to "share" an unprotected copy with other users without suffering any direct impairment of the software's use by the sharing user. Indeed, for some kinds of software products, such as multiplayer games, sharing with another prospective user may actually enhance the sharing user's enjoyment of the product.[43]

The character of information products as potential public goods has effects that are highly relevant to intellectual property law. As Christopher Yoo explains, "[t]he market failures associated with nonexcludability have traditionally provided one of the central justifications for copyright."[44] And the zero marginal cost (or "ZMC") of producing additional copies of

---

42. *See* UNIFORM TRADE SECRETS ACT § 1(4), which defines a "trade secret" as "information, including a formula, pattern, compilation, program, device, method, technique, or process, that: (i) derives independent economic value, actual or potential, from not being generally known to, and not being readily ascertainable by proper means by, other persons who can obtain economic value from its disclosure or use, and (ii) is the subject of efforts that are reasonable under the circumstances to maintain its secrecy."

43. *Cf.* CARL SHAPIRO & HAL R. VARIAN, INFORMATION RULES: A STRATEGIC GUIDE TO THE NETWORK ECONOMY 173–225 (1999) (describing network effects and "positive feedback").

44. Christopher S. Yoo, *Copyright and Public Good Economics: A Misunderstood Relation,* 155 U. PA. L. REV. 635, 645 (2007)

digital works, which creates the potential for information products to be nonrivalrous, has become part of the debate over the optimal level of copyright protection. The ZMC conundrum is that, to maximize welfare, price should fall to the level of marginal cost, because otherwise people who would pay more than the cost of producing an additional unit of a good would be deprived of the good even though they are willing to pay more than it costs to produce. When marginal cost is zero, this means that price should be zero. But pricing at zero, obviously, would leave the producer with "no incentive to produce the work in the first place."[45] The upshot is that "providing authors with sufficient incentive to produce creative works requires giving them the means to set prices that exceed marginal cost," which in turn "necessarily reduce[s] access below efficient levels. . . ."[46]

Despite the relevance of such questions in determining the scope of copyright and other forms of intellectual property protection, however, they imply neither that information products are intangible nor that such products are defined by, or consist of, the terms of customizable private licenses. The public good character of "pure" information, and the potential public good character of tangible information products if they are not made excludable by law, technology, or both, does not mean that complex contracts are necessary or desirable to regulate such products.

Ultimately, if software can be copied at minimal cost by users without legal or technical restrictions, then the software provider may be able to sell only one copy—the first—and conventional economics predicts that the software will be produced only if there is a single buyer willing to pay a price high enough to cover all the provider's costs. Although free and open source software presents an obvious challenge to this prediction, there are undoubtedly many software providers that would refrain from producing software in such a case. But this fact is at most a rationale only for recognizing property rights of some kind in software. It is not a rationale for using licenses that privatize the definition of such rights.

In contrast to software providers, suppliers of toasters—the good often contrasted with software by advocates of the "intangibility" view—do not have to worry that one person will buy the product and share copies of it for free with the rest of the world. This difference is because not everyone can use the same toaster at the same time—toaster consumption is

45. *Id.* at 646.

46. *Id.*

rivalrous—and because there is no practical way for other consumers to copy the toaster. Toasters are efficiently supplied because the benefits of owning a toaster can be largely confined to those who buy them. The effect of intellectual property rights and DRM is to make proprietary software products as excludable as toasters.

Information products have other economic characteristics that differentiate them in certain respects from other types of products, but these differences are a matter of degree and also do not make the license somehow necessary or inevitable. For example, the low cost to the software provider of producing copies means that most of the costs are fixed, whether the provider distributes one copy or one hundred. But as Carl Shapiro and Hal Varian point out, "Large fixed costs and small incremental costs—that is, substantial economies of scale—are hardly unique to information goods."[47] For example, one of the key characteristics of the pharmaceutical industry is that fixed costs (including R&D) "tend to be high relative to its variable costs in the sense that the variable or *incremental* cost of producing and packaging an additional batch of product tends to be quite small. . . ."[48] Pharmaceutical patents are intangible property, but pharmaceutical products are not.

The UCITA preface effectively summarizes the multiple misconceptions about software that underlie the "intangibility" rhetoric. The preface states, "A software product may be provided in the same form in two transactions, but in one case the user is authorized to make 100,000 copies and in the other merely to use a single copy at home. The value of the transaction inheres not in the tangible medium (if, indeed, any is used), but rather inthe license grant terms." Both the premises and the conclusions are erroneous.

The quoted statement assumes, contrary to fact, that software can be provided in a transaction in which not *any* "tangible medium" is "used." Software cannot be provided without the use of any tangible medium. Software must be "fixed in a tangible medium of expression," not only to be eligible for copyright protection but also to be stored and used in a machine. If the software is transmitted over the Internet, tangible media will be

47. *Id.* at 22.

48. Uwe E. Reinhardt, *The Pharmaceutical Sector in Health Care, in* PHARMACEUTICAL INNOVATION: INCENTIVES, COMPETITION, AND COST-BENEFIT ANALYSIS IN INTERNATIONAL PERSPECTIVE 34 (Frank A. Sloan & Chee-Ruey Hsieh, eds., 2007) (emphasis in original).

required at the origin and destination of the transmission, and the software will be sent in data packets that will be copied multiple times onto various tangible media, albeit for short periods of time, in the course of transmission. Software does not travel by extrasensory perception.

In addition, the assertion that the transaction's value "inheres not in the tangible medium . . . but rather in the license grant terms" erroneously assumes that these are the only two possibilities. In fact, the value of software lies neither in the disk or other medium on which it is stored nor in the license terms under which it is distributed, but in the physical copy of the software that produces physical effects in the computer.

Finally, the UCITA preface is also mistaken in suggesting that, because "[a] software product may be provided in the same form in two transactions, but in one case the user is authorized to make 100,000 copies and in the other merely to use a single copy at home," the two transactions involve two different "products." If the copies of the software product are all the same, then the two transactions do not involve two products. Rather, they involve one product in two different quantities. One can buy one toaster or one hundred thousand toasters of the same design, but the toaster is still the product. The same is true for software. In both cases, one hundred thousand tangible physical artifacts are required.

2.4 No Ghost in the Machine

The view that software is intangible asks us to believe that software (literally) is a "ghost in the machine." The philosopher Gilbert Ryle introduced this term in 1949—not, of course, in relation to software, but to describe the doctrine that "[w]ith the doubtful exception of idiots and infants in arms every human being has both a body and a mind," which are "harnessed together" until the body dies, after which the mind "may continue to exist and function."[49] According to this doctrine, "[h]uman bodies are in space and are subject to the mechanical laws which govern all other bodies in space . . . [b]ut minds are not in space, nor are their operations subject to mechanical laws."[50] In other words, the body is tangible, but the mind is not.

49. GILBERT RYLE, THE CONCEPT OF MIND 11 (2000) (first published 1949).

50. *Id.*

Ryle contends that the "dogma" of the ghost in the machine is "entirely false," because it rests on a "category-mistake."[51] To illustrate, Ryle tells the following story:

> A foreigner visiting Oxford or Cambridge for the first time is shown a number of colleges, libraries, playing fields, museums, scientific departments and administrative offices. He then asks 'But where is the University? I have seen where the members of the Colleges live, where the Registrar works, where the scientists experiment and rest. But I have not yet seen the University in which reside and work the members of your University.' It has then to be explained to him that the University is not another collateral institution, some ulterior counterpart to the colleges, laboratories and offices which he has seen. The University is just the way in which all that he has already seen is organized.[52]

Like the mind-body dichotomy, the doctrine of software as intangible reflects a kind of dualism. Rustad suggests, "[T]hink of the difference between the price paid at Coconuts record store for a blank compact disk and the latest Oasis or Jewel release. The physical medium is incidental to the transfer of information which is the value being transferred. The information embedded upon a CD-ROM constitutes value not CD-ROM as a physical medium."[53] The commentator who argues that software is intangible because most of the value does not reside in the media is a like a person who sees the encoded disk and asks, "But where is the software?" The assumption is that "software" is an extra member of a class of which the encoded disk is a member. In fact, however, "software" is to the encoded disk as "the University" is to its colleges, laboratories, and offices. One is as tangible as the other.

If most of the value of a software product resides in the "information," rather than in the medium, software is not unique in this respect. In keeping with the mind-body analogy, consider the body itself. In a 1973 episode from the first season of the television series *M*A*S*H,* Hawkeye Pierce remarks, "Without love, what are we worth? 89 cents. 89 cents worth of chemicals

---

51. *Id.* at 15–16.

52. *Id.* at 16.

53. Michael L. Rustad, *The Uniform Commercial Code Proposed Article 2B Symposium: Commercial Law Infrastructure for the Age of Information,* 16 J. MARSHALL J. COMPUTER & INFO. L. 255, 267 n.54 (1997).

walking around lonely."[54] Perhaps because of inflation, the cost of the raw elements in the human body has increased, according to a 2003 article in *Wired,* to $17.18.[55] But the same article—entitled *How to Sell Your Body for $46 Million*—reports that you could sell the "reusable" parts of your body, such as bone marrow and various organs, antibodies, and enzymes, for vastly larger sums.[56] These body parts derive this considerably enhanced value from the "information" that, through evolution, is encoded in DNA and expressed in proteins, giving them their structure and function. The "medium" may be $17.18 worth of chemicals, but the "product" is worth (even just in monetary terms) far more. This does not mean that humans are "intangible."

Consider also the contingent nature of the relationships between software and media and between mind and body. Ryle pointed out that, in mind-body dualism, the belief is that the person's "body and his mind are ordinarily harnessed together, but after the death of the body his mind may continue to exist and function. . . ."[57] But in fact, each person infers the existence of other "minds" from observation of the behavior of other bodies, and in every case we observe, the behavior of other bodies after death provides no basis to infer that the mind continues to exist or function. The consistent absence of evidence that the mind survives the body's death supports the conclusion that mind and body are not independent.

Applying the same analysis to software, we find that, if you destroy the physical copy, the software cannot function. In a series of tax cases regarding eligibility for the investment tax credit, which applies only to "tangible" property, federal courts have relied on this observation to reject the idea that software is "intangible" because its value does not primarily reside in the media in which it is fixed. In *Comshare, Inc. v. United States,*[58] the Sixth Circuit held that "what matters . . . is that the value of the source code and the associated intangible rights was entirely dependent upon the existence of the tapes and discs."[59] The software "could not exist in usable form without

---

54. The Quote Garden, Quotations from *M*A*S*H,* http://www.quotegarden.com/mash.html.

55. Start, *How to Sell Your Body for $46 Million,* WIRED 11.08, Aug. 2003.

56. *Id.*

57. GILBERT RYLE, THE CONCEPT OF MIND 11 (2000) (first published 1949).

58. 27 F.3d 1142 (6th Cir. 1994).

59. *Id.* at 1149.

the tangible medium."[60] In *Norwest Corp. v. Commissioner*,[61] the Tax Court held on similar grounds that software acquired without any associated exclusive intellectual property rights constituted tangible personal property eligible for the ITC.[62]

There is, of course, a difference between software and minds. Software can be reproduced in multiple copies. For now, at least, minds cannot be reproduced in multiple bodies. But ease of reproduction is analytically distinct from the duality question. When software is first written, before a second copy is made, the software cannot survive its physical destruction any more than the human mind can survive the destruction of the brain. If a computer crashes immediately after the code is written and stored in volatile memory, before the code has been saved to disk or backed up, there is no code. Any attempt to recreate the code depends on human memory, and even if the author's memory is photographic, re-creation is required. It would be unwise to tell the software author who has just spent two hours writing a program, only to have it disappear because of a hardware failure, that—because software is intangible—nothing has been lost.

In 2003, revisions were proposed in Article 2 of the Uniform Commercial Code, which applies to transactions in goods, to exclude "information" from "goods." Nimmer writes, "The Official Comments to the proposed revisions of Article 2 explain that Article 2 would not apply to digital copies, even though they are on a diskette. The information, not the plastic, counts."[63] But consider the toaster with which Rustad and the UCITA prefatory note both contrast software. The toaster presumably is made of plastic and metal. Does anyone, to paraphrase Nimmer, "truly believe" that the plastic and metal "matters more than" the design and arrangement of the plastic and metal? If the toaster were melted down, its value would be little more than the value of the plastic in a disk. Any number of products that are indisputably tangible derive their value primarily not from the raw materials used in their manufacture but from the information embodied in their design. In this respect, software is no different.

---

60. *Id.*

61. 108 T.C. 358 (1997).

62. *Id.* at 375.

63. Raymond T. Nimmer, *Emerging Trends in Commercial Law: Surviving Tomorrow's Challenges: Panel 1: A Modern Template for Discussion*, 2 DePaul Bus. & Comm. L.J. 623, 648 (2004).

2.5 Software as a Service

Not to be confused with software intangibility is the emergence of "software as a service"—or SaaS—and the rise of Web-based and other remotely hosted software applications. When software applications are stored and executed on network servers and accessed through remote client software, the user does not necessarily install or even run a copy of the primary applications software on a local disk at all. Access to SaaS may be priced on the basis of usage or other metrics.

Running software remotely in no way implies that the software is intangible. Processing occurs mainly on a remote server, rather than on the user's machine, and SaaS more readily accommodates central management of applications and data. But the software is just as tangible as in any other distribution arrangement. Because the user does not install or even receive a complete copy of the software, the concept of ownership of a copy may be more difficult to apply, but it does not follow that complex licensing is necessary.

Merely granting access to copyrighted content, whether or not it is interactive, does not require a copyright license. The viewer of a pay-per-view film needs no license to watch it, even when watching includes interacting with menus. The fragmentary and transient partial copying that occurs in streaming the film is not, at least so far, regarded as the equivalent of the copying that occurs when software is installed on a computer disk or copied into a computer's memory.[64] And if such copying, when it occurs in connection with remote access to SaaS, rises to the level that would be potentially infringing without a license, the fragmentary local copies that result can be viewed as having been sold to the user, obviating any license.

UCITA uses the term "access contract," which it defines in Section 102(a)(1) as "a contract to obtain by electronic means access to, or information from, an information processing system of another person, or the equivalent of such access." UCITA provides, by definition, that an access contract is a kind of "license." But UCITA does not say which intellectual property rights, if any, are being licensed in such a contract. Apart from defining the access

---

64. *See* Cartoon Network LP, LLLP v. CSC Holdings, Inc., 536 F.3d 121, 129-30 (2d Cir. 2008) (holding, in a challenge to remote storage digital video technology, that there is no copying for purposes of the Copyright Act when copyrighted works remain in the buffers for only a transitory period).

contract as a license, UCITA offers no particular justification for treating it as one or for viewing licensing as inevitable for providing access to software.

Section 601(a) of UCITA states that, "[i]f an access contract provides for access over a period of time," then the "licensee's rights of access are to the information as modified and made commercially available by the licensor from time to time during that period." The only circumstance in which a "change in the content of the information" is regarded under UCITA as a breach of contract is if "the change conflicts with an express term of the agreement." Therefore, as long as the "access contract" does not specifically prohibit a particular change in the information content, the licensor can change the information in any way the licensor may choose. This is one reason among many that UCITA is regarded as pro-vendor.

There is, of course, a time dimension involved as well. Whereas selling a copy of software confers on the owner of the copy a perpetual right, under Section 117(a)(1), to engage in the copying necessary to use the software, providing access credentials has no automatic permanent effect under the Copyright Act. The credentials, in fact, are often provided by monthly subscription. In that sense, some form of "access contract" may be required. But it does not follow that the access contract is "the product," and it definitely does not follow that a privately written set of rules necessarily must govern access terms. With some inclusion of the time dimension in the definition of software copies that can be owned and therefore used pursuant to Section 117(a)(1) of the Copyright Act, SaaS and other time-limited software is tangible and could be distributed largely or entirely within the statutory framework without additional license terms.

2.6 Implications of Tangibility

If software products are tangible, then the license is not the product. Rather, the tangible product is the product. There is nothing inevitable about the license. There is no reason, in principle, why selling of copies of software must be different from selling toasters. One can buy one software copy or one toaster, and one can buy one hundred software copies or one hundred toasters. As a practical matter, if the software is not protected by DRM measures, then the software is easier to copy than the toaster. But if the EULA is justified, it must be justified on grounds other than software "intangibility."

THREE

Very Long Text

The Reality of the EULA

AN ARTICLE IN UNCYCLOPEDIA ("the content-free encyclopedia that anyone can edit") provides the best practical description of the software license.[1] The article defines "license" as "a synonym for *very long text.*" It adds, "Another synonym for license is legalese or *lawyer-readable code.*" Although rarely considered in legal analysis, the sheer impenetrability of license text is highly pertinent.

Defenders of the proprietary end user license agreement argue that the EULA promotes—and indeed is essential for—efficiency.[2] According to this argument, the transaction costs to software providers would be far too high if separate licenses were negotiated with every user. The argument assumes, however, that any kind of license is required. As discussed in Chapter 2, software is not "intangible," and the software, not the license, is the product. Licenses remain an option, but there is reason to believe that EULAs as they exist today actually reduce efficiency. They do this by creating a legal regime that is known to and understood (more or less) by the software provider but that is effectively hidden from the user. In other words, the license is the *problem.*

Contract law imposes a "duty to read" in the sense that not having read a contract is not a defense to its enforcement.[3] And standard-form contracts are nothing new. An official comment to the Restatement (Second) of Contracts, issued nearly thirty years ago, frankly acknowledges that "[a] party who makes regular use of a standardized form of agreement does not ordinarily expect his customers to understand or even to read the standard terms."[4] Vendors use standard-form agreements "to eliminate bargaining over details of individual transactions, and that purpose would not be served

1. "License," Uncyclopedia, http://uncyclopedia.org/wiki/License.

2. *See* Gomulkiewicz & Williamson, *Brief Defense,* at 338.

3. *See* Restatement (Second) Contracts § 23 Comment e (1981).

4. *Id.* § 211 Comment b.

if a substantial number of customers retained counsel and reviewed the standard terms."[5]

Contrary to the comment's apparent assumption, being able to read and understand the terms is relevant to more than just a possible negotiation. Even when the basis on which terms are presented is "take-it-or-leave-it," understanding them can inform the customer's decisions regarding whether to take or leave. But the Restatement makes clear that, as a matter of contract law, assent is no less effective merely because a party does not read or understand the terms. People who agree without reading "understand that they are assenting to the terms not read or not understood, subject to such limitations as the law may impose."[6]

So one can blame the user for clicking "agree" to license terms without reading them. But the EULA effectively creates private intellectual property and commercial law, and as far as the objectives of such law are concerned, a "duty-to-read" argument misses the point. Users act quite rationally in declining to read the license, because the cost of attempting to understand the legal significance of the license outweighs the prospective benefit. The result is information asymmetry between the provider and the user. The software provider, as creator of the terms, knows what they say and generally understands their significance. The user, on the other hand, lacks such knowledge. The problem with this asymmetry is that it drives "good" software licenses, from the user's perspective, out of the market. Because users are not able, at reasonable cost, to discriminate among licenses, software providers are left with no incentive to provide more favorable licenses to attract users. Like used cars, software licenses quite naturally tend to be "lemons."

The Internet does not, in this case, come to the rescue. Blogs and Web sites occasionally comment on objectionable EULAs, and on rare occasions such comments produce EULA changes. Such cases, however, are the exception. They are likely to remain so, because—as loquacious as bloggers are on other topics—the incentive to comment on EULAs is low. And because many of those who would otherwise make such challenges instead are active in the free and open source software movement and do not devote significant

5. *Id.*

6. *Id.*

efforts to changing proprietary EULAs (an activity that would probably be futile in any event).

EULA defenders maintain that the "flexibility" of the EULA makes it superior to the more limited set of rights defined by the Copyright Act (and other intellectual property law). In making this contention, they rely in part on the assertion that most users know little about the Copyright Act. But most users have no more understanding of the EULA, and the complexity and multiplicity of EULAs makes it even less likely that anyone will acquire that understanding. As between a solution that relies on public law and a solution that relies on the private law of the license, even at this late date, the case for the EULA remains unmade.

3.1 Software License Readability

The linguist Rudolf Flesch found that shorter sentences and sentences with shorter words are easier for people to understand.[7] Based on this seemingly obvious but often unrecognized insight, Flesch developed numerical scales, or "yardsticks," for measuring the readability of texts. The Flesch "reading ease" formula is based on the average number of words per sentence (average sentence length, or ASL) and the average number of syllables per word (average word length, or AWL). The formula is as follows:

$$\text{Reading Ease} = 206.835 - (1.015 \times \text{ASL}) - (84.6 \times \text{AWL})$$[8]

Take the first three paragraphs of *The Pet Goat.*[9] This is the story that former president George W. Bush continued reading to a group of school children at Emma E. Booker Elementary School in Sarasota, Florida, on September 11, 2001, for more than seven minutes after being informed that the United States was under attack. The first three paragraphs contain 12 sentences, 82 words, and 83 syllables, making average sentence length equal to 6.833 words and average word length equal to 1.012 syllables—every

7. *See* RUDOLF FLESCH, THE ART OF PLAIN TALK 56–57 (1951).

8. *See* Rudolf Flesch, *A New Readability Yardstick,* 32 JOURNAL OF APPLIED PSYCHOLOGY 221, 225 (1948).

9. Siegfried Engelmann & Elaine C. Bruner, *The Pet Goat,* in READING MASTERY II, STORYBOOK 1 153 (1995).

word but one has only one syllable. The readability score is calculated as follows:

$$\text{Reading Ease} = 206.835 - (1.015 \times 6.833) - (84.6 \times 1.012)$$
$$\text{Reading Ease} = 206.835 - 6.935 - 85.615 = 114.285$$

The maximum possible reading ease score is 121.2. The story's reading ease score of 114.3 is extremely high, as one would expect.

The Flesch-Kincaid "grade level" formula uses the same variables—words per sentence and syllables per word—but with a different result. Rather than calculating a readability value in which higher scores are better, Flesch-Kincaid results in a number that corresponds to the educational grade level at which readers are more likely than not to understand the text. The Flesch-Kincaid formula is as follows:

$$\text{Grade Level} = (0.39 \times \text{ASL}) + (11.8 \times \text{AWL}) - 15.59$$ [10]

For the first three paragraphs of *The Pet Goat,* the grade level score is as follows:

$$\text{Grade Level} = (0.39 \times 6.833) + (11.8 \times 1.012) - 15.59$$
$$\text{Grade Level} = 2.665 + 11.942 - 15.59 = -0.983$$

This grade level score, which rounds to -1.0, means that even a kindergartener would be likely to understand the text.

A 2004 op-ed column in the *New York Times* by Paul Krugman includes a paragraph about Bush's reading of the pet goat story on 9/11.[11] This paragraph in Krugman's column contains 2 sentences, 50 words, and 75 syllables, making average sentence length equal to 25 words and average word length equal to 1.5 syllables. The result is a Flesch-Kincaid grade level score of 11.9. A college student would be likely to understand the paragraph. Considering that Krugman is a college professor, this score seems about right.

10. J. Peter Kincaid, Robert P. Fishburne, Jr., Richard L. Rogers, & Brad S. Chissom, Derivation of New Readability Formulas (Automated Readability Index, Fog Count and Flesch Reading Ease Formula) for Navy Enlisted Personnel, Research Branch Report 8-75, Naval Air Station Memphis, Feb. 1975, at 14.

11. Paul Krugman, *Moore's Public Service,* NEW YORK TIMES, July 2, 2004.

Software marketing and support materials tend to fall somewhere between *The Pet Goat* and Krugman's commentary on Bush's reading of it. For example, the product screen for the Adobe Acrobat family on the Adobe Web site features a series of choices accompanied by short sentences: "Share your ideas/Control your work/Work better with everyone/Simplify form creation/What's new." These five sentences contain 15 words with 25 syllables. The Flesch-Kincaid grade level score is 5.3. Sixth-graders should understand the choices. The User Guide for Adobe Reader is only modestly more difficult. The preface to the User Guide's second chapter, which explains the basic use of the software, receives a Flesch-Kincaid score of 7.1. By the eighth grade, most readers should understand this language from the User Guide.

The EULA for Adobe Reader, on the other hand, is much different. The Reader EULA begins with an all-capital-letters notice admonishing that, by using, copying, or distributing all or part of the software, the recipient accepts all the terms and conditions of the contract, "INCLUDING, IN PARTICULAR THE LIMITATIONS ON: USE CONTAINED IN SECTION 2; TRANSFERABILITY IN SECTION 4; WARRANTY IN SECTION 7; AND LIABILITY IN SECTION 8." The use limitations in Section 2 appear in one paragraph, and each of Sections 4, 7, and 8 is one paragraph. These four paragraphs, to which the EULA draws special attention, contain a total of 667 words, with 30.3 words per sentence and 1.8 syllables per word. As a result, the Flesch-Kincaid grade level for the four "limitations" paragraphs is a whopping 17.3—more than ten grades of formal education higher than for the text from the Adobe User Guide.

The Flesch-Kincaid score of 17.3 means that, to be likely to understand these four key paragraphs of the Adobe Reader EULA, the user must have at least 17.3 years of formal education—12 years of education through high school, plus four years of college, plus another 1.3 years of graduate or professional school. Even a first-year law student, having completed fewer than 17 years of formal education, could be expected to have difficulty with the sheer complexity of the text. The paragraph in Section 2 that states what "you may not" do with the software contains 169 words, with 33.8 words per sentence and 1.8 syllables per word, for a Flesch-Kincaid Grade Level score of 19.3. Even a law school graduate, with only 19 years of formal education, could be forgiven for having trouble with this key portion of the license.

Apple's iTunes software license is only slightly more readable than Adobe's license for Reader. The iTunes license as a whole receives a Flesch-Kincaid grade level score of 16.0. This score suggests that only on graduation from

TABLE 1 Readability of Selected Texts

Text	*Flesch-Kincaid Grade Level Score*	*Reader Likely to Understand*
The Pet Goat—first three paragraphs	−1.0	Kindergartener
Paul Krugman op-ed—paragraph about Bush reading *The Pet Goat* on 9/11	11.9	College Student
Adobe Acrobat Product Screen—sentences describing Web site choices	5.3	Sixth Grader
Adobe Reader User Guide—second chapter preface explaining basic use	7.1	Eighth Grader
Adobe Reader EULA—four "limitations" paragraphs	17.3	Second-Year Graduate Student
Adobe Reader EULA—use limitations paragraph	19.3	Post-Doctoral Student

college (which represents the completion of 16 years of formal education) is a student finally likely to understand the terms on which he or she has been using iTunes throughout his or her youth. Section 2 of the license, which grants permission to use the software, receives a Flesch-Kincaid grade level score of 18.4—indicating that the reader must be more than two years into graduate or professional school to be likely to understand this essential clause.

Robert Gomulkiewicz and Mary Williamson assert that "EULAs provide valuable information to end users."[12] Given the extremely low readability of such licenses, however, it seems highly doubtful that EULAs are informative to anyone. Even attempting to read a EULA often involves scrolling through dense text in a small window. Indeed, in a more recent article, Gomulkiewicz himself comes closer to the reality of the EULA:

> Under . . . real world circumstances, the EULA stands little chance of being eloquent, stylish, or even particularly readable. No one systematically re-thinks the business-deal points that are reflected in the words of the EULA, especially the boilerplate at the end of the document. Some say

12. Gomulkiewicz & Williamson, *Brief Defense*, at 338.

> that that is just fine with software publishers, maybe even their goal—that they are intent on obfuscation not clarity. However, in my experience, software business-people and their legal counsel seldom cynically connive to create an impenetrable EULA. It just happens naturally.[13]

The result, he acknowledges, is the software license as lengthy "legalese":

> End-users, of course, only see the net result—a wordy license, written in legalese, crammed onto a small piece of paper or displayed electronically with little thought given to its presentation. A curious user may read a bit of it. He or she may quickly skim the document for onerous terms. On rare occasions the user will ask a lawyer to help interpret the license. Usually, however, the user does not read the license at all.[14]

3.2 Software License Efficiency

Gomulkiewicz and Williamson maintain that EULAs "promote efficient software transactions"[15] by enabling software providers to distribute software with "very low transaction costs."[16] But in fact, EULAs reduce efficiency by creating and exacerbating an information gap between the software provider and the user. Although EULAs may lower the transaction costs of software providers as compared to individually negotiated licenses, they impose high transaction costs for any customer wishing to understand the EULA's legal effect. And in making the costs of such an understanding prohibitive, they give the software provider an asymmetric information advantage. This asymmetry results in transaction terms that are inefficient.

There is, of course, nothing to stop the user from retaining legal counsel to review the license terms before the user clicks "agree." The Apple Software License Terms for OS X, after affirming that the licensed software can be used to reproduce materials, states that it is licensed only for reproduction of

---

13. Robert W. Gomulkiewicz, *Getting Serious about User-friendly Mass Market Licensing for Software,* 12 Geo. Mason L. Rev. 687, 693–94 (2004) [hereinafter Gomulkiewicz, *Getting Serious*] (footnotes omitted).

14. *Id.* at 694 (footnote omitted).

15. Gomulkiewicz & Williamson, *Brief Defense,* at 341.

16. *Id.* at 342.

materials that the user has the right to copy and advises: "If you are uncertain about your right to copy any material, you should contact your legal advisor." For most consumers, however, and for many business firms with a relatively small investment in the software in question, the cost of consulting a legal advisor over a question of license interpretation exceeds the amount the user is willing to pay for the software. Even in a substantial corporation, the cost of reviewing every license that any employee is asked to click in the course of employment may be prohibitive.

For commercial software products, as between individually negotiated licenses and standard-form licenses, the argument of Gomulkiewicz and Williamson for the standard-form license is not without merit. Through mass distribution, the large costs of developing a complex piece of software are spread across thousands or millions of users. Because of this cost spreading, an individual user, for only a few hundred dollars, can gain access to software that may have cost tens of millions of dollars to develop. The ability of software providers to charge such relatively low prices depends on keeping transaction costs low. If the provider were required to enter into individually negotiated contracts with each user, causing transaction costs to be substantially increased, then the software would cost much more or would not be available.

But the efficiency problem with EULAs does not result from the absence of individual negotiation Rather, it results from a disparity of information regarding the transaction terms. As Michael Meyerson, writing about form contracts in general, observed in a 1990 article, "The characteristic of form contracts that raises the greatest concern for efficiency is not . . . that they are offered on a take-it-or-leave-it basis."[17] Rather, "inefficient transactions occur because consumers do not read form contracts, or do not understand the terms, and are thus unaware of their contents."[18] Indeed, "the businesses that draft these contracts do so knowing that they will not be read by the typical consumer."[19] Moreover, consumers often have good reason not to read standard-form contracts, because "the benefit to be derived from acquiring adequate knowledge of contract terms is usually low and is likely

---

17. Michael I. Meyerson, *The Efficient Consumer Form Contract: Law and Economics Meets the Real World,* 24 GA. L. REV. 583, 595 (1990).

18. *Id.*

19. *Id.*

to be far exceeded by the significant costs of acquiring that information."[20] As a result, "it is rational for even a conscientious consumer to pay little, if any, attention to subordinate contract terms."[21]

For contracts to yield efficient terms, it is not necessary that consumers be able to negotiate them, but it is necessary for consumers to be able, at acceptable cost, to understand them, so that they can make informed choices in the marketplace. Richard Posner, in earlier editions of his classic treatise on law and economics, described the idealized process in which such choices should occur:

> If one seller offers unattractive terms, a competing seller, wanting sales for himself, will offer more attractive terms. The process will continue until the terms are optimal. All the firms in the industry may find it economical to use standard contracts and refuse to negotiate with purchasers. But what is important is not whether there is haggling in every transaction but whether competition forces sellers to incorporate in their standard contracts terms that protect the purchasers.[22]

In the most recent edition of Posner's treatise, the confident assertion that the terms will be optimal has become, instead, a question. Posner now asks, "[I]f one seller offers unattractive terms, won't a competing seller, wanting sales for himself, offer more attractive terms, the process continuing until the terms are optimal?"[23] The question may be rhetorical, but Posner seems less certain of the result. The most recent edition acknowledges that "the form contracts used in consumer transactions *do* tend to be one-sided against the consumer; evidently, competition cannot be relied upon to yield the optimal form."[24] Posner concludes only that "the one-sided form contract *may be* optimal. . . ."[25]

Even in the idealized form described by Posner in earlier versions of his book, the process can produce optimal terms only if the buyer understands the terms so as to be able to identify and evaluate the terms

20. *Id.* at 600.

21. *Id.*

22. Richard A. Posner, Economic Analysis of Law § 4.7 at 127–28 (5th ed. 1998).

23. Richard A. Posner, Economic Analysis of Law § 4.9 at 116 (7th ed. 2007).

24. *Id.*

25. *Id.* (emphasis added).

being offered. This assumption becomes clear in Posner's discussion of terms and monopoly:

> [S]ince a monopolized product will be priced higher than it would be under competition, prospective buyers will invest more time and effort in search rather than less; and *one form of consumer search is careful reading of the terms of a contract.* It pays the consumer to read the contract even if he knows the monopoly seller will not bargain (haggle) with him, for he must still decide whether to buy the product or do without.[26]

For the consumer to have a real choice in this scenario, however, "careful reading of the terms of a contract" must in fact suffice. Whether or not there is a monopoly, the consumer may rationally decide not to read the contract, not because "he knows the . . . seller will not bargain (haggle) with him," but because he cannot understand the contract without incurring prohibitive costs for legal advice. Posner himself acknowledges, in a different context, "The presumption that a contemplated exchange is value-maximizing is valid only when the parties actually agree on its terms."[27] He focuses on failures of communication of the terms, but the exchange also cannot be value-maximizing if one party does not understand the terms and cannot acquire that understanding at acceptable cost.

3.3 Effects of Information Asymmetry

Posner notes that, under *ProCD,* a contract is created even though the buyer is required "to agree to detailed contract terms that will be revealed to him only after he indicates his acceptance."[28] Focusing not on the complexity or obscurity of the terms, but on the point in the process at which they are presented, Posner asks how a contract can be formed when the buyer does not know the terms of the offer.[29] He then answers his own question with another: "Well, but can't you agree to buy a pig in a poke?"[30]

26. *Id.* (emphasis added).

27. *Id.* § 4.3 at 101.

28. *Id.* § 4.3 at 103.

29. *Id.*

30. *Id.*

The phrase "pig in a poke" refers to "the folly of buying something that one has not seen."[31] The reference is to a suckling pig "small enough to be carried to market slung over the shoulder in a stout 'poke,' the old-fashioned name for a bag smaller than a sack."[32] In "ancient days," unscrupulous sellers would replace the advertised pig with a runt or even a cat, refusing to open the poke for the buyer's inspection because "everyone knew how hard it would be to catch the piglet if it got loose."[33] Since that time, the word has gone out—through proverbs in many languages—that buying a pig in a poke, or a cat in a sack, is not a good idea.

More people at one time or another have purchased a grab bag—"a bag or other receptacle holding small articles which are to be drawn (as at a party or fair) without being seen often on payment of a small sum."[34] Clearly it is legitimate to sell a grab bag, although the buyer might reasonably complain if the bag turned out to be empty or contained only sand. There is, perhaps, an implied-in-fact warranty that the bag contains *something* that *someone* might find to have value commensurate with the price. And even with this implied warranty, as the dictionary notes, the payment is typically "a small sum." Few people would take the risk of paying very much without knowing what was inside the bag.

If someone nevertheless chooses to make a substantial payment for a pig in a poke or for a grab bag, the choice seems foolish. Courts have construed contracts to avoid reaching the result that someone was buying "a pig in a poke," on the assumption that the contracting parties would not have intended such a result.[35] Indeed, Posner himself, as a circuit judge, used this reasoning in the software context in *Sutter Insurance Co. v. Applied*

---

31. Charles E. Funk, A Hog on Ice & Other Curious Expressions 105 (1948).

32. *Id.*

33. *Id.* at 105–06.

34. Webster's Third New International Dictionary, Unabridged (2002), http://unabridged.merriam-webster.com.

35. *See, e.g.,* Seymour v. Coughlin Co., 609 F.2d 346, 350 (9th Cir. 1979) ("were the agreement construed otherwise, Coughlin would, so to speak, be purchasing 'a pig in a poke'"); Carter v. Rary, 311 F. Supp. 1386, 1390 (D. Ga. 1969) ("Investors in a modern commercial world do not pay earnest money for a 'pig in a poke.'") *But see* Adamson v. Alexander Milburn Co., 275 F. 148, 153 (2d Cir. 1921) (district judge was influenced too "greatly by the thought that a man would not, to use his expression, 'buy a pig in a poke'"). There is, of course, also a sense in which any purchase of information, before it has been revealed, is a purchase of a pig in a poke.

Systems, Inc.[36] Sutter, the software buyer, was "a commercially sophisticated enterprise" and "an experienced user" of the type of software at issue.[37] Judge Posner's opinion observed, "It is . . . *possible* that it bought a pig in a poke for \$360,000—a piece of software that, usable only for Sutter's smallest line of business, was absurdly overpriced. But how plausible is the suggestion? Commercial reasonableness is a useful guide to the interpretation of an ambiguous contract."[38]

All the same, if the person who chooses to buy the pig in the poke is otherwise competent, it does not seem illegitimate for the law to enforce the contract. As Judge Easterbrook, the author of the *ProCD* decision, stated in *Hill v. Gateway 2000, Inc.*,[39] "[a] contract need not be read to be effective; people who accept take the risk that the unread terms may in retrospect prove unwelcome."[40] A more difficult question is whether this type of transaction, if it dominates the market for an important type of product such as software, produces economically efficient results. The problem is that one party knows what is in the bag—that is, what the license means—but the other party does not. The results is "adverse selection,"[41] which defeats efficient allocation.

To illustrate, consider a poke that contains either a wriggling piglet, which will produce juicy pork chops, or a writhing cat, which will serve only as a meal of last resort. Assume that there is a market for each type of animal, but that the cat is worth much less than the pig. Sellers will accept \$20 or more for the pig, and buyers will pay \$25 or less for the pig. The pig should sell for a price between \$20 and \$25, and each party will be better off as a result of the exchange. The cat is worth much less. Sellers will accept \$5 or more for the cat, and buyers will pay \$10 or less for the cat. The cat should sell for a price between \$5 and \$10, and at such a price, each party will also be better off. For example, if a cat sells for \$7.50, the buyer receives something for which he or she was willing to pay \$10 for \$2.50 less—giving the buyer \$2.50

---

36. 393 F.3d 722 (7th Cir. 2004).

37. *Id.* at 726.

38. *Id.* (emphasis in original).

39. 105 F.3d 1147 (7th Cir. 1997).

40. *Id.* at 1148.

41. Inés Macho-Stadler & J. David Pérez-Castrillo, An Introduction to the Economics of Information: Incentives and Contracts 103 (2001).

of "consumer surplus"—and the seller receives $2.50 of producer surplus. At any price between $5 and $10, the social surplus is $5.

Now assume that the seller knows whether the poke contains a pig or a cat, but the buyer does not. The seller's position is unchanged. The seller will accept $20 or more for a pig and $5 or more for a cat. But the buyer must adjust what the buyer is willing to pay by taking into account the risk that the poke contains a cat rather than a pig. If the buyer will pay up to $25 for a pig and up to $10 for a cat, and if the chance of getting a pig is 50 percent and the chance of getting a cat is 50 percent, then the buyer—assuming he or she is also neutral toward risk—will be willing to pay up to $17.50 for the unknown animal. The $25 that the buyer would pay for a pig is multiplied by 0.5, which is the probability that the animal is a pig, and the $10 that the buyer would pay for a cat is multiplied by 0.5, which is the probability that the animal is a cat. Adding the resulting values, $12.50 and $5, yields $17.50.

If the buyer offers $17.50 for the animal in the bag, and the animal is in fact a cat, then the seller will accept it, because the seller will accept anything equal to or greater than $5 for a cat. But if the buyer offers $17.50 and the animal is a pig, the seller will not accept it, because the seller will not accept less than $20 for a pig. Soon pokes will not contain pigs, but only cats. Almost as soon, buyers will learn that a "pig in a poke" is always really a cat. Once this "cat is out of the bag," the buyer—knowing that the probability of the animal being a cat is not 0.5 but 1—will not pay up to $17.50 but will pay only up to $10. The "pig in a poke" will not be a pig at all. The market for pigs in pokes will become a market for cats.

This phenomenon of adverse selection was first described not for pigs but for "lemons." In 1967, George Akerlof, then an assistant professor of economics at Berkeley, published a paper in which he examined the market for used cars.[42] Akerlof observed that used cars, even when they have "just left the showroom," tend to sell at prices far below new cars.[43] His explanation was that the seller of a used car knows whether it is a "lemon," but the buyer does not. The seller will accept a low price if the car is a lemon, but will part with a good car only for a high price. The buyer, not knowing the quality of the car, must decide in ignorance how much he is willing to pay. At first, the buyer

---

42. George A. Akerlof, *The Market for "Lemons": Quality Uncertainty and the Market Mechanism*, *in* AN ECONOMIC THEORIST'S BOOK OF TALES 7 (1984). In 2001, for this article, Akerlof received the Nobel Prize in Economics.

43. *Id.* at 8.

might offer to pay a price somewhere between what he would pay for a good car and what he would pay for a lemon. That price is likely to be enough for the lemon, but not enough for the good car. Over time, only lemons will be supplied.[44]

This scenario damages the chance for an efficient market and may entirely eliminate the market for good used cars. If the buyer and seller had equal knowledge, then the price of a used car would reflect its quality. Good used cars would sell at higher prices, and lemons would not drive (so to speak) the good cars out of the market. The resulting additional sales of good used cars would make both parties to each transaction better off. Information asymmetry destroys the opportunity to make the prospective parties better off, because the asymmetry prevents the transaction from occurring. Accordingly, the allocation of used cars is not efficient.

In the four decades since Akerlof wrote his paper, economists have debated whether empirical evidence supports this analysis in the case of used cars. In addition, as Akerlof himself acknowledged, the market itself can provide remedies for information asymmetry.[45] New developments in technology have helped reduce the disparity in information between sellers and buyers of cars and other products. For example, buyers can obtain, at relatively low cost, reports that show the accident history of a car based on its vehicle identification number or have the car inspected by a third party. Other factors that promote a market for used cars that are not lemons include the certified reseller programs that some manufacturers offer.

But the contemporary software license shows—at least as well as used cars—how information asymmetry can indeed create a market for lemons. And this economic effect, in turn, explains a great deal about software licenses and the software to which they apply. As seen in Chapter 1, the vast majority of the terms in the typical proprietary EULA "legislate" in favor of the software provider and restrict the software user. But this imbalance is possible only because of the impenetrability of the legislative license, which thwarts a market solution that would result in the availability of more favorable terms. In the case of used cars, the lemon is the used car. In the case of EULAs, the lemon is the license itself. The typical EULA is a lemon, from the standpoint of the user, because the quality of its terms, for the user, is low. A license that the software provider understands, but most users find

44. *See id.* at 8–9.

45. *See id.* at 21.

inscrutable, is inherently likely to be one-sided in favor of the provider. Unable to assess its quality, users will accurately assume that the license disfavors them. Lacking the ability to differentiate between good and bad licenses, users will pay only what they would pay for a bad license, and that is what they will get.

This conclusion applies to all the terms of the license, not only those that relate to the quality of the software. But the quality of the license also affects the quality of the software. Proponents of UCITA contended that "the complexity of software products makes them inherently imperfect."[46] They say "[i]t could be argued that the state of the art in software is that all products contain bugs, and it is impossible to produce a software program without them."[47] There is, however, a contrary point of view:

> Software has matured to the point where it can and does operate safely. Millions of people travel safely every day to and from their destinations in automobiles loaded with software. Legions of patients are monitored accurately and receive appropriate treatment with medical software. Millions of airline passengers fly safely in planes controlled by software. The state of the art is such that software that performs properly and safely is a reality, not a dream. Consequently, the state of the software art and technology has evolved to a point where we can expect it to do what it is supposed to do.[48]

It may not be necessary for a word processing or spreadsheet program to meet the same standards of software reliability as software for controlling medical devices or jet planes. But the fact that high-reliability software does exist demonstrates that high reliability is possible. If ordinary software contains numerous bugs, this fact is not unavoidable. Rather, it is a consequence of a given level of investment in software reliability. This level of investment, in turn, is a matter of choice.

Except in transactions involving software of great enough value that the licensee has reason to retain legal counsel to interpret and negotiate license

---

46. Carlyle C. Ring, Jr., & Raymond T. Nimmer, *Series of Papers on UCITA Issues,* http://www.nccusl.org/nccusl/uniformact_qanda/uniformacts-q-ucita.asp.

47. Frances E. Zollers, Andrew McMullin, Sandra N. Hurd, & Peter Shears, *No More Soft Landings for Software: Liability for Defects in an Industry That Has Come of Age,* 21 Santa Clara Computer & High Tech. L.J. 745, 780 (2005).

48. *Id.*

terms, virtually all software licenses disclaim all implied warranties to the maximum extent permitted by law. Even when they offer limited express warranties, they limit liability to, at most, the price of the product. The effect of such terms is to make the legal risk of producing unreliable software extremely low. To the extent legal risk influences the software provider's investment in product reliability, the effect is to provide little or no incentive for such investment.

Software providers have other incentives, such as reputation, to provide some level of software quality. But by immunizing themselves in the EULA from most potential legal actions for software quality problems, they reduce the cost they might otherwise incur because of software failure. In turn, they can be expected to invest less than they otherwise would in avoiding such failure. If information asymmetry causes the license to provide less quality protection than is optimal, then this investment in quality is also likely to be less than optimal.

In a 2006 article, Lucian Bebchuk and Richard Posner acknowledge that the "usual assumption in economic analysis of law is that in a competitive market without informational asymmetries, the terms of contracts between sellers and buyers will be optimal. . . ."[49] They argue that there could also be "cases in which 'one-sided' contracts . . . would be found in competitive markets even in the absence of fraud, prohibitive information costs, or other market imperfections. . . ."[50] They contend that sellers are deterred by reputational concerns from acting "opportunistically," but that consumers are not, and they suggest that one-sided contracts are merely "a way of redressing the balance."[51]

According to Bebchuk and Posner, asymmetric information between consumer and seller is accompanied by asymmetric reputational concerns. The seller has a reputation to protect, but the buyer, as far as his dealings with sellers are concerned, does not. The result, they conclude, is that "seemingly one-sided terms may not be one-sided after all."[52] The expected cost of the one-sided term to the buyer "must be discounted by the likelihood that

49. Lucian A. Bebchuk and Richard A. Posner, *Boilerplate in Consumer Contract: One-Sided Contracts in Competitive Consumer Markets,* 104 Mich. L. Rev. 827, 827 (2006).

50. *Id.*

51. *Id.*

52. *Id.* at 830.

reputational considerations will induce the seller to treat the buyer fairly even when such treatment is not contractually required."[53]

Bebchuk and Posner suggest that their approach "can explain the large number of cases in which sellers dependably treat consumers much better than their contracts require them to do."[54] As an example, they assert that "hotels usually do not charge a guest for checking out of his room shortly after the check-out time. . . ."[55] The contract reserves this right, they say, to protect the hotel against the opportunistic guest "who decides cavalierly to stay in the room, watching TV, until the evening news."[56]

But apart from the authors' assertion, presumably based on their own experience checking out of hotels, there is no empirical evidence that sellers in general, or software providers in particular, reliably do better by their customers than their contracts require. There will be cases in which both sellers and buyers forego legal rights they might otherwise have, but it does not follow that sellers are consistently less opportunistic or better behaved than buyers. Anyone who has checked into a hotel has witnessed complaints by guests who reserved particular types of rooms—with a king bed, or a particular view, for example—and have been given a different type of room. Hotel clerks often respond that, even if the customer paid for a guaranteed reservation, the hotel does not guarantee a particular type of room, but promises only to make an effort to satisfy the customer's request. In short, hotels invoke one-sided terms all the time. That on occasion they may forbear does not make the terms any more "optimal."

One might argue that the availability of "free" automatic updates, consisting of "patches" to correct security vulnerabilities and other software problems, demonstrates that software providers in fact have strong incentives to improve the reliability of their products even with the exculpatory language in software licenses. But the patch argument is double-edged. Patch management is itself a major challenge for information technology departments, imposing substantial costs of its own. And the need for frequent patches is itself a commentary on the reliability of the software before the patch was applied. Imagine an inflatable raft that had to be patched once a week to avoid sinking. If the raft manufacturer mailed a patch kit once a week to

53. *Id.*,

54. *Id.* at 834.

55. *Id.*

56. *Id.* at 835.

make it easy for the user to patch the raft, the user might be grateful. But most users would prefer a raft constructed of material sufficiently strong that weekly patching was not required.[57]

Of course, software development necessarily involves debugging throughout the development cycle. With large custom software systems, both unit and system testing by the developer are often followed by user acceptance testing. The user ordinarily will find shortcomings during this testing. But the purpose of user acceptance testing is to identify such problems so that they can be solved *before* the user accepts and starts using the product. For mass market software, there is usually no user acceptance testing. The software provider decides when to declare the product completed and ready for use. Unlike the custom software developer, the provider of mass market software—because of the exculpatory terms of the typical EULA—has no contractual responsibility to deliver software that satisfies any particular set of acceptance criteria. As a result, the software can be commercially distributed despite significant residual errors.

The software industry has long used the concept of beta testing to refer to the testing of an unfinished software product by users. Some users volunteer to be beta testers, and in return they receive early access to new products. These volunteers place a higher value on the opportunity to try the new software than they do on the disadvantages of dealing with a potentially error-prone program that is not yet a finished product. But the growing practice of distributing software that requires constant ongoing fixes—facilitated by EULA terms—means that, in a real sense, we have become a nation of beta testers, like it or not. Those who have not volunteered for this status nevertheless must live with the costs it presents.

3.4 Does the Internet Come to the Rescue?

Another argument is that an "informed minority" of consumers will obtain and share enough information to protect the uninformed majority: "If a large enough group of consumers is informed, there may be a 'pecuniary externality'

57. Moreover, even with constant patching, many leaks are missed. An IBM research report concluded that "[m]ore than half of the security vulnerabilities disclosed during 2008 had no patches available from the vendor by the end of the year . . . ." Elinor Mills, *Majority of Vulnerabilities Go Unpatched, IBM*, CNET NEWS, Feb. 3, 2009, http://news.zdnet.com/2100-9595_22-265701.html.

protecting the uninformed. This protection will be derived from the competition of sellers for the marginal buyers who are informed and base their purchase decisions on this information."[58] But there are problems with such an argument. "While adventurous consumers may research to find the best price, the far greater costs of searching for, reading, understanding and finally comparing the aggregate value of different sets of contract terms will overwhelm any benefit from doing so. . . . [T]here generally will be too few informed consumers to produce a competitive market for contract terms."[59]

These comments were written in 1990, before the World Wide Web made it possible for "adventurous consumers" to share their research findings with the world at minimal cost. On occasion, such consumers have taken on the EULA. When Google released its Chrome Web browser in late 2008, the original EULA seemed to give Google free reign to use any content the user might submit, post, or display on or through any Google product, software, service, or site.[60] Blog postings critical of the EULA appeared as soon as Chrome was released, and within hours, Google removed the offending language. But it is unclear that Google actually intended to use any content a user might submit—the term, in other words, might have been a mistake in the first place—and changing it might not have deprived Google of any right it had planned to assert.

Just a few months later, despite the controversy over the Chrome EULA, the social networking site Facebook amended its terms of use to expand its rights relating to user content. The terms already granted Facebook a license to do essentially anything it chose with user content, but the license expired when the user removed the content from the site. In early 2009, Facebook amended the terms so that the license would never expire, giving Facebook the right to use the content in perpetuity[61] The change provoked a storm of user protest, and Facebook reversed it, promising to seek user input before making further changes.

---

58. Michael I. Meyerson, *The Efficient Consumer Form Contract: Law and Economics Meets the Real World,* 24 GA. L. REV. 583, 601 (1990) (footnotes omitted).

59. *Id.*

60. Tap the Hive, http://tapthehive.com/discuss/This_Post_Not_Made_In_Chrome_Google_s_EULA_Sucks.

61. Chris Walters, *Facebook's New Terms Of Service: "We Can Do Anything We Want With Your Content. Forever."* THE CONSUMERIST, Feb. 15, 2009, http://consumerist.com/5150175/facebooks-new-terms-of-service-we-can-do-anything-we-want-with-your-content-forever.

But Facebook was a community of users to begin with, whereas most software licenses and terms of use apply to more diffuse user populations. In such cases, user reaction tends to have less influence, as seen in the case of Microsoft's license terms relating to the use of Windows Vista in virtual machines. Since Apple began using Intel microprocessors, one of the selling points of the Mac has been that, with products such as Parallels Desktop, users can run Windows and Windows applications in a virtual machine within the OS X operating system. When Microsoft released Windows Vista in January 2007, the license terms for less expensive home versions prohibited the use of Vista in virtual machines. As a result, Mac users who wanted to run Vista without violating the license were required to pay for more expensive versions, such as Vista Ultimate. In mid-2007, Microsoft publicly considered making a change, but it decided not to do so.

In January 2008, Microsoft reversed course, changing its license terms to permit the use of Vista Home Basic and Home Premium in a virtualized environment. Microsoft's refusal to license the less expensive versions of Vista had been discussed in various Web forums. According to press reports, however, the decision to change the license terms ultimately resulted from "a complaint filed with antitrust regulators."[62] In addition, Microsoft may have had business reasons for making the change. In December 2007, PC World called Vista the number one "tech disappointment" of 2007, and in February 2008, just a month after the virtualization change, Microsoft lowered Vista prices across the board.[63] Enabling Mac users to add Vista at lower cost might have been considered a method of promoting Vista adoption. In any case, the change does not seem to have resulted from the activism of an informed minority.

There are both logical and practical reasons why an informed minority alone is unlikely to transform the EULA any time soon. The first type of reason relates to the logic of collective action. As discussed above, the cost to the user of acquiring a legally sufficient understanding of the EULA terms is likely in most cases to exceed any potential benefit to the user. If all the users

62. Gregg Keizer, *Vista Virtualization Rules Relaxed to Quash Antitrust Probes: Microsoft Eases Virtualization Agreement to Avoid Antitrust Fight,* MACWORLD, March 11, 2008, http://www.macworld.co.uk/business/news/index.cfm?RSS&NewsID=20684; Dan Tynan, The 15 Biggest *Tech Disappointments of 2007,* PC WORLD, Dec. 17, 2007, http://www.pcworld.com/article/140583-5/the_15_biggest_tech_disappointments_of_2007.html.

63. Bill Ray, *Microsoft Cuts Vista Price,* THE REGISTER, Feb. 29, 2008, http://www.theregister.co.uk/2008/02/29/vista_price_cut/.

shared the cost, this might no longer be the case. Just as the software provider spreads the cost of legal advice on the license across all the units of the software being supplied, users, by sharing the cost among them, could do the same. But because users cannot be forced to participate in such an arrangement, and because there is no one to offer them selective incentives to do so, they are unlikely to share the costs.[64]

There are users who are motivated by benefits other than the direct benefit of understanding the license text, such as reputation or a sense of having contributed to the community, but this leads to the practical reason why an informed minority is unlikely to have a major effect on most EULAs. Most users lack legal training and, even if otherwise motivated to comment on EULAs, may not be able to advance general user understanding of EULA terms. Beyond that, the users most motivated to scrutinize license terms from a consumer perspective are likely to be those who are more focused on the free and open source software movement. Thus, dissemination to users of actionable information about EULA terms is ad hoc and sporadic at best.

3.5 Common Standards and Implicit Legal Knowledge

Would there be any less information asymmetry between the software user and the software provider without the EULA? Defenders of the EULA contrast the use of EULAs with a distribution model based on copyright law alone. In such a model, the software provider would simply sell copies of its products, and the Copyright Act would determine what the user was permitted to do. The EULA defenders maintain that EULAs lead to more informed choices than do copyright-based models because "most purchasers of mass market software have little knowledge of their rights under copyright law."[65]

> Most of these customers have probably never heard of the doctrine of first sale, the doctrine of fair use, or section 117 of the Copyright Act. . . . Unsophisticated end users also lack information describing what copyright law does not allow them to do with software. For example, most

64. *See* MANCUR OLSON, THE LOGIC OF COLLECTIVE ACTION: PUBLIC GOODS AND THE THEORY OF GROUPS 44, 51 (1971).

65. Gomulkiewicz & Williamson, *Brief Defense*, at 347.

> software purchasers could not differentiate between an impermissible public and a permissible private performance or display, or distinguish a 'fair use' from an infringing use. Many end users do not know whether they may rent the software which they have acquired.[66]

The supposed public ignorance of copyright law is a weak justification for the primacy of a legal regime ruled by privately written and variable terms of multiple licenses. Even if license terms were more readable than they are, the user would still be required to understand not just one set of legal standards, but each of the various different sets of license terms, as well as the intellectual property and contract law principles that provide the context in which such terms are construed. If users have little knowledge of copyright law, it is difficult to see why they should be expected to have any more knowledge of the law of the license.

On the contrary, it seems likely that the use of a copyright model similar to the one used for printed books would increase the ability of users to make an informed choice. A copyright regime such as that used for printed books relies on a common set of standards and requires less consideration of variations in terms from one transaction to the next. In most cases, the only term that varies is the price. People choose between books based on the content of the books themselves, confident—at least with traditional printed books—that a particular book will not be sold under a special set of terms that skews the comparison.

Moreover, people are not required to have an explicit knowledge of copyright law doctrines to have a generally sound idea of what the law does and does not permit them to do with a book. Although people may not be familiar with the first sale doctrine, they understand that they are free to lend or resell books they have bought, and although they may not know the intricacies of the idea/expression dichotomy, they recognize the significance of the difference between copying a concept and copying the particular wording in which the concept is stated. But because each software license is different, understanding must be acquired anew for each set of license terms.

In other words, people gain implicit knowledge of copyright law through experience with a common body of copyright law over time and across a range of situations and experiences. One of the paradoxes of legal compliance is that we expect the law to affect the behavior of people who are not

---

66. *Id.* at 347–48 (footnotes omitted).

schooled in the law and are unlikely to be aware of what the law says. For activities that have enough value or risk to justify the cost of legal counsel, such as making a will or divorcing a spouse, people may rely on expert advice. But for many activities, people rely on implicit knowledge of the law. Implicit legal knowledge arises through the diffusion of relevant legal norms into the broader culture and through long-term exposure to them. Effective dissemination of implicit legal knowledge requires relative stability and simplicity. It seems reasonable to assume that, if rules of liability are straightforward and unchanging, they are more likely to influence behavior than are rules that are complex and variable.

3.6 Virtues of Simplicity

In 1999, the Ninth Circuit remarked that "the intersection of copyright and contract law" was "an area of law that is not yet well developed."[67] Thomas Merrill and Henry Smith, in exploring more broadly the interface between contract and property, have identified a key principle that differentiates the law's treatment of contract from its treatment of property. They call this principle the "numerus clausus," which means, "the number is closed."[68] Under this principle, "[g]enerally speaking, the law will enforce as property only those interests that conform to a limited number of standard forms," such as the fee simple, the defeasible fee simple, the life estate, and the lease.[69] Moreover, "[p]ersonal property is restricted to fewer available forms of ownership than real property."[70] In contrast, the law permits an infinite range of interests to be created and regulated by contract.[71]

As Merrill and Smith explain, the parties to a contract have "the freedom to 'customize' legally enforceable interests,"[72] and they can be "as whimsical or fanciful as they like in describing the promise to be performed, the consideration to be given in return for the promise, and the duration of

---

67. Sun Microsystems, Inc. v. Microsoft Corp., 188 F.3d 1115, 1122 (9th Cir. 1999).

68. Thomas W. Merrill & Henry E. Smith, *Optimal Standardization in the Law of Property: The Numerus Clausus Principle,* 110 Yale L.J. 1, 4 (2000).

69. *Id.* at 3.

70. *Id.* at 17.

71. *Id.* at 3.

72. *Id.*

the agreement."[73] Such customization of interests is easy to see in the software license terms we have reviewed. Ironically, although EULAs are "standard-form" contracts, the freedom of each licensor to customize the legally enforceable interests in the license means that, in comparison with the property framework of the Copyright Act, EULAs represent an absence of standardization.

Merrill and Smith offer an economic theory to explain "why property rights, unlike contract rights, are restricted to a limited number of standardized forms."[74] The root of the *numerus clausus* principle, they assert, is that, "[w]hen property rights are created, third parties must expend time and resources to determine the attributes of these rights, both to avoid violating them and to acquire them from present holders."[75] They explain, "The existence of unusual property rights increases the cost of processing information about all property rights. Those creating or transferring idiosyncratic property rights cannot always be expected to take these increases in measurement costs fully into account, making them a true externality."[76] The *numerus clausus* principle, by eliminating idiosyncratic property rights, standardizes property rights and in doing so reduces the measurement costs.

Merrill and Smith focus on the measurement costs to third parties, rather than on costs incurred by parties to the transaction, because "explanations based on classes of individuals within the zone of privity have difficulty identifying costs that are not impounded into the price facing those who make the decision whether to create the fancy in the first place."[77] In other words, when two parties voluntarily choose to create a "fancy," they take into account, with regard to how much they will pay or accept, respectively, any costs imposed on them by the custom definition of rights. But the price does not reflect the third-party costs their fancy may later create. "The need for standardization in property law stems from an externality involving measurement costs: Parties who create new property rights will not take into account the full magnitude of the measurement costs they impose on strangers to the title."[78]

---

73. *Id.*

74. *Id.* at 8.

75. *Id.*

76. *Id.*

77. *Id.* at 28.

78. *Id.* at 26–27.

In the case of the proprietary EULA, "strangers to the title" may be less likely to bear such measurement costs.[79] First, because EULAs sharply restrict transfers of the interests in them to third parties, and because such restrictions increasingly are backed by digital rights management techniques, there is less occasion for strangers to the title to attempt to determine the attributes of the license rights for purposes of a potential exchange. Second, because of these restrictions, there is little need for "measurement" by third parties to avoid violating the rights because there is little a third party can do, other than outright piracy, with the licensed materials. Nevertheless, if someone considers, for example, buying a used Autodesk package on eBay, there is a measurement cost not present when buying most other used items.

In addition, when EULAs purport to restrict what one can do with the output from proprietary software, as they sometimes do, third-party measurement costs can be substantial. For example, if the user creates digitally synthesized voice files and shares them with a third party, the third party may not be able readily to determine whether the EULA for the voice synthesis software asserts control over the output. If it does, then the third party may not be able to use the files as planned—even if the third party pays for them in reliance on the licensee's claim to have the right to distribute them.[80]

Perhaps most important in the case of EULAs is that, contrary to Merrill and Smith's assumption, the costs of creating the "fancy" are not likely to be "impounded into the price facing those who make the decision whether to create the fancy in the first place." With a EULA, only the software provider makes the decision whether to "create the fancy." The user rationally does not read the license and therefore cannot attach any particular positive or negative value to the fancy. In this respect, the user is like the used car purchaser who is unable to measure the car's quality, and therefore will not incur measurement costs, but still suffers from the unavailability of good used cars

79. The first Merrill and Smith article on the *numerus clausus* does not discuss the EULA. In a follow-up article, Merrill and Smith cite shrinkwrap contracts as an example of how "corporate lawyers" have "extend[ed] the scope of protection for intellectual property," but do not otherwise comment on EULAs. Thomas W. Merrill & Henry E. Smith, *The Property/Contract Interface,* 101 COLUM. L. REV. 773, 774–75 (2001).

80. *See* UCITA § 506(b), comment 3 ("neither copyright nor patent recognize concepts of protecting a buyer in the ordinary course (or other good faith purchaser) by giving that person greater rights than were authorized to be transferred"), *quoted in* Rhone-Poulenc Agro, S.A. v. DeKalb Genetics Corp., 271 F.3d 1081, 1085 (Fed. Cir. 2001), *vacated, en banc, and remanded,* 284 F.3d 1323, 1334 (Fed. Cir. 2002).

in a "market for lemons." The software user bears no measurement costs, but the fancy in the EULA still imposes costs—namely, the costs of receiving a "lemon" license and being unable to choose a license the user might otherwise prefer.

3.7 What Can Be Done?

Observing that the proprietary EULA is inherently inefficient does not in itself provide a solution. There may not be one, or if there is, it may be worse than the problem. The common law is inherently conservative, and few principles are more deeply entrenched than freedom of contract. Moreover, declining to enforce contracts that people sign without understanding them leads to unacceptable results. If such contracts are not given effect, then evading contractual obligations becomes as easy as feigning ignorance.

Nevertheless, we should not go forward with an inefficient distribution method for software without at least exploring ways to improve it. One possibility is that proprietary software providers themselves might be persuaded, at least in some cases, simply to sell copies—rather than using licenses at all—in the hope of attracting more users. Robert Gomulkiewicz has not supported the sale of software copies as a distribution model, but he has stated, "The licensing model for many software products is simple: you can use the product in any way that it is capable of being used."[81]

If the license authorizes the use of one copy in any way it can be used, and the license is perpetual, then the rights the license conveys are substantially the same as the use rights enjoyed by the owner of a copy under Section 117(a)(1) of the Copyright Act. Under Section 202, the software provider would not be giving up any intellectual property rights in the software by selling copies, and ownership of a copy would give the user the needed use rights. As we saw at the outset, some software licenses go overboard with disclaimers, but even if the software provider wants to disclaim warranties in the sale of a copy, Section 2-316 of the UCC makes it possible to do so in a few specified words. In such cases, a simple sales contract would suffice.

The main right found in some EULAs that is not also held by the owner of a copy is a right to use the software on more than one computer. If the software provider wanted to choose a distribution approach based on selling copies, however, then the provider could simply agree to sell not one copy

---

81. Gomulkiewicz, *Getting Serious*, at 699.

but two or more copies to the user. This would not require actually providing multiple copies. As a matter of product delivery, the user could be the one to make the extra copies from one distribution disc or download, but the user would still be the owner of two copies, with use rights for each.

A simple sales approach works less well if the second copy can only be used on a portable computer or can only be used by the same person who uses the first copy. And because of the first sale doctrine and the arbitrage problem, the sale of copies will not work for software providers that want to charge different prices in different markets, such as OEM and academic. In addition, if the software uses DRM that requires the user's permission for accessing the user's computer, then the provider will need to obtain that permission in some sort of contract.

Notwithstanding the paean to license-based price discrimination in *ProCD*, however, there are many ways to achieve targeted pricing other than by license. Publishers of traditional books use hard cover and paperback versions to charge different prices according to the relative value different types of purchasers attach to the product. Shapiro and Varian describe how versioning—"offering [an] information product in different versions for different market segments"—can achieve differential pricing in a manner that does not rely on license restrictions.[82]

Even when a license is necessary, software providers could make EULAs simpler and more readable or, as Gomulkiewicz proposes, "user-friendly."[83] He suggests that, for products the user is permitted to use in any way they can be used, "the license grant, at most, needs to say that the user may use the software as described in the product documentation."[84] Actually, a license grant that said "the user may use the software as described in the product documentation" would not necessarily be simple at all. It would incorporate by reference the entire "product documentation," which, if lengthy, could make the license even more complex than the typical EULA. Moreover, saying that you can use the product as described in the product documentation is not the same as saying that "you can use the product in any way that it is capable of being used." The product is likely to be capable of being used in ways that are not described in the documentation. And the worse the documentation, the fewer the rights.

---

82. Carl Shapiro & Hal R. Varian, Information Rules: A Strategic Guide to the Network Economy 53-55 (1999).

83. Gomulkiewicz, *Getting Serious*, at 688.

84. *Id.* at 699.

But it seems clear that software providers, if they were so inclined, could adopt a minimal EULA, with terms that were short and sweet. In fact, the Microsoft Office 2004:Mac software Student and Teacher Edition came in a box that states, on the front, "Includes 3 installs." The box also contains the following language: "This product is licensed to be used on three personal computers or other devices in your household for non-commercial use by people who reside in your household." Additional information about eligibility requirements appears on the back of the box. Notwithstanding the assumption of the Seventh Circuit in *ProCD* that placing complete terms on the outside of a box would require "using microscopic type," these boxes appear to demonstrate that the most important terms can in fact be stated on the box without necessarily "removing other information that buyers might find more useful."

Might software providers come to see the option of a concise and readable license as offering potential competitive benefits? Starting in the 1980s, Borland licensed its computer language products under a "No-Nonsense License Statement." The Borland license stated, "You must treat this software just like a book, except that you may copy it onto a computer to be used and you may make archival copies of the software for the sole purpose of backing up our software and protecting your investment from loss." The idea was to win customers from competitors by demonstrating that Borland did not play games with its EULAs.

As today's EULAs demonstrate, however, the "no-nonsense license" concept did not catch on for long. Borland's No-Nonsense License Statement has gone the way of Borland itself. In part, the reason may be that the approach was somewhat self-contradictory. If Borland had truly wanted to require only that the user treat the software "just like a book," except for copying as part of use and except for archival copying, then Borland could have simply sold a copy and achieved the same result under the Copyright Act. But the license statement also contained other terms, including terms that limited the warranty to one that the "physical diskettes" and "physical documentation" would be "free of defects in materials and workmanship" for sixty days from purchase, along with a disclaimer of all other warranties, express and implied.

A Danish provider of unmanaged hosting services, EasySpeedy ApS, offers "No nonsense Terms of Agreement."[85] They begin, "Tired of complex,

---

85. http://easyspeedy.com/support/dedicated_hosting_terms.jspx.

incomprehensive contracts? If you experience any problems with the server hardware, it's our responsibility. If you experience any problems with your operating system, software or applications within your server, it's your responsibility." The terms are stated in relatively simple declarative sentences (in English), and in total the terms and the "No nonsense Acceptable Use Policy" are stated in fewer than one thousand words. But even these "no-nonsense" provisions conclude, "This page is subject to change without any notice." And industry-wide, simplicity of terms is clearly the rare exception.

Although software providers may not intentionally make EULAs difficult to understand, they have no obvious economic incentive to reduce the information asymmetry that results from license unreadability. That is because the asymmetry favors the provider, which is the better-informed party regarding the effects of the license. If licenses were easier for users to understand, then the process that Posner describes could occur and providers would be required to compete over license terms. This prospect, along with uncertainty about the prospective benefits, may be what deters providers from making a serious attempt to clarify the EULA.

If software providers will not make changes on their own, consideration should be given to enacting legislation requiring that license terms be readable. An example of readability legislation is found in Florida law concerning insurance policy forms, which must be submitted to the state's Office of Insurance Regulation before being used.[86] Each such policy "shall be readable," which includes achieving a minimum score of 45 on the Flesch reading ease test (or an equivalent score on another approved test).[87] The statute provides a detailed specification for how the Flesch test must be applied.[88] Recognizing that such a test can produce arbitrary results, the statute provides that the office may authorize a lower Flesch test score if "it finds that a lower score will provide a more accurate reflection of the readability of a policy form, is warranted by the nature of a particular policy form or type or class of policy forms, or is the result of language which is used to conform to the requirements of any law."[89]

---

86. Fla. Stat. § 627.410(1).

87. *Id.* § 627.4145(1).

88. *Id.* § 627.4145(5).

89. *Id.* § 627.4145(2).

As Gomulkiewicz points out in a 2004 article, objective standards such as the Flesch reading ease test can be somewhat arbitrary and "cannot evaluate the overall effectiveness of communication."[90] SEC readability rules are more subjective, focusing on "plain English principles."[91] As Gomulkiewicz also notes, subjective standards are just that, and they make it very difficult for the drafter to know in advance whether a document complies.[92] The Florida statute combines an objective approach—the minimum Flesch score requirement—with an escape valve that allows the state insurance office to permit a lower Flesch score based on a subjective review. Unlike insurance policy forms, EULAs are not submitted to a state agency for approval, and the potentially high cost of establishing a procedure for administrative pre-approval of EULA forms makes such an approach unattractive.[93] But the absence of a perfect solution does not mean that nothing can be done.

Although the precise form of the legislation would require further study, there is much to be said for a truth in licensing in licensing act. Rather than attempting to set detailed substantive rules or defaults on numerous topics, as did UCITA, and thus encouraging the trend toward legislative licenses, an act aimed at promoting truth and transparency in licensing would be entirely procedural and itself short and sweet. It could provide that standard-form mass-market licenses would not be enforceable unless they met specific requirements for Flesch test scores, font size, and the like, or a court otherwise determined that they were not unnecessarily verbose and were reasonably understandable to an ordinary user.[94] A software provider could be assured of compliance with the act by meeting the quantitative requirements, but could depart from them if absolutely necessary and still be able to enforce license terms with the requisite showing.

A further possibility is to add provisions to the Copyright Act that make it possible to confer the right to use software on multiple computers, to limit

---

90. Gomulkiewicz, *Getting Serious,* at 711.

91. 17 C.F.R. § 230.421(d)(1).

92. *Id.*

93. *See id.* at 713.

94. A truth in licensing act could require that, when software is distributed in boxes, the license terms (if any) appear with a minimum font size on the outside of the box. This approach would force software providers to find a way to be succinct. When software is not delivered in a box, but is downloaded, the act could require that the license terms appear with a minimum font size, in their entirety, "above the fold" of a Web page of a given resolution.

time periods, and to prohibit some transfers, without using a license at all. If the reason for licensing rather than selling copies is that the sale-of-a-copy model is "one-size-fits-all," then a potential solution is to introduce additional sizes, but with due regard for the *numerus clausus* principle. In other words, there could be small, medium, and large, but not twenty different sizes and half-sizes. Such relatively simple changes in copyright law could obviate the use of licenses in the relatively few cases in which current mass-market software licenses provide rights that go beyond the rights already enjoyed under the Copyright Act by the owner of a copy.

One difference between books and software is that, with a traditional book, the copy you buy is the copy you read. In contrast, with software, the copy you buy, ordinarily, is the copy you install. Even Section 117(a)(1) of the Copyright Act, which addresses the reproduction of software as part of its use in a machine, does not fully reflect this fact. But the Act could be revised with only modest changes to provide for these different kinds of copies. The copy of a digital work that is actually executed in a machine is one we can call the execution copy or *active copy.* The active copy in the memory of the machine is the copy that acts on the machine and produces results. Ironically, the active copy is the most transient, and sometimes it is also fragmentary, because portions of code may not be loaded unless a particular execution of the program requires them. Nevertheless, the active copy is the one with the greatest practical significance for the user. The other types of copies are useless without an active copy.

At the same time, there is no active copy without a *storage copy.* The storage copy is stored, typically on disk, and is the copy from which the *active copy* is made. For example, when Adobe Reader runs, the storage copy on a hard disk is copied into RAM to create the active copy that runs on the machine. Each active copy implies a storage copy, so ownership of an active copy could carry with it, by default, ownership of the corresponding storage copy. But there could be circumstances in which one storage copy, such as one on a network server, is associated with several active copies.

The storage copy, in turn, is usually created from a *distribution copy.* The distribution copy may be distributed on an optical disc enclosed in a software package, or it may be created by download from another distribution copy on a server. To guard against the risk that the *storage copy* on disk will be lost or corrupted because of a disk error, the user may also make an *archival copy* on a backup medium.

Neither the copyright laws nor, for that matter, most software licenses draw distinctions between these different kinds of copies. The doctrine of

MAI Systems—that "a 'copying' for purposes of copyright law occurs when a computer program is transferred from a permanent storage device to a computer's RAM"[95]—assumes that, for purposes of copyright law, a copy is a copy is a copy. The Copyright Act itself does the same. Section 101 defines "copies" as "material objects, other than phonorecords, in which a work is fixed by any method now known or later developed, and from which the work can be perceived, reproduced, or otherwise communicated, either directly or with the aid of a machine or device." The Act draws no distinction between the different types of copies used in digital systems. Nor does the Copyright Act account for the fact that most storage copies and all active copies of digital works (whether or not they are "computer programs") are necessarily made by the user.

A relatively simple change in the Copyright Act would be to provide for the sale of different types of copies and to provide that the sale of one distribution copy includes, by default, one storage copy, one active copy, and one archival copy. The seller could, alternatively, designate the sale of a distribution copy as a sale of two storage and active copies. The Act would then further provide that, when a copy is sold, if it is not provided to the user (as with a distribution copy on DVD or a storage copy pre-installed on a hard drive), then the user is entitled to create (and, as necessary, to recreate) the copy. The sale of copies could be permanent or for a specified time period, creating ownership of a copy that would be analogous to an estate for a term of years. By this means, distribution of time-limited versions could occur.

For such a change in the law to have any prospect of being enacted, it almost certainly would have to present an optional framework that software providers would not be required to adopt. And for an optional framework to be voluntarily used, it would have to offer benefits that were available only when the copyright owner sold copies rather than licensing them. For example, the sale of software copies could carry an implied-in-law authorization to use DRM to prevent the creation of additional copies. This would obviate the provisions of the software license that provide consent for such use.

There would remain the problem that the owner of a copy can resell the copy, and this ability would interfere with price discrimination strategies in which different versions, such as an OEM and academic versions, are licensed to different types of users. Here a possible solution would be to expand the software rental amendments to prohibit not only rental but also resale of

---

95. MAI Systems Corp. v. Peak Computer, Inc., 991 F.2d 511, 518 (9th Cir. 1993).

copies without permission of the software provider. This would not affect the right of the owner of a copy to give away a copy, but it would prevent someone who bought an OEM copy at a reduced price from reselling it on eBay.

Of course, legislative efforts often lead to unintended results, and any such legislation could be seen by some as an opportunity to increase the restrictions on users. Even if the legislation prevailed, there would be no assurance that software providers would change the distribution model. Perhaps because the prospects for changing proprietary software licensing seem so faint, most effort by those who support a different approach to software access has been focused on free and open source licensing. To this option we turn in Part 2 of this book.

PART II

The Free and Open Source Alternative

FOUR

GPL

A Private Copyleft Act

AS DISCUSSED IN PART 1, one possible alternative to the EULA is to distribute software in largely the same way that publishers distribute printed books, under rules provided in the Copyright Act. Compared to the complexity and variability of EULAs, the Copyright Act is a model of simplicity and uniformity. If the software provider instead wishes to permit the use of an unlimited number of copies and the unrestricted transfer of copies, copyright law proides an even simpler concept. This concept is dedication of works to the public domain.

Some of the most influential software works of our time are already in the public domain. Tim Berners-Lee invented the World Wide Web while working at CERN, the European Organization for Nuclear Research. In 1993, Berners-Lee persuaded his employer to dedicate the Web client and server software and the Web library of common code to the public domain.[1] As we will see in Chapter 6, this decision played a key role in the emergence of the World Wide Web as a global phenomenon that lived up to its name.

Before choosing the public domain approach, Berners-Lee considered asking CERN to license the Web technology to the public under the GNU General Public License. The GPL—which Berners-Lee decided against using—is to dedication to the public domain as the EULA is to the sale of a copy. Although the GPL seeks to promote software "freedom," it does so as a license that rivals its proprietary counterparts in complexity and conditionality. Weighing in at more than 5500 words in its current version, the GPL serves different values than the EULA but is no less "legislative" than the most far-reaching proprietary license.

---

1. JAMES GILLIES & ROBERT CAILLIAU, HOW THE WEB WAS BORN: THE STORY OF THE WORLD WIDE WEB 261 (2000); CERN European Organization for Nuclear Research, *Statement Concerning CERN W3 Software Release Into Public Domain,* April 30, 2003, at 2, http://tenyears-www.web.cern.ch/tenyears-www/.

Indeed, the term that describes the GPL's core principle—"copyleft"—reveals not only the GPL's reversal of some of the normal effects of copyright, but also the GPL's legislative character. The GPL is a private "copyleft act." It provides that anyone who distributes modified versions of GPL-licensed software must do so under the GPL. The resulting chain reaction multiplies the GPL so that, over time, it becomes a kind of legislative regime. Whereas works in the public domain are completely free, works licensed under the GPL and derivatives of those works can only be distributed as the GPL permits.

Although Berners-Lee decided against using the GPL for the Web technologies, Linus Torvalds chose the GPL for Linux, and the GPL is the most widely used "free and open source" software license today.[2] The current chapter addresses the GPL and the ideology of its creator, Richard Stallman, as well as some of the practical effects of its terms. The GPL is an anti-EULA that challenges proprietary software on ideological grounds. Whereas the use of the proprietary EULA has become an industry practice associated with no particular individual, the GPL remains closely linked to its creator's personal views and life story, and its creator continues to play a leading role in its application and development.

4.1 License Ideology: Stallman, Gates, and the Ethics of Copying

If clicking assent to a proprietary end user license brings to mind a religious ritual, Richard Stallman's fight for free software resembles a religious crusade. Stallman has been "[a]n atheist since early childhood" and once had a button made that said "Impeach God."[3] Nevertheless, as Sam Williams explains, "Like a Jew keeping kosher or a Mormon refusing to drink alcohol, Stallman paints his decision to use free software in the place of proprietary in the color of tradition and personal belief."[4] According to Williams, Stallman does not force his beliefs on his listeners, but "a listener

---

2. Software Freedom Law Center, *Free Software Foundation Releases Guidelines for Revising the Widely Used GNU GPL*, Nov. 30, 2005, http://www.softwarefreedom.org/news/2005/nov/30/gplv3-process/.

3. SAM WILLIAMS, FREE AS IN FREEDOM: RICHARD STALLMAN'S CRUSADE FOR FREE SOFTWARE (2002), http://oreilly.com/openbook/freedom/ch08.html at http://oreilly.com/openbook/freedom/ch04.html.

4. *Id.* at http://oreilly.com/openbook/freedom/ch08.html.

rarely leaves a Stallman speech not knowing where the true path to software righteousness lies."[5]

Stallman, who founded the GNU project and wrote the GNU Emacs text editor, has the shoulder-length hair and beard one associates with a biblical prophet. Williams describes an "unusual ritual" in a speech that Stallman gives:

> Pulling a black robe out of a plastic grocery bag, Stallman puts it on. Out of a second bag, he pulls a reflective yellow computer disk and places it on his head. The crowd lets out a startled laugh.
>
> "I am St. Ignucius of the Church of Emacs," says Stallman, raising his right hand in mock-blessing. "I bless your computer, my child."[6]

Stallman developed his fervor for free software when he began working at the MIT Artificial Intelligence Lab in 1971 and "became part of a software-sharing community that had existed for many years."[7] Unfortunately, from Stallman's point of view, the beginning of the 1970s was also the dawn of the "proprietary" software era. Until that time, most software was provided at no additional charge by the computer manufacturer or was developed by users. Martin Goetz, who helped start a small company called Applied Data Research, has suggested that "software products, as a business, began in 1964" when ADR started selling a program called Autoflow.[8] But Goetz acknowledges that IBM's announcement in 1969 that it would "unbundle" hardware and software "was what turned a nascent business into the software industry."[9]

Another software industry pioneer, Ernest Keet, believes that the 1969 unbundling announcement was meaningful, but "only over a 10-year period"[10]—that is, the decade of the 1970s. Keet explains, "IBM gave customers the message that buying software is not only OK, it's required.

---

5. *Id.*

6. *Id.*

7. Richard M. Stallman, Free Software, Free Society: Selected Essays of Richard M. Stallman 17 (2002) [hereinafter Stallman, *Selected Essays*].

8. Martin Goetz, *Memoirs of a Software Pioneer: Part 1,* IEEE Annals of the History of Computing 43, 43 (2002).

9. *Id.*

10. Luanne Johnson, *Creating the Software Industry: Recollections of Software Company Founders of the 1960s,* IEEE Annals of the History of Computing 14, 27 (2002).

The customer had to start justifying the expenditure for IBM software as well as ours."[11] Except for the operating system, software was no longer included in the price of the machine. The most immediate driving force behind unbundling appears to have been the threat of antitrust actions against IBM, and despite the unbundling announcement, such actions were brought.[12] Efforts to enhance competition thus contributed to the undoing of a software sharing ideology that, Stallman remarks, was "as old as computers."[13]

According to Stallman, the halcyon software-sharing days persisted at the MIT AI Lab into the 1970s, but not beyond. Stallman recalls that, "[i]f you saw someone using an unfamiliar and interesting program, you could always ask to see the source code, so that you could read it, change it, or cannibalize parts of it to make a new program."[14] The people who worked in this environment considered themselves "hackers" in the best sense of the term. Stallman was an AI Lab hacker who worked to improve the timeshare operating system of a Digital Equipment Corporation PDP-10 computer.[15] For Stallman, "[t]he situation changed drastically in the early 1980s," when the PDP-10 was discontinued.[16] Manufacturers of successor machines required that customers execute nondisclosure agreements even to receive executable code and provided no source code at all.

To Keet, IBM's message that "buying software" was "not only OK" but "required" was a step in the development of an industry, but in Stallman's view, this approach gave rise to a new "proprietary-software social system," which he regards as "antisocial" and "unethical."[17] Stallman explains, "[T]he first step in using a computer was to promise not to help your neighbor. A cooperating community was forbidden. The rule made by the owners of proprietary software was, 'If you share with your neighbor, you are a pirate. If you want any changes, beg us to make them.'"[18] While others of his generation

11. *Id.*

12. *See* Burton Grad, *A Personal Recollection: IBM's Unbundling of Software and Services,* IEEE ANNALS OF THE HISTORY OF COMPUTING 64, 65 (2002).

13. Stallman, *Selected Essays,* at 17.

14. *Id.*

15. *Id.*

16. *Id.*

17. *Id.* at 18.

18. *Id.*

sought to make their fortunes in the emerging software business, Stallman deplored this system and vowed to create a new one.

Bill Gates also came of age around the time of IBM's 1969 unbundling announcement. As a student at an exclusive Seattle preparatory school in the late 1960s, Gates, like Stallman at the AI Lab, used a PDP-10.[19] The machine belonged to a local company. Among other things, Gates and friends exploited security flaws in a monitor program to give themselves the run of the system. If Stallman was a "hacker" in the best sense, Gates and his friends may have been hackers of a slightly more mischievous type.[20] Later, as a Harvard sophomore, Gates saw a January 1975 *Popular Electronics* cover that featured the "Altair 8800" microcomputer kit, offered by company in New Mexico known as MITS. Gates and Paul Allen developed a BASIC interpreter for the Altair and moved to Albuquerque, where they formed the company then known as "Micro-Soft."[21]

Whereas Stallman considered it unethical *not* to copy software, Gates's ethical views on copying were the opposite. In Gates's famous "letter to hobbyists" of February 3, 1976, he complained that many computer hobbyists were using software without paying for it. He wrote, "As the majority of hobbyists must be aware, most of you steal your software. Hardware must be paid for, but software is something to share. Who cares if the people who worked on it get paid?"[22] Gates asked, "Is this fair?" He also provided the answer: "Most directly, the thing you do is theft."[23] More than thirty years later, industry organizations supported by Microsoft and others continue to advance the essentially moral argument that to copy software is to steal it.

Stallman contends that this position is based on the assumption "that software companies have an unquestionable natural right to own software and thus have power over all its users."[24] Stallman maintains that "the U.S. Constitution and legal tradition reject this view; copyright is not a natural right, but an artificial government-imposed monopoly that limits the users'

---

19. *See* STEPHEN MANES & PAUL ANDREWS, GATES: HOW MICROSOFT'S MOGUL REINVENTED AN INDUSTRY—AND MADE HIMSELF THE RICHEST MAN IN AMERICA 29 (1994).

20. *See id.* at 33–34.

21. *See id.* at 63–64, 92.

22. Bill Gates, *An Open Letter to Hobbyists,* Feb. 3, 1976, *reprinted in id.* at 91–92, also http://en.wikipedia.org/wiki/Image:Bill_Gates_Letter_to_Hobbyists.jpg.

23. *Id.*

24. Stallman, *Selected Essays,* at 18.

natural right to copy."[25] The Constitution empowers Congress "[t]o promote the Progress of Science and useful Arts, by securing for limited Times to Authors and Inventors the exclusive Right to their respective Writings and Discoveries. . . ."[26] The purpose of copyright and patent law is thus explicitly utilitarian.

But the Constitution does not mention "the users' natural right to copy." And even if it did, or if such a right could somehow be found in the Bill of Rights, it is unclear how a "natural right" can exist in a Stallmanist world. Just as Gates's letter to hobbyists gives no philosophical rationale for its assertions, Stallman does not identify the source of this "natural right." He says that, "[a]s an atheist," he does not "follow any religious leaders,"[27] so the natural right to copy software apparently is not God-given. But his comments do not make clear how else this "natural right" might arise.

Stallman simply asserts that, if we "judge these issues based on ordinary common-sense morality while placing the users first," we conclude that "[c]omputer users should be free to modify programs to fit their needs, and free to share software, because helping other people is the basis of society."[28] Different people, however, have different views about what "ordinary common-sense morality" requires, and some of these people, unlike Richard Stallman, are conservative Republicans. As Albert Einstein reportedly once said, "[c]ommon sense is nothing more than a deposit of prejudices laid down in the mind before you reach eighteen."[29] Nor is it obvious why users should be placed "first," ahead of everyone else (including creators). Apparently, however, if you have doubts on these points, you are not one of the people to whom Stallman's views are addressed.

4.2 UNIX, GNU, and Linux

The "GNU" in "GNU General Public License" is a "recursive acronym" for "GNU's Not Unix."[30] The UNIX operating system was created in 1969 by

---

25. *Id.*

26. U.S. Const. art. 1, § 8, cl. 8.

27. Stallman, *Selected Essays.*, at 19.

28. *Id.* at 18.

29. Fred R. Shapiro & Joseph Epstein, The Yale Book of Quotations 230 (2006).

30. Stallman, *Selected Essays*, at 19.

Ken Thompson and other computer scientists at Bell Labs.[31] Bell Labs was the research arm of what was then the largest monopoly in the world—American Telephone and Telegraph Company (AT&T)—or the Bell System, sole operator of the U.S. telephone network. AT&T shared UNIX source code with academic institutions across the country and offered them licenses at very low cost. Much of what has followed in free and open source software is related, in one way or another, to the UNIX system.

In the mid-1960s, IBM used microcode in its System/360 to provide software compatibility across a line of computers.[32] Nevertheless, systems from different manufacturers still had different instruction set architectures and therefore could not run the same machine code. UNIX initially was written in assembly language for the machine on which it was first designed to run. But in 1972, Dennis Ritchie of Bell Labs invented the C programming language, and in the summer of 1972, Thompson and Ritchie rewrote UNIX in C. By writing an operating system in a high-level language, the Bell Labs scientists made UNIX portable across different machine architectures. As long as a C compiler was available for a given machine, a version of UNIX could be created for that machine with relative ease. UNIX became popular in part because of this portability and a "timesharing" capability that supported multiple users, a key ingredient in its eventual use as a leading operating system for Internet servers.

In 1976 and 1977, UNIX creator Thompson taught computer science at the University of California at Berkeley. UCB students and faculty members began developing UNIX enhancements. These enhancements were incorporated into the Berkeley Software Distribution (BSD or "Berkeley Unix"). The BSD components—which soon supplanted most of the original code—were licensed under an open source license before the term "open source" had been invented. But the original UNIX code remained proprietary and required a license from AT&T.

---

31. "UNIX" was a play on "Multics," the name of a timeshare operating system that Bell Labs, General Electric, and MIT had been working to develop. "Multics" was short for "Multiplexed Information and Computing Service." Bell Labs withdrew from the Multics project in 1969. Today, UNIX is a trademark of The Open Group, a nonprofit industry consortium.

32. As explained in Chapter 2, microcode enables processors to run in "emulation" mode, which allows multiple processor designs to be compatible with a single instruction set architecture.

Stallman started the GNU project in 1983 to provide a free alternative to UNIX. To return to a world in which software was freely shared, "what was needed first was [a free] operating system."[33] According to Stallman, "[a]s an operating system developer, [he] had the right skills for this job."[34] But "operating system," he says, "does not mean just a kernel, barely enough to run other programs."[35] Operating systems of the day included "command processors, assemblers, compilers, interpreters, debuggers, text editors, mailers, and much more," and "[t]he GNU operating system would include them too."[36]

As it turned out, despite Stallman's self-recognized skills for operating system development, the GNU project never did produce a successful operating system kernel. That achievement fell to Linus Torvalds, a Finnish developer who released the first version of Linux in 1991. Linux was a Unix-like operating system for Intel and compatible microprocessors. Linux was not part of the GNU project, but Torvalds decided early on to license Linux under the GPL.[37] Linux soon became the most famous GPL-licensed program.

Stallman has insisted ever since that "Linux" be referred to as the "GNU/Linux operating system."[38] He explains, "If you call our operating system 'Linux,' that conveys a mistaken idea of the system's origin, history, and purpose. If you call it 'GNU/Linux,' that conveys (though not in detail) an accurate idea."[39] According to an article in OSWeekly.com,

> [O]ne of Richard Stallman's criteria for giving an interview to a journalist was that the journalist agrees to use his terminology throughout his article. Sometimes he even makes sure that the journalist has read the GNU philosophy before interviewing him, for 'efficiency's sake.' He has been known to turn down speaking requests over some terminology issues.[40]

---

33. Stallman, *Selected Essays,* at 19.
34. *Id.*
35. *Id.*
36. *Id.*
37. See Linus Torvalds & David Diamond, Just for Fun: The Story of an Accidental Revolutionary 96 (2001).
38. Stallman, *Selected Essays,* at 53.
39. *Id.*
40. Puru Govind, The *"GNU/Linux" and "Linux" Controversy,* OSWeekly.com, May 5, 2006, http://www.osweekly.com/index.php?option=com_content&Itemid=&task=view&id=2242.

For his part, Torvalds—who created Linux—says that "calling Linux in general 'GNU Linux' I think is just ridiculous."[41]

4.3 Free Software, Copyleft, and the GPL

The Free Software Foundation, of which Stallman is president, defines a "free software" license as one that protects four freedoms (numbered beginning with zero): (0) the freedom to run the program, (1) the freedom to study and change the source code, which in turn requires access to the source code, (2) the freedom to distribute exact copies, and (3) the freedom to distribute modified copies.[42] FSF identifies more than thirty free software licenses currently in use that, according to it, satisfy this definition.[43] FSF also notes that, although dedication to the public domain is not a license, public domain status is consistent with the GPL.[44] The four freedoms do *not* include the freedom of a user to charge others a fee for the right to use a modified version of the software that the user creates.

There is no freedom to charge a license fee under the GPL because it is not only a "free software" license: it is also a free software license that embodies the concept Stallman calls "copyleft." As Stallman tells the story, in the mid-1980s, one of his friends sent him a letter in an envelope marked "Copyleft—all rights reversed."[45] Stallman adopted the word "copyleft" to describe the "distribution concept" that became embodied in the GPL.[46] Stallman first implemented the copyleft concept in 1989, in version 1 of the GPL. Version 2 of the GPL appeared in 1991, and version 3 in 2007.[47]

---

41. *Id.*

42. The Free Software Definition, http://www.gnu.org/philosophy/free-sw.html. The zero-based numbering of the four freedoms follows the zero-based indexing of arrays in modern programming languages.

43. FSF, at http://www.fsf.org/licensing/licenses/.

44. *Id.*

45. Stallman, *Selected Essays,* at 23.

46. *Id.*

47. The GNU Lesser General Public License (LGPL) is a free software license, but does not include the copyleft condition. FSF designed the LGPL for use with software libraries in "special circumstances only" and generally discourages its use. See Licenses—Free Software Foundation, http://www.fsf.org/licensing/licenses/.

TABLE 2 Copyleft and Permissive Free Software Licenses

Freedom	*"Copyleft"*	*"Permissive"*
0. Freedom to run	The licensee is free to run the program.	
1. Freedom to study and change source code.	The licensee receives and is free to modify the program's source code.	
2. Freedom to distribute copies.	The licensee is free, and may not be charged a royalty, to distribute copies of the program.	
3. Freedom to distribute modified copies.	The licensee is free, and may not be charged a royalty, to distribute modifications of the program . . .	
	If and *only if* the modifications are also distributed on these terms.	*Whether* or *not* the modifications are distributed on these terms.

As shown in Table 2, the fundamental differen ce between copyleft and other forms of free and open source licensing is in the conditions that attach to freedom 3 in the Free Software Definition, namely the freedom to distribute modified copies. Under a copyleft license, the licensee is free to distribute modifications of the program, but only if the licensee distributes the modifications on the same terms.[48] Under a non-copyleft license, also referred to as a "permissive" free software license, the licensee is free to distribute modifications whether or not the licensee does so on the same terms. As a result, the licensee under a permissive license is free to distribute a modified version under a license that is not only non-copyleft but, if the licensee so chooses, is proprietary—one in which source code need not be provided and a royalty may be charged.

In contrast to the proprietary EULA, the GPL is the subject of relatively little case law. FSF maintains an active "enforcement" arm, but it appears that compliance with GPL conditions has been achieved largely without reported decisions.[49] In *Progress Software Corp. v. MySQL, AB*,[50] the court

48. The GNU Affero General Public License extends the copyleft concept by requiring the operator of a network server that runs a modified version of licensed software to provide source code for the modified version to users even if the modified version is not itself being distributed. *See* GNU Affero General Public License, http://www.fsf.org/licensing/licenses/agpl.html.

49. *See* Mike Gunderloy, *Will We Ever Have a GPL Test Case?*, OSTATIC, May 29, 2008, http://ostatic.com/163417-blog/will-we-ever-have-a-gpl-test-casess.

50. 195 F. Supp. 2d 328 (D. Mass. 2002).

ruled on motions that did not address whether the conditions of the GPL would be given effect.[51] According to FSF, the judge "made clear" in a hearing "that she sees the GNU GPL to be an enforceable and binding license. . . ."[52] A Munich court prohibited distribution of a Dutch company's product without GPL-required source code.[53] Other overseas decisions have been reported. But in the courts of the United States, the GPL remains largely unlitigated.[54]

Wallace v. IBM

The first GPL case to make its way to a federal appellate court was an antitrust action. In *Wallace v. International Business Machines Corp.*,[55] Judge Frank Easterbrook—author of the *ProCD* decision ten years earlier—broadly declared, "The GPL and open-source software have nothing to fear from the antitrust laws."[56] The plaintiff, Daniel Wallace, alleged that he was unable to compete with Linux because IBM, Red Hat, and Novell conspired "to eliminate competition in the operating system market by making Linux available at an unbeatable price"—namely, under the GPL, "free *forever*."[57] The court rejected Wallace's predatory pricing claim, noting that "[p]redatory pricing is a three-stage process: Low prices, followed by the exit of producers who can no longer make a profit, followed by monopoly prices."[58] If there is no prospect of monopoly prices, there is no antitrust concern. *Wallace* appears to assume that the GPL will be applied in accordance with the GPL's terms, in

---

51. *See id.* at 329.

52. FSF, *Judge Saris defers GNU GPL Questions for Trial in MySQL vs. Progress Software*, March 1, 2002, http://www.gnu.org/press/2002-03-01-pi-MySQL.html.

53. Stephen Shankland, *GPL Gains Clout in German Legal Case*, CNET News, April 22, 2004, http://news.cnet.com/2100-7344-5198117.html.

54. In December 2008, FSF filed a copyright infringement lawsuit against Cisco Systems alleging that, in distributing products under the Linksys brand, Cisco failed to comply with the GPL and the LGPL. FSF, *Free Software Foundation Files Suit Against Cisco for GPL Violations*, Dec. 11, 2008, http://www.fsf.org/news/2008-12-cisco-suit. As of this writing, the *Cisco* case remains unresolved.

55. 467 F.3d 1104 (7th Cir. 2006).

56. *Id.* at 1108.

57. *Id.* at 1106 (emphasis in original).

58. *Id.*

the sense that it will cause Linux to remain free "forever," but does not directly address the question.

Wallace challenged the GPL as a potential competitor of Linux providers, not as a user. Perhaps for that reason, he does not appear to have presented any antitrust challenge to the agreement of all GPL licensors to disclaim warranties. Section 15 of the current version of the GPL states that, to the extent permitted by applicable law, "THERE IS NO WARRANTY FOR THE PROGRAM." The same section adds, "SHOULD THE PROGRAM PROVE DEFECTIVE, YOU ASSUME THE COST OF ALL NECESSARY SERVICING, REPAIR OR CORRECTION."[59] In addition, Section 16 disclaims liability for damages.

Section 4 states that, if you distribute a modified version, "you may offer support or warranty protection for a fee," but in so stating it seems to rule out the possibility that "you" might offer warranty protection other than "for a fee." Of course, the fee could be as little as 1 cent, but as a practical matter, the GPL seems to embody an understanding that the licensor will not provide a warranty as part of the basic license. Unlike an agreement to charge a zero license fee, an agreement not to provide warranties could be seen, at least arguably, as one that has anticompetitive effects. But *Wallace* did not address this point.

The SCO Group v. IBM

In 2003, The SCO Group, Inc. (hereinafter SCO), sued IBM in the U.S. District Court for the District of Utah. SCO alleged that, "[t]hrough a series of corporate acquisitions," SCO owned "all right, title and interest in and to UNIX," including UNIX System V, and to various license agreements under which AT&T had licensed UNIX to customers.[60] SCO also alleged that Linux was a "variant or clone of UNIX" and that it was, "in material part, based upon UNIX source code and methods."[61] SCO stated that all commercial UNIX

---

59. This clause, contained in all three versions of the GPL (in Sections 9, 11, and 15, respectively), appears to have been taken nearly verbatim from a 1980s-era IBM proprietary license (or both were taken from a common source). *See* Julie A. Mark, *Software Copying Policies: The Next Step in Piracy Prevention?*, 2 J.L. & Tech. 43, 54 n.88 (1987) (quoting an IBM license with almost identical language).

60. Second Amended Complaint of SCO ¶ 2, filed Feb. 27, 2004, http://www.sco.com/scoip/lawsuits/ibm/.

61. *Id.* ¶ 3.

versions in use, including Linux, were "modifications of and derivative works based on the UNIX System V Technology."[62]

According to SCO, IBM had violated a 1985 license agreement by contributing UNIX System V code to Linux for general public use.[63] SCO also claimed that IBM had violated other UNIX-related agreements and had committed unfair competition, interference with contract, and misappropriation of trade secrets.[64] In addition, SCO alleged that IBM had infringed SCO's claimed UNIX copyrights by "incorporating (and inducing, encouraging, and enabling others to incorporate) SCO's proprietary software into Linux open source software offerings."[65] The SCO action against IBM was followed by IBM counterclaims against SCO and other lawsuits by and against SCO, including a 2004 suit by SCO against a Linux user, AutoZone, for alleged infringement of UNIX copyrights.

For a software licensing dispute, the case attracted an unusually high level of publicity. SCO was quoted in the news media as stating that Linux contained UNIX source code owned by SCO, but it refused to identify the code.[66] In 2005, the district court observed that, "[v]iewed against the backdrop of SCO's plethora of public statements concerning IBM's and others' [alleged] infringement of SCO's purported copyrights to the UNIX software," it was "astonishing" that SCO had "not offered any competent evidence to create a disputed fact" regarding such infringement.[67] Although the court did not grant IBM's requested summary judgment on the issue, it made clear its considerable skepticism about SCO's claims.[68]

But the most significant blow against SCO came in 2007, in a separate action in the same court, *The SCO Group, Inc. v. Novell, Inc.*[69] The *Novell* case concerned SCO's claim to ownership of UNIX. In 1993, Novell purchased a number of UNIX-related assets, including UNIX System V, from an AT&T subsidiary, UNIX System Laboratories. In 1995, Novell sold certain UNIX

---

62. *Id.* ¶ 30.

63. *Id.* First Cause of Action.

64. *Id.* Second through Ninth Causes of Action.

65. SCO Group, Inc. v. IBM, 2005 U.S. Dist. LEXIS 4493, *8 (D. Utah Feb. 8, 2005).

66. Stephen Shankland, SCO: Unix Code Copied into Linux, CNET NEWS, May 1, 2003, http://france-zdnet.com.com/2100-3513_22-999371.html.

67. *Id.* at *17.

68. See *id.*

69. 2007 U.S. Dist. LEXIS 58854 (Aug. 10, 2007).

assets to The Santa Cruz Operation, Inc. (hereinafter Santa Cruz). In 2001, Caldera Systems, Inc. (hereinafter Caldera), purchased the UNIX assets of Santa Cruz, and in 2002, Caldera changed its name to The SCO Group, Inc. SCO's claimed ownership of UNIX thus depended on Novell's having transferred the rights to Santa Cruz.

After SCO sued IBM and threatened other Linux distributors and users, Novell sued SCO for "slander of title," later adding other claims.[70] Novell maintained that the UNIX copyrights were not among the UNIX assets that were transferred to Santa Cruz in 1995 and that Novell, not SCO, owned the UNIX copyrights. In an August 2007 summary judgment ruling, the district court agreed with Novell.[71] Just over a month after this decision, SCO filed a petition for reorganization under Chapter 11 of the Bankruptcy Code.[72] The bankruptcy court permitted Novell's claims against SCO to proceed, and in July 2008, after a bench trial, the court awarded Novell damages of more than $2.5 million against SCO for unjust enrichment, breach of fiduciary duty, and conversion.[73]

SCO's litigation campaign against IBM and other distributors and users of Linux prompted an intense negative reaction in the free and open source software community. Some companies that distribute Linux offered to indemnify users against possible suits by SCO. For example, Hewlett-Packard announced that it would offer "full legal indemnification to customers buying Linux on HP hardware with a standard support package after they sign an addendum to their sales contract. . . ."[74] Notably, however, the indemnification came with a decidedly non-free condition: "No modifications to the source code can be made under the contract, but desired changes can be discussed with HP on a case-by-case basis."[75] And IBM flatly declined to provide such an indemnification. An IBM spokesperson explained, "Linux is open-source code. No single company provides it. Users understand that there are no warranties or indemnities that come with Linux. . . ."[76]

---

70. *Id.* at *4.

71. *Id.* at *90, *97–*98.

72. *SCO Files for Chapter 11 Protection,* Sep. 14, 2008, http://www.sco.com/chapter_11/.

73. The SCO Group, Inc. v. Novell, Inc., 2008 U.S. Dist. LEXIS 54282, *61–*62 (D. Utah July 16, 2008).

74. Todd Weiss, *Update: HP to Indemnify Its Corporate Linux Users against SCO: The Move to Protect Customers Will Take Effect Oct. 1,* COMPUTERWORLD, Sep. 24, 2003, http://www.computerworld.com/softwaretopics/os/linux/story/0,10801,85288,00.html.

75. *Id.*

76. Daniel Lyons, *IBM Refuses to Indemnify Linux Users,* FORBES.COM, Aug. 5, 2003, http://www.forbes.com/2003/08/05/cz_dl_0805ibmlinux.html; Todd R. Weiss, *LinuxWorld: A*

SCO is a case in which clear evidence of copying has not emerged. But the case does highlight a potential vulnerability of free software. Nearly all free and open source licenses disclaim all warranties. There are, accordingly, no express or implied warranties that the person granting the license or contributing to the software has the authority to do so. Nor do contributors agree to indemnify users for losses or lawsuits that may result from claims that contributions are infringing. "[B]eginning in May 2004, Linux contributors were required to attest that they have the right to make that contribution,"[77] but without warranties and indemnifications, there is still potential user risk. Problems of infringement are not, of course, limited to free and open source software, and proprietary licenses often also disclaim noninfringement warranties and indemnifications. But it seems possible that, at some point, the open nature of the development process could give rise to stronger infringement claims than those of SCO.

4.4 GPL "Enforceability"

Given that questions about the enforceability of the EULA were relatively common in the early years of its use, it is not surprising that people ask similar questions about the GPL. Like the EULA, the GPL is a nonnegotiable standard form, and a user becomes a licensee as a result of conduct rather than by signing anything. But the GPL, unlike the EULA, does not claim to be an agreement. According to Eben Moglen, a professor at Columbia Law School who chairs the Software Freedom Law Center and who played a key role in drafting version 3 of the GPL, the GPL is a "unilateral permission," which requires no assent by the user.[78] Accordingly, the questions about the significance of user manifestations of assent that have dogged the EULA do not arise, or at least are not the same, for the GPL. On the other hand, the unilateral permission theory raises questions of its own.

The distinction on which Moglen insists requires closer attention to the nature of a license. In one sense, a license is simply permission to do that

---

Defiant IBM Says Linux Indemnification Is Unnecessary: It Asserts That SCO's Legal Claims Have No Merit, COMPUTERWORLD, Jan. 21, 2004, http://www.computerworld.com/softwaretopics/osnux/story/0,10801,89269,00.html.

77. Josh Lerner & Jean Tirole, *The Economics of Technology Sharing: Open Source and Beyond*, 19 JOURNAL OF ECONOMIC PERSPECTIVES 99, 114 n.15 (2005).

78. Pamela Jones, *The GPL Is a License, Not a Contract*, LWN.net, Dec. 3, 2003, http://lwn.net/Articles/61292/.

which is otherwise forbidden. James Bond has a "license to kill" because the criminal law generally looks askance at killing. Issuance of a driver's license grants the recipient permission to operate a motor vehicle, an act the law otherwise prohibits. Professional licenses are required to practice "learned" professions. James Bond's license to kill, which places him in the highly select double-0 section of Her Majesty's Secret Service, presumably derives from the authority of Her Majesty herself. Lesser public authorities grant driver's licenses, professional licenses, and the like.

In some cases, a license grants permission to do that which is forbidden not by public law but by private right. In those cases, the license comes not from the government, but from the owner of the private right. For example, a copyright license grants permission to do that which is otherwise forbidden by copyright law, such as reproducing a protected work. Apart from the private nature of the grant and the act for which permission is granted, a license to copy is not, analytically, unlike a license to kill.

Nevertheless, the Nimmer copyright treatise states that a copyright license is not only a grant of permission but "an agreement not to sue the licensee for infringement."[79] And a leading information licensing treatise, *Modern Licensing Law,* by Raymond Nimmer and Jeff Dodd, states,

> A license is an agreement that deals with, and grants or restricts, a licensee's contractual right, power[,] privilege or immunity with respect to uses [of] (including allowing access to) information or rights in information made available by a licensor. The agreement includes a focus on what rights, immunities, or uses are given or withheld in reference to use of the information as well as what the licensee has agreed to do or not to do with respect to the information.[80]

If a license is, as these authorities state, an agreement, and if the agreement is enforceable, then the agreement forms a contract between the parties.[81]

---

79. 3–10 Melville Nimmer & David Nimmer, Nimmer on Copyright § 10.01[C][5] n.73.1 (2008).

80. Raymond T. Nimmer & Jeff C. Dodd, Modern Licensing Law § 1:2 at 3 (2008–09 ed.).

81. *See* Restatement (Second) Contracts § 1 (a "contract" is "a promise or a set of promises for the breach of which the law gives a remedy, or the performance of which the law in some way recognizes as a duty"); Uniform Commercial Code § 1-201(12) (a "contract" is "the total legal obligation that results from the parties' agreement . . .").

In this respect, it is not merely a grant of permission by one person to another, but a contract that binds both parties to its terms.

In disputing the view of such treatises and asserting that "[l]icenses are not contracts," Moglen states that "the work's user is obliged to remain within the bounds of the license not because she voluntarily promised, but because she doesn't have any right to act at all except as the license permits.[82] In contrast, a contract is "an exchange of obligations, either of promises for promises or of promises of future performance for present performance or payment."[83] Moglen maintains that "[t]he idea that 'licenses' to use patents or copyrights must be contracts" is merely "an artifact of twentieth-century practice. . . ."[84] That practice is to make access to the copyrighted work contingent on paying and "promis[ing] to enter into certain obligations concerning the work."[85] With respect to software, such obligations by users include promises not to decompile or reverse engineer the software, and not to transfer the software.[86]

Consistent with Moglen's outlook, the GPL states in Section 9,

> You are not required to accept this License in order to receive or run a copy of the Program. . . . However, nothing other than this License grants you permission to propagate or modify any covered work. These actions infringe copyright if you do not accept this License. Therefore, by modifying or propagating a covered work, you indicate your acceptance of this License to do so.

Although the significance of "acceptance" of a unilateral grant of permission is unclear, if there is no valid license, and if the user's actions would otherwise infringe copyright, then it appears that Moglen is correct in saying that a user who violates the conditions of the license is potentially liable for copyright infringement. As discussed in Part 1, the Ninth Circuit held in *Sun*

---

82. Eben Moglen, *Enforcing the GNU GPL*, Sep. 10, 2001, http://www.gnu.org/philosophy/enforcing-gpl.html.

83. Pamela Jones, *The GPL Is a License, Not a Contract*, LWN.net, Dec. 3, 2003, http://lwn.net/Articles/61292/.

84. *Id.*

85. *Id.*

86. *Id.*

Microsystems, Inc. v. Microsoft Corp.[87] that a licensee becomes liable for copyright infringement rather than merely for breach of contract if the terms violated "are limitations on the scope of the license rather than independent contractual covenants."[88] If the GPL is not a contract, then there can be no contractual covenants. In that case, the GPL requirements, such as the requirement that modifications be distributed, if at all, under the GPL, can only be conditions of the license and, accordingly, can only operate as limitations on license scope. The GPL thus effectively accomplishes the "comply or forfeit" strategy also found in the typical EULA.

A case that involved not the GPL but another free software license known as the Artistic License appears to confirm the effectiveness of conditions similar to the ones that appear in the GPL. In *Jacobsen v. Katzer,*[89] Jacobsen managed an open source software group called Java Model Railroad Interface, or JMRI.[90] The association between model railroad enthusiasts and the "hacker" community behind the open source movement is longstanding. Eric Raymond writes that "[t]he beginnings of the hacker culture as we know it today can be conveniently dated to 1961, the year MIT acquired the first PDP-1," when "[t]he Signals and Power committee of MIT's Tech Model Railroad Club adopted the machine as their favorite tech-toy and invented programming tools, slang, and an entire surrounding culture that is still recognizably with us today."[91] It is therefore fitting that a model railroad case, albeit one decided almost fifty years later, has provided one of the first tests at the appellate level of the effectiveness of open source license conditions.

JMRI created an application known as DecoderPro for programming the decoder chips that control model railroad trains and made it available for download it under the Artistic License.[92] A competitor used portions of DecoderPro source code in its own software without complying with the Artistic License, including terms requiring attribution, copyright notices, and descriptions of changes.[93] Jacobsen sought a preliminary injunction on the basis of copyright infringement, but the district court denied it,

---

87. 188 F.3d 1115 (9th Cir. 1999).

88. *Id.* at 1121.

89. 535 F.3d 1373 (Fed. Cir. 2008).

90. *Id.* at 1376.

91. Eric S. Raymond, A *Brief History of Hackerdom, in* OPEN SOURCES: VOICES FROM THE OPEN SOURCE REVOLUTION 20 (Chris DiBona, Sam Ockman & Mark Stone, eds., 1999).

92. 535 F.3d at 1376.

93. *Id.*

apparently concluding that the competitor had, at most, committed a breach of contract, for which no injunction was available.[94] Applying Ninth Circuit law as set forth in *Sun Microsystems,* the Federal Circuit vacated the district court's ruling, holding that the terms of the Artistic License were not merely contractual covenants, but "enforceable copyright conditions."[95]

Although *Jacobsen* did not involve the GPL, there is no obvious reason why the same analysis would not apply to the GPL. If the issue is GPL "enforceability" against licensees, then the question is not whether the GPL creates an enforceable contract, but whether the violation of the conditions set forth in the GPL actually does, as FSF asserts, make the user a copyright infringer. *Jacobsen* suggests that it does. Like the Artistic License, the GPL expressly conditions its permissions on compliance with its terms.

Given Moglen's insistence that the GPL is a unilateral license, however, and given that the GPL itself does not purport to form a contract, the question of "enforceability" has a different meaning in the GPL context than in the EULA context. In this context, the less obvious but more difficult question becomes whether the GPL is enforceable against the licensor. If there are grounds for doubt about the GPL's "enforceability," this question is the one to which they relate.

Moglen has been quoted as explaining that "[t]he word 'license' has, and has had for hundreds of years, a specific technical meaning in the law of property."[96] This meaning, he states, is that "[a] license is a unilateral permission to use someone else's property."[97] Moglen explains, "The traditional example given in the first-year law school Property course is an invitation to come to dinner at my house. If, when you cross my threshold, I sue you for trespass, you plead my 'license,' that is, my unilateral permission to enter on and use my property."[98] The story seems correct as far as it goes. But suppose that Professor Moglen invites me to dinner at his house, and after I cross the threshold, he discovers that I am wearing a Microsoft T-shirt. And suppose (more plausibly) that, on seeing the shirt, he demands that I leave at once. I might have been able to plead his original invitation as a defense to a suit for trespass when I initially crossed his threshold, but if I do not leave now, he

94. *Id.* at 1377.

95. *Id.* at 1383.

96. Pamela Jones, *The GPL Is a License, Not a Contract,* LWN.net, Dec. 3, 2003, http://lwn.net/Articles/61292/.

97. *Id.*

98. *Id.*

will prevail in a suit based on my refusal to leave after being told to go. The law is clear that "[a] license, within the context of real property law, grants the licensee a *revocable* non-assignable privilege to do one or more acts upon the land of the licensor, without granting possession of any interest therein."[99] The invitation to dinner is revocable at will.

The operative principle, which may have been omitted from the first-year property course but will certainly be covered in first-year contracts, is that promises must be supported by consideration, or a consideration substitute, to be binding. Indeed, as the Nimmer treatise on copyright points out, consideration "undoubtedly" is "[t]he most well-known aspect of Anglo-American contract law. . . ."[100] The treatise specifically affirms that "consideration is necessary to render a nonexclusive license irrevocable."[101] Although the doctrine of promissory estoppel may permit enforcement of a promise that is not supported by consideration if the promisee reasonably relies on the promise to his detriment, the doctrine is an exception to the general rule, and the reasonableness of reliance depends on the circumstances.

It follows that, although violation of the GPL's conditions by a licensee may give rise to a copyright infringement action, a key question of enforceability for the GPL is whether the "unilateral permissions" granted in the GPL are enforceable against the licensor—so that compliance with the GPL's conditions actually does insulate the licensee from infringement liability. Section 2 of the GPL states that "[a]ll rights granted under this License are granted for the term of copyright on the Program, and are irrevocable provided the stated conditions are met." But the statement that the rights are irrevocable is itself a promise, which, as a matter of law, may well be revocable at will if it is not part of a contract.

A potential exception to the consideration requirement, promissory estoppel, might apply, but whether and how it would apply is far from certain. Section 90 of the Restatement (Second) of Contracts provides:

> A promise which the promisor should reasonably expect to induce action or forbearance on the part of the promisee or a third person and

---

99. Ark Bryant Park Corp. v. Bryant Park Restoration Corp., 730 N.Y.S.2d 48, 55 (App. Div. 2001) (emphasis added).

100. 3-10 Melville Nimmer & David Nimmer, Nimmer on Copyright § 10.03[A][8] (2008).

101. *Id.*

> which does induce such action or forbearance is binding if injustice can be avoided only by enforcement of the promise. The remedy granted for breach may be limited as justice requires.[102]

The doctrine of Restatement Section 90 might be invoked by a GPL licensee to assert that a licensor should not be permitted to revoke the unilateral permission granted in the GPL. The standard, however, is inherently vague. For example, whether a licensor "should reasonably expect" that GPL licensees will rely on the promise depends in part on whether it is reasonable to assume that the ordinary requirement of consideration will not apply. There is also no assurance that a court would determine in every case that "injustice can be avoided only by enforcement of the promise." And in limiting any remedy "as justice requires," a court could stop far short of giving full effect to the GPL's terms even under such a theory.

Applying the analogy to real property licenses that Moglen advances, consider the Connecticut Superior Court decision in *Margaitis v. Deacon.*[103] Margaitis alleged that Deacon gave him a license to farm fifteen acres of Deacon's land for five years.[104] After Margaitis took possession of the property and made preparations to farm it, however, Deacon advised Margaitis that he had "changed his mind" and asked Margaitis to vacate the land.[105] Margaitis sued Deacon to recover his expenses for labor, materials, and equipment, and his lost revenues and profits.[106]

Striking Margaitis's complaint, the court stated that "a license does not create a contractual obligation between the parties and is freely revocable."[107] Moreover, licenses to enter real property are revocable "regardless of whether expenditures have been made by the licensee."[108] The court rejected not only the breach of contract claim, but also a promissory estoppel claim. The court quoted a Washington decision, which stated, "Implicit in the nature of a license is the licensee's presumed knowledge that permission may be withdrawn. Consequently, funds expended in reliance on a mere license do not

---

102. Restatement (Second) Contracts § 90(1).

103. 2005 Conn. Super. LEXIS 504 (Feb. 15, 2005).

104. *Id.* at *1.

105. *Id.*

106. *Id.* at *1–*2.

107. *Id.* at *7.

108. *Id.*

create a valuable, compensable property right."[109] On this basis, despite the allegation of an expressly granted five-year license, the court concluded that the facts alleged had "fail[ed] to establish the existence of a clear and definite promise by which the defendant could reasonably have expected to induce reliance on the part of the plaintiff."[110]

If, as Moglen maintains, the GPL is a unilateral license of the same kind as a license to enter real property, then the GPL, like Deacon's license to Margaitis, may well be freely revocable, regardless of whether licensees have spent money or taken other actions in reliance on it. The statement in the GPL that it is irrevocable, like the Deacon's alleged statement that the license to Margaitis would last for five years, presumably would give way under such authority to "the licensee's presumed knowledge that permission may be withdrawn." If these principles apply to the GPL, the consequences could be profound.

For example, suppose that a programmer we'll call Sam creates a new work—Sam's Spreadsheet. Sam chooses to distribute Sam's Spreadsheet under the GPL, and users create modified versions, which they distribute under the GPL. Sam's was only an alpha version, but users have created Sam's Plus, and Sam's Plus is a big hit. Now Sam, in light of the positive reaction to Sam's Plus, has a change of heart. If Moglen is correct and the GPL is a non-contractual unilateral permission, then Sam can freely revoke the permissions he granted when he licensed the original Sam's under the GPL. And under the principle recognized in *Margaitis v. Deacon,* Sam's Plus is now infringing Sam's copyright despite the investments that users have made in it in reliance on the original GPL license grant.

The risk is greatest if the original GPL licensor revokes the license grant. The creators of Sam's Plus who distribute it are GPL licensees who have also become GPL licensors. They, too, can revoke their license grants, but if they do, they will violate the conditions of the GPL under which they are licensees. As a result, if it is one of the creators of Sam's Plus rather than Sam who has a change of heart, then Sam will have a potential copyright infringement action against the revoking licensee. This is no guarantee that the licensee will not revoke, but it makes the risk lower than it would be if Sam himself decided he wanted to take a different licensing approach.

---

109. *Id.* at *11 (quoting Showalter v. City of Cheney, 76 P.3d 782, 785 (Wash. App. 2003)).

110. *Id.* at *11.

4.5 Permissions and Patents

Perhaps the most likely area for eventual litigation over the effectiveness of the GPL is in connection with patents. The GPL and its copyleft principle are rooted in copyright. Version 1 of the GPL (GPLv1) did not even mention patents. But FSF and other Stallman groups have long been concerned that software patents are having a pernicious effect. One approach, by groups such as the Open Invention Network, is to identify prior art to oppose "poor quality" software patents and to build a portfolio of patents that can be licensed only to companies that do not use their own patents to attack free software.[111] But such efforts face many challenges and in any event are not likely to be a complete answer. As a result, the two more recent versions of the GPL have tried to use terms of the license to address the patent problem. In doing so, they have created significant potential issues of license interpretation.

If a third party holds patents that apply to GPL-licensed software, the third party can thwart the GPL regime by selectively granting non-"free" licenses only to certain users, such as those who agree to pay patent royalties for any further distribution. For example, if a GPL licensee creates a modified version of a GPL-licensed work, and the modified version requires a license under a third party's patent, then the third party can grant a license to the creator of the modified work but not to that person's licensees. Even though the creator of the modified work distributes the modification under the GPL, it will not be free, because those who receive it will still have to pay for a license from the third-party patent holder.

Of course, this problem can exist regardless of whether the GPL licensee accepts a patent license from the third party or is even aware of the third party's patent. But version 2 of the GPL (GPLv2)—under which Linux is still licensed—takes the position that GPL licensees should not affirmatively avail themselves of patent licenses in such circumstances. Section 7 of GPLv2 provides that, "if a patent license would not permit royalty-free redistribution of the Program by all those who receive copies directly or indirectly through you, then the only way you could satisfy both it and this License would be to refrain entirely from distribution of the Program."

This clause discourages GPL licensees from redistributing software that they know could expose downstream GPL licensees to patent royalty

111. *See* About Open Invention Network, http://www.openinventionnetwork.com/about.php.

obligations for using software that the downstream licensees expect to be free. Stallman calls it the "liberty or death" clause—"since it ensures the program will remain free or die."[112] Actually, the clause "ensures" only death, and only if the licensee accepts a patent license—the licensee who is unaware of third-party patents or ignores them can still distribute the software, and the third-party patents, if they apply at all, will still apply.

Microsoft has maintained that a number of Microsoft patents apply to Linux. Rather than suing Linux users, Microsoft has sought to persuade companies that distribute Linux to pay patent royalties. Eventually, if enough Linux distributors agree, those who decline may be vulnerable to infringement suits. Microsoft entered into an arrangement with Novell in 2006 in which Microsoft agreed not to sue Novell's customers under the Microsoft patents for their use of SUSE Linux, which Novell distributes. As part of the arrangement, Microsoft also issued certificates to some of its own customers that entitled them to free support from Novell for SUSE Linux. Microsoft customers who wanted to use Linux for some purposes thus could obtain the software and support from Novell without worrying about possible patent infringement.

Under Section 7 of GPLv2, if Microsoft had granted a patent license to Novell that did not permit royalty-free distribution by "all those who receive copies" of Linux "directly or indirectly through" Novell, then the patent license would have precluded Novell from distributing Linux. Microsoft was not prepared to grant a broad patent license to all Linux recipients. But the parties were able to bypass this problem by having Microsoft agree not to sue Novell's customers, while refraining from granting a patent license to Novell itself. The effect was that Novell became a favored distribution channel for Linux because customers who obtained it from Novell would not face the potential Microsoft patent threat that others might.

FSF regarded the Microsoft-Novell deal as exploitation of a GPLv2 "loophole." In version 3 of the GPL (GPLv3), FSF sought not only to close the loophole but also to force Microsoft to grant a broad patent license to all Linux users. Section 11 of GPLv3 defines "patent license" broadly as "any express agreement or commitment, however denominated, not to enforce a

---

112. Richard M. Stallman, *Microsoft's New Monopoly,* July 5, 2005, http://www.fsf.org/licensing/essays/microsoft-new-monopoly.html, *cited in* Lothar Determann, *Dangerous Liaisons—Software Combinations as Derivative Works? Distribution, Installation, and Execution of Linked Programs under Copyright Law, Commercial Licenses, and the GPL,* 21 Berkeley Tech. L.J. 1421, 1484 & n. 239 (2006).

patent (such as an express permission to practice a patent or covenant not to sue for patent infringement)," whether addressed to the GPL licensee or to the licensee's customers—thus extending the concept to undertakings such as those of Microsoft in relation to Novell's customers. And aiming at the Microsoft-Novell certificate arrangement, Section 11 states that, if "you convey, or propagate by procuring conveyance of, a covered work, and grant a patent license to some of the parties receiving the covered work . . . , then the patent license you grant is automatically extended to all recipients of the covered work and works based on it."

By distributing certificates redeemable for free Linux support from Novell, Microsoft was arguably "procuring conveyance" of Linux, a GPL-licensed work. If at least part of Linux came to be licensed under GPLv3 rather than GPLv2, and if Microsoft continued to distribute the certificates, then FSF could argue that Microsoft had granted a license under Microsoft's patents "to all recipients of the covered work." Presumably such a license would extend to all recipients of Linux, whether from Novell or a third party, and to all recipients of future Linux versions. Microsoft chose not to take the risk that such a term would be given effect and announced on July 5, 2007, shortly after GPLv3 was released,

> At this point in time, in order to avoid any doubt or legal debate on this issue, Microsoft has decided that the Novell support certificates that we distribute to customers will not entitle the recipient to receive from Novell, or any other party, any subscription for support and updates relating to any code licensed under GPLv3. We will closely study the situation and decide whether to expand the scope of the certificates in the future.[113]

What if Microsoft had ignored the new GPL provision? The challenge for FSF would then be to show how the GPL could cause a patent license granted by Microsoft to third parties to be "automatically extended." Section 11 of GPLv3 applies to "you," the GPL licensee. Section 9 states that you "indicate your acceptance" of the license "by modifying or propagating a covered work. . . ." Section 0 defines propagation as an act that would be infringing without a copyright license. It is not clear that "procuring conveyance," in this case distribution, of a copyrighted work requires a license. The exclusive

113. Microsoft Statement about GPLv3, July 5, 2007, http://www.microsoft.com/presspass/misc/07-05statement.mspx.

right under the Copyright Act is to distribute works, not to "procure" their distribution.

And even if "procuring" the distribution of a copyrighted work could be infringing, "you"—as the person to whom the GPL's "unilateral permission" is granted—are free to choose whether or not to rely on this grant. If you comply with the conditions that the GPL attaches to the permission, you can invoke the GPL as a defense to a copyright infringement action. If you do not comply with those conditions, you cannot invoke the GPL as such a defense. Those are the only possible consequences of a unilateral permission. It follows that the GPL cannot cause Microsoft—or any other prospective licensee—"automatically" to do anything. For that reason, the clause is likely to be given no effect at all.

If the GPL did not claim to make third-party patent license grants "automatically" extend to everyone, but instead stated that the GPL licensee, as a condition of the permissions granted in the GPL, is required to extend the third-party patent license grants, then the clause could be given effect. But in that case, even if procuring conveyance was otherwise infringing, it would still be up to Microsoft to decide whether to comply with the condition. If Microsoft procured conveyance and did not comply with the condition requiring it to extend its patent license grants, then Microsoft might be vulnerable to a copyright infringement action. But Microsoft's legal relations with third parties could not be affected. The third parties would still be liable to Microsoft for patent infringement if they required a patent license and did not have one. Any possible copyright infringement liability of Microsoft for procuring distribution could not affect the third parties' patent infringement liability to Microsoft.

Unlike GPL licensees, GPL licensors do make promises, but it is even less clear how Microsoft, merely by "procuring conveyance" of Linux, could become a GPL licensor. There is no provision in the GPL that purports to make anyone a GPL licensor by conduct alone. In dismissing concerns about becoming an inadvertent GPL licensor as "FUD" ("fear, uncertainty, and doubt"), GPL advocates insist that no one becomes a GPL licensor without deciding to do so. And if it were possible to become an inadvertent GPL licensor, the issue of revocability would arise. Indeed, the issue of revocability of the unilateral permission granted in the GPL is perhaps most likely to arise in a case, should one present itself, in which a party is deemed to have become a GPL licensor without intending to do so, and the party therefore takes advantage of the free revocability of unilateral permissions. As a result, even if Microsoft somehow became an inadvertent GPL licensor, enforceability of any promise that might be attributed to it would be far from assured.

4.6 No More Readable Than the EULA

The patent provisions are just one way in which GPLv3 seeks to address "threats" to free software, while also reinforcing the GPL's basic copyleft provisions and making them as broadly applicable as possible. But in the course of doing so, FSF has created a license document that resembles the proprietary EULA in length and complexity. And so the GPL, which in many ways attempts to be the most complete repudiation of the proprietary EULA, in at least one way has become what it so vehemently opposes—a legislative license that, as far as readability is concerned, out-EULAs the EULA.

Section 4 of GPLv3, which contains the basic permission-granting terms, receives a Flesch-Kincaid grade level score of 23.6—higher than the scores of the most complex major EULAs. To be likely to understand these terms, a reader would require more than 23 years of formal education—12 years through high school, 16 years through college, 20 years through a doctoral degree, and nearly all the way through a second doctoral degree. Only a permanent student or (possibly) a licensing lawyer could be reliably expected to comprehend their meaning.

As an example, consider how the GPL expresses the right to modify the software. Because the feature that perhaps best distinguishes free software from proprietary software is the grant of permission to change the source code and to distribute modified copies, modification provisions are key. GPLv2 grants permission, on stated conditions, to "modify your copy or copies of the Program or any portion of it, thus forming a work based on the Program, and copy and distribute such modifications or work. . . ." The most important condition of the permission to "copy and distribute" modifications is Section 2(b), which states, "You must cause any work that you distribute or publish, that in whole or in part contains or is derived from the Program or any part thereof, to be licensed as a whole at no charge to all third parties under the terms of this License." This is the copyleft condition, and in GPLv2 it is at least reasonably understandable.

For GPLv3, released in 2007, FSF has rewritten these terms. GPLv3 deletes the GPLv2 statement that "[y]ou may modify your copy or copies of the Program or any portion of it, thus forming a work based on the Program, and copy and distribute such modifications or work. . . ." And in Section 8, GPLv3 provides, "You may *not* propagate or modify a covered work except as expressly provided under this License."[114] In other words, there is no implied license to modify a covered work.[115] Permission to modify a covered work must be found in a provision of GPLv3 that expressly grants it.

Section 2 of GPLv3 expressly grants permission to "make, run and propagate covered works *that you do not convey,* without conditions. . . ."[116] Section 0 states that to "propagate" a work means to do anything with the work that, without permission, would make the licensee liable for copyright infringement, except running it or "modifying a private copy." Section 0 also states that to "modify" a work means "to copy from or adapt all or part of the work in a fashion requiring copyright permission, other than the making of an exact copy." Because modifying a work means copying from it or adapting it in a way that requires copyright permission, propagation appears to include modification (as long as it is modification of something other than a "private copy"). Therefore, the unconditional permission granted in Section 2 of GPLv3 includes permission to modify "covered works that you do not convey."

Nowhere, however, does GPLv3 state that it permits the licensee—with or without conditions—to modify covered works that the licensee *does* convey. Section 0 states, "To 'convey' a work means any kind of propagation that enables other parties to make or receive copies." Accordingly, if the licensee shares the work with others in any manner that enables them to make or receive copies—and thus conveys the work—then the licensee does not fall within the express permission to modify the work granted under Section 2, which is limited to modification of works that the licensee does not convey. And as noted above, GPLv3 expressly prohibits any modification that it does not expressly permit. As a result, taken literally, GPLv3 expressly prohibits one of the essential freedoms it is designed to protect—the right to modify works that you then share.[117]

---

114. (Emphasis added.) Section 8 continues, "Any attempt otherwise to propagate or modify it is void, and will automatically terminate your rights under this License (including any patent licenses . . .)."

115. Section 0 states, "A 'covered work' means either the unmodified Program or a work based on the Program."

116. (Emphasis added.)

117. One might argue that "works that you do not convey" means "works that you do not simultaneously (at the time of modification) convey." Of course, that is not what the language says. And the alternative language would not make much sense, because

The terms and conditions of GPLv3 do permit the licensee to convey a modified work, once the work has been modified, but the right to convey a work that has been modified is not the same as the right to modify the work in the first place. Section 5 states that the licensee, on stated conditions, may convey "a work based on the Program, or the modifications to produce it from the Program, in the form of source code." Section 6 permits the licensee to convey a covered work in object code if source code is also provided. But to "convey" refers only to propagation "that enables other parties to make or receive copies," and modifying a work does not, in and of itself, so enable others. Moreover, under the Copyright Act, the right to distribute copies of works to the public, provided in Section 106(3), is separate and distinct from the right to prepare derivative works based on the copyrighted work, provided by Section 106(2).[118] A license to do one is not a license to do the other.

GPLv3 is obviously *intended* to permit the licensee to modify even those works that the licensee *does* convey. For example, the Preamble states, "The GNU General Public License is intended to guarantee your freedom to share and change all versions of a program." As Lawrence Rosen has noted, however: "The preamble, of course, is not an operative part of the GPL license. It is not among its *terms and conditions.* There is nothing in its words that must be obeyed."[119] The apparent omission of express permission for the licensee to modify a covered work that the licensee conveys can only be a drafting error—some might even call it a blunder. Nevertheless, the difficulty tracking this core concept through the complex new language of

---

it is difficult to see how modification and conveying of modified works could occur simultaneously as a practical matter. In addition, the permission to modify "works that you do not convey" is granted "without conditions." If this permission applied to works that you *subsequently* convey, it would remove the essential conditions of the GPL, including the copyleft condition. For these reasons, "works that you do not convey" can only be read to apply to works that you do not convey at *any* time. The authorization to modify works that you do not convey does not provide authorization to modify works that you convey after modifying them.

118. 17 U.S.C. § 106(2), (3). Section 10 of GPLv3 states, "Each time you convey a covered work, the recipient automatically receives a license from the original licensors, to run, modify and propagate that work, subject to this License." But this clause (which is part of a section that deals with patents) does not grant any license to the conveying licensee—the "you" addressed in the clause. Nor does it grant a license from the conveying licensee to the recipient permitting the recipient to modify the conveying licensee's contribution, if any.

119. Lawrence Rosen, Open Source Licensing: Software Freedom and Intellectual Property Law 109 (2004) (emphasis in original).

GPLv3 reinforces the conclusion that merely understanding the GPL is a serious challenge.

In Part 1, we saw how EULA impenetrability creates information asymmetry that predictably produces a "lemon license." One might assume that the GPL, designed as it is to "plac[e] users first," is the opposite of a lemon from the user's point of view. In fact, however, the GPL places more restrictions on users than does dedication to the public domain, and by disclaiming warranties and liability, it establishes at least a default rule that leaves the user holding the bag for any software problems. One difference from the EULA is that the licensor often has no information advantage in understanding the GPL, because the licensor often is not FSF, its drafter. But the cost of determining the legal effect of the GPL in any particular set of circumstances remains potentially high, and this cost results in inefficiency.

It is presumably frustration with the EULA-like verbosity of the GPL and other free and open source software licenses that led to the creation of the "Do What the Fuck You Want to Public License."[120] Version 2 of the WTFPL, dated December 2004, contains only 79 words. Its operative provision contains only nine: "You just DO WHAT THE FUCK YOU WANT TO." The WTFPL surpasses all other software licenses in readability. As discussed in Chapter 3, the Flesch-Kincaid grade level score is determined as follows:

$$\text{Grade Level} = (0.39 \times \text{ASL}) + (11.8 \times \text{AWL}) - 15.59$$

For the WTFPL, the score is as follows:

$$\text{Grade Level} = (0.39 \times 9) + (11.8 \times 1) - 15.59$$
$$\text{Grade Level} = 3.51 + 11.8 - 15.59 = -0.28$$

This score means that a child with less than a first grade education is likely to be able to understand the WTFPL (apart from one word that a few first-graders still may not yet know). Given the difference between the 23.6 years of formal education required for the main permission-granting section of the GPL and the −0.28 years required for the WTFPL, there is something to be said for the latter.

120. WTFPL, http://sam.zoy.org/wtfpl/.

4.7 Free as in Free Beer

The word "free" in "free software," according to Stallman, refers to "freedom, not price"—"free" as in "free speech," not as in "free beer."[121] Indeed, he says, "it has *nothing* to do with price."[122] But clearly free software does have *something* to do with price. And clearly it does include a "free beer" component. Free software is *royalty*-free. Under the GPL, there is and can be no royalty to run, change, or redistribute the licensed software. Moreover, the royalty-free character of free software is a core element of Stallman's ideology. He states,

> Extracting money from users of a program by restricting their use of it is destructive because the restrictions reduce the amount and the ways that the program can be used. This reduces the amount of wealth that humanity derives from the program. When there is a deliberate choice to restrict, the harmful consequences are deliberate destruction.[123]

Of course, "[e]xtracting money from users of" a product "by restricting their use of it" if they do not pay for it is how a market economy manages access to all products—other than true public goods, which are not "excludable." If such a restriction impermissibly "reduces the amount of wealth that humanity derives," then all products should be freely available. Even if the argument is limited to "non-rivalrous" information, it seems to suggest that no property rights in information should be recognized. But Stallman appears to believe that someone who creates a work of authorship does have the right to withhold the work altogether, even if doing so reduces humanity's wealth. It is not clear why this is not also impermissible "hoarding."

The "free as in free speech, not as in free beer" motto also points to a more immediate problem with Stallman's ideology, which is that he regards charging for *copies* of free software, as opposed to charging for the right to use them, as not only permissible but laudable. And according to Stallman, not only is it ethical to charge for copies of free software, but one can and should charge as much as the market will bear. He specifically rejects the idea that "you should not charge money for distributing copies of software, or that you

121. Stallman, *Selected Essays,* at 43.

122. *Id.* at 20 (emphasis added).

123. *Id.* at 38.

should charge as little as possible—just enough to cover the cost."[124] Rather, Stallman says, "we encourage people who redistribute free software to charge as much as they wish or can."[125] In fact, "You can charge nothing, a penny, a dollar, or a billion dollars."[126]

One might assume that, if software should be usable without "[e]xtracting money from users" through licensing restrictions, then *copies* of software should not be sold or should be sold only at cost. Withholding a copy from one who does not pay for it can completely preclude the use of the program (and will, if there are no other copies). If "the desire to be rewarded for one's creativity does not justify depriving the world in general of all or part of that creativity," then how can it be ethical to withhold any valuable work one creates? One need not look beyond the GPL itself to see that free software presents this conundrum.

GPL proponents dismiss as "FUD"—"fear, uncertainty, and doubt"—the suggestion that the GPL is a viral "infection" that can force users to distribute their software under the GPL's terms. A GNU FAQ explains, "The GPL does not require you to release your modified version, or any part of it. You are free to make modifications and use them privately, without ever releasing them. This applies to organizations (including companies), too; an organization can make a modified version and use it internally without ever releasing it outside the organization."[127] It is only if the user chooses to distribute the modified program that it must be distributed under the GPL.[128] But if it is unethical, as Stallman maintains, to deprive the world of all or part of one's creativity, then how can it be ethical to permit the user to withhold a modified GPL-licensed program? Why not require that modifications be distributed?

Stallman says that the GPL promotes "pragmatic idealism,"[129] and it may be that not requiring distribution of modified GPL-licensed programs is a necessary compromise to make the license palatable to a sizable number of users. But it also appears that Stallman regards it as entirely ethical, even

---

124. *Id.* at 65.

125. *Id.*

126. *Id.* at 66.

127. Frequently Asked Questions about the GNU Licenses, http://www.gnu.org/licenses/gpl-faq.html.

128. *Id.*

129. Stallman, *Selected Essays,* at 93.

without regard to pragmatic considerations, to deprive the world of access to one's work product except on one's own terms and to charge the world for such access by charging for at least the first distributed copy. Stallman opposes charging fees for use of software, but—in addition to encouraging free software developers to charge fees for copies of the software—he approves of charging fees for providing services related to software, such as developing and consulting. Once again, it is fine to "depriv[e] the world in general of all or part of [one's] creativity" by charging for creative services, as long as no royalty is paid.

The reasons for such distinctions seem to lie as much in Stallman's own personal biography as in any ethical theory. In the mid-1980s, when Stallman developed the GNU Emacs text editor, many people who wanted it were not yet on the Internet and could not get copies by FTP. Because he "had no job" and "was looking for ways to make money from free software," Stallman charged $150 to mail a tape with the software to anyone who wanted one.[130] Extracting money from potential users of a product by restricting their use of it is unethical, but withholding copies from people who did not pay $150 was not an impermissible form of hoarding.

As Stallman points out, the ability to charge for a copy is of limited value when the recipient of any copy is free to redistribute it. This is especially so in the Internet age, when there is no longer any need to mail a tape. In providing reassurance for those who "sometimes worry that a high distribution fee will put free software out of range for users who don't have a lot of money," Stallman says, "The difference is that free software naturally tends to spread around, and there are many ways to get it."[131] Charging $150 for a copy of GNU Emacs may no longer be economically viable. But if it were, under Stallman's ethics, doing so would be perfectly appropriate.

One argument for the distinction between charging a royalty and charging for a copy of free software is that consumption of the "information" embodied in the software is nonrivalrous, whereas consumption of any one copy of the software is at least potentially rivalrous. In other words, any number of people can use Emacs without interfering with each other, but if any one person uses a tape on which Emacs is stored, use of the same tape by others is necessarily more limited. Lawrence Lessig, a Stallman admirer, asserts that "[f]ree code . . . builds a commons in knowledge," and that "[t]his

---

130. *Id.* at 164.

131. *Id.* at 66.

commons is made possible by the nature of information."[132] Lessig explains, "My learning how a Web page is built does not reduce the knowledge of a how a Web page is built. Knowledge . . . is nonrivalrous; your knowing something does not lessen the amount that I can know."[133]

In fact, as noted in Part 1, consumption of information can be rivalrous even when a different copy is being consumed. If a competitor consumes a different copy of a company's trade secret, the company's knowledge may not be lessened, but the secret nevertheless loses value and may even cease to be a trade secret. Even if the information is not a trade secret, its value to a person who uses it may be lessened as it becomes available to others. For example, business software that enhances one's productivity is less valuable when one's competitors also use it than when they do not. And consumption of the same copy can be at least partially nonrivalrous, as in the case of a tape that is reused or software that is used by multiple users on a network. But we can assume for the sake of argument that one person's consumption of any one copy of software is likely to affect other persons' potential consumption of that one copy in ways that the one person's consumption does not affect other persons' consumption of other copies.

On this assumption, the GPL prohibits charging for the nonrivalrous information content of software, but permits charging for the rivalrous copies of the software. Perhaps it is ethical to charge for consumption that precludes consumption by others, whereas it is unethical to charge for consumption that does not preclude consumption by others. Or, in Lessig's less moralistic terms, "With ordinary property, the law must both create an incentive to produce and protect the right of possession; with intellectual property, the law need only create the incentive to produce."[134]

Leaving aside the possible effects on the incentives of potential creators, and focusing only on rivalry in consumption, one can see that not charging for consumption of rivalrous goods does seem problematic in a way that not charging for consumption of nonrivalrous goods may not be. If rivalrous goods are free, they may be consumed by persons who do not value them, or do not need them, as much as others, and those who value or need them more will be deprived of them, precisely because they are rivalrous.

---

132. Lawrence Lessig, The Future of Ideas: The Fate of the Commons in a Connected World 57 (2001).

133. *Id.*

134. Lawrence Lessig, Code Version 2.0 183 (2006).

In contrast, if nonrivalrous goods are free, then those who value them or need them most will be able to consume them (assuming they are produced in the first place) even if others also consume them as well.

For example, if the grocery store has 25 cartons of eggs, giving them away at no charge will mean that those who value them most will not necessarily receive them. The first customers to arrive, even though they might not have been willing to pay more than a few cents for a carton of eggs, will take as many cartons as they want, and subsequent customers, even though they might have been willing to pay full price, will be confronted with empty shelves and perhaps a few stray yolks. Charging for eggs allocates scarce supplies of a rivalrous good to those who value the good most. One can dispute whether those who value the good most in terms of being able and willing to pay the most are those who need or deserve the good most, but there is at least a basis for allocating rivalrous goods on the basis of price.

On the other hand, if the store posts on its Web site a recipe for making omelets that customers can download at no charge, giving away the information content of the recipe for free will not prevent any customer from "consuming" the information, because consumption by those who value the information less will not in and of itself reduce the supply of the information to those who value it more. Those who want the recipe most intensely will still be able to download it no matter how many others have already downloaded it. If charging for a copy of software is like charging for a carton of eggs, and providing the software royalty-free is like giving away the omelet recipe at no charge, then perhaps the distinction between selling copies and charging royalties makes some sense.

But in the case of information goods, consumption of copies can be made *effectively* nonrivalrous, at minimal cost to the producer, simply by not charging for additional copies. In fact, this is exactly what is happening in the grocery store example. The eggs cannot be "copied," but the store is providing each customer who logs onto the Web site with a copy of the recipe. Using any one copy of a recipe is potentially rivalrous, but consumption is effectively nonrivalrous because the grocery store provides multiple copies for free. And the cost of each additional copy is negligible to the provider. If it is unethical to charge a royalty and ethical to charge for copies only because copies are rivalrous, then the copying charge is essentially self-justifying—because it is only the existence of a fee for copies that makes any copy effectively rivalrous. Charging for eggs is necessary to provide eggs to those who value them most, but charging for copies is not necessary to provide copies to those who value them most, because in the absence of a charge, it costs little or nothing to provide copies to everyone. If it is unethical to charge for the "information" through a license fee, one might reasonably conclude that it is also unethical to charge for cost-free copies.

The Internet made it more difficult, as a practical matter, to charge for copies, but Stallman found "another way to make a living . . . in selling services relating to the free software" he had developed.[135] "This included teaching, for subjects such as how to program GNU Emacs and how to customize GCC, and software development, mostly porting GCC to new platforms."[136] He apparently considered it ethically permissible to withhold the benefits of access to teaching and development from those who would not pay for it.

Of course, there is nothing wrong with making a living. In fact, making a living is generally a good idea. But the rather large loophole in Stallman software ethics that permits, when it comes to making a living, withholding services and copies of software from people who do not pay for them reminds us that economic constraints cannot be avoided. It also enters into the evaluation of free and open source licensing, because no matter how generous development collaborators are, they, too, must make a living. How they do so is important.

---

135. *Id.* at 24.

136. *Id.*

FIVE

From "Free" to "Open Source"

IN 1998, AT LEAST IN PART as a response to the moralism of the free software movement, a group of people who believed in providing access to source code and rights to modify it coined the less politically charged term "open source" to describe these concepts.[1] As Eric Raymond recalls,

> It seemed clear to us in retrospect that the term 'free software' had done our movement tremendous damage over the years. Part of this stemmed from the well-known 'free-speech/free-beer' ambiguity. Most of it came from something worse—the strong association of the term 'free software' with hostility to intellectual property rights, communism, and other ideas hardly likely to endear themselves to an MIS manager.[2]

Raymond and others in the open source movement asserted more pragmatic values. What was needed, they concluded, was better marketing. "Our success after Netscape would depend on replacing the negative FSF stereotypes with positive stereotypes of our own—pragmatic tales, sweet to managers' and investors' ears, of higher reliability and lower cost and better features."[3] Their ideas included the view that the transparency and collaborative character of open source software produces software of higher quality. Raymond's dictum, which he calls "Linus's law," is that "[g]iven enough eyeballs, all bugs are shallow."[4] Less dramatically, "[g]iven a large enough

---

1. Michael Tiemann, *History of the OSI* (Sep. 19, 2006), at http://www.opensource.org/history.

2. Eric S. Raymond, *The Revenge of the Hackers, in* OPEN SOURCES: VOICES FROM THE OPEN SOURCE REVOLUTION 212 (Chris DiBona, Sam Ockman, & Mark Stone, eds., 1999) [hereinafter Raymond, *Revenge*].

3. *Id.*

4. Eric S. Raymond, *The Cathedral & the Bazaar, in* THE CATHEDRAL & THE BAZAAR: MUSINGS ON LINUX AND OPEN SOURCE BY AN ACCIDENTAL REVOLUTIONARY 30 (1999) [hereinafter Raymond, *Cathedral*].

beta-tester and co-developer base, almost every problem will be characterized quickly and the fix obvious to someone."[5]

A crucial element of this pragmatism is at least a partial rejection of the "copyleft" concept, in which distribution of modified versions must occur on the same royalty-free terms as distribution of the original. Although the Open Source Initiative (OSI) approves the GPL and other copyleft licenses as "open source," OSI also recognizes permissive licenses as valuable instantiations of the open source model. These licenses vary in terms and complexity but do not require that all derivative works be licensed on the same terms.

For example, the BSD license, which originated as the license from the University of California for Berkeley Unix, permits the user to do essentially anything with the software, as long as the licensor's copyright notice is retained. The license provides, "Redistribution and use in source and binary forms, with or without modification, are permitted," provided that three conditions are met: first, redistributions of source code must retain the copyright notice, the list of conditions, and a warranty disclaimer; second, redistributions in binary form must also reproduce the copyright notice, the list of conditions, and the disclaimer; third, neither the name of the licensor "nor the names of its contributors may be used to endorse or promote products derived from [the] software without specific prior written permission."[6] An "advertising" clause in the original BSD license requiring credit to the University of California no longer appears. Under the BSD license, the software can be incorporated into proprietary software without any violation of the license terms.

5.1 A Focus on Process

Because "open source" software overlaps with "free" software, people often refer to "free and open source software," "FOSS," or "F/OSS." To make the acronym more interesting, they sometimes refer to "free/libre and open source software," or "FLOSS." Proponents of the term "open source," as opposed to "free," have shown less interest in ideology and more interest in defining a process for creating software that performs tasks well. Whereas Stallman is an avowed activist, both Eric Raymond and Linus Torvalds, in

---

5. *Id.*

6. BSD License, http://www.opensource.org/licenses/bsd-license.php.

the subtitles of their books, refer to themselves as "accidental revolutionaries."[7] (An earlier book on the history of the personal computer industry was entitled *Accidental Empires,*[8] suggesting that many things happen by accident in this field.)

Although Eric Raymond calls Linux "subversive," Raymond's most famous essay, reprinted in his book by the same name, *The Cathedral & the Bazaar,* focuses on the process of open source development rather than on ideology. Raymond remarks, "I think Linus's cleverest and most consequential hack was not the construction of the Linux kernel itself, but rather his invention of the Linux development model."[9] This "bazaar" model, in Raymond's view, is to "release early and often, delegate everything you can, be open to the point of promiscuity," replacing "quiet, reverent cathedral-building" with "a great babbling bazaar of differing agendas and approaches . . . , out of which a coherent and stable system could seemingly emerge only by a succession of miracles."[10]

Raymond contrasts the "bazaar" model of open source development with the more traditional model in which development is similar to building a "cathedral." Frederick Brooks, Jr., was a leading designer of IBM's OS/360, the operating system for the System/360 series, and author of *The Mythical Man-Month,* a classic series of essays on software engineering. Brooks's law posits that "[a]dding manpower to a late software project makes it later."[11] Brooks should know ; as Paul Ceruzzi writes, "System/360 was a success for IBM and redefined the industry . . . , but the operating system OS/360 . . . was a failure and its troubles almost sank the company."[12]

In one of the essays in the book, Brooks compares the design of a software system to the design of a great cathedral.[13] Although Brooks was talking

---

7. *See* LINUS TORVALDS & DAVID DIAMOND, JUST FOR FUN: THE STORY OF AN ACCIDENTAL REVOLUTIONARY (2001); ERIC S. RAYMOND, THE CATHEDRAL & THE BAZAAR: MUSINGS ON LINUX AND OPEN SOURCE BY AN ACCIDENTAL REVOLUTIONARY (1999).

8. ROBERT X. CRINGELY, ACCIDENTAL EMPIRES: HOW THE BOYS OF SILICON VALLEY MAKE THEIR MILLIONS, BATTLE FOREIGN COMPETITION, AND STILL CAN'T GET A DATE (1996).

9. Raymond, *Cathedral,* at 27.

10. *Id.* at 21–22.

11. Frederick P. Brooks, Jr., *The Mythical Man-Month, in* THE MYTHICAL MAN-MONTH: ESSAYS ON SOFTWARE ENGINEERING 25 (1975).

12. PAUL E. CERUZZI, A HISTORY OF MODERN COMPUTING 101 (1998).

13. Frederick P. Brooks, Jr., *Aristocracy, Democracy, and System Design, in* THE MYTHICAL MAN-MONTH: ESSAYS ON SOFTWARE ENGINEERING 41, 42 (1975).

about proprietary software, Raymond makes clear that he also finds the Free Software Foundation approach to be closer to a "cathedral"-building model.[14] According to Raymond, "[o]ne unexpected side-effect of FSF's policy of trying to legally bind code into the GPL is that it becomes procedurally harder for FSF to use the bazaar mode. . . ."[15]

The GPL's ethical purity, if not rigidity, is inconsistent with "a great babbling bazaar of differing agendas and approaches," not only because the GPL embodies and requires a single agenda and approach but also because the very concept of a "bazaar" seems alien to the GPL philosophy. As noted in the preceding chapter, Stallman's ethical views permit charging for copies of software, as opposed to charging royalties for use of software, but Stallman and the GPL reject any mixing of free software with "proprietary" software for which license fees are charged. Under the GPL, if you combine another program with a GPL-licensed program, the other program must also be distributed under the GPL.

Section 2 of GPLv2 provides that, if "identifiable sections" of a modified work are not "derived from" the covered work and "can be reasonably considered independent and separate works in themselves," then the GPL does not apply to those sections "when you distribute them as separate works." In addition, Section 2 of GPLv2 provides that "mere aggregation" of a separate work with a covered work "on a volume of a storage or distribution medium does not bring the other work under the scope of this License." These provisions have made it possible for Linux "distributions" to include works that are not licensed under the GPL and even works that are not free software at all, as long as they are independent and separate works. Section 5 of GPLv3 revises this language, but uses similar terms.

Considerable controversy, but little or no guiding case law, has arisen over the circumstances in which combining a GPL-licensed work with another work brings the other work within the GPL. One potential dividing line is static versus dynamic linking, but the real picture is more complex. Static linking occurs when a source code file is linked with another file, before

14. Raymond, *Cathedral,* at 29.

15. Eric S. Raymond, *The Cathedral and the Bazaar,* FIRST MONDAY, Feb. 16, 1998, http://www.firstmonday.org/issues/issue3_3/raymond/. Interestingly, the quoted passage, which appears in the version of Raymond's essay in the online journal *First Monday,* does not appear in the version of the same essay in Raymond's 1999 book or in the online version on Raymond's Web site. *See* http://www.catb.org/~esr/writings/cathedral-bazaar/cathedral-bazaar/ar01s03.html.

compiling, so that the compiled binary file contains code from the other file.[16] Dynamic linking, on the other hand, occurs when a compiled binary file, while running, calls functions that instruct the processor to execute a separate binary file in a separate address space.[17] Although static linking generally seems more likely to give rise to a combined work that is subject to the GPL, Linus Torvalds asserts that the dynamic versus static linking debate is a "red herring,"[18] and Eben Moglen says that the line depends not on whether the linking is static or dynamic, but on "copyright law."[19] Without judicial decisions that say where "copyright law" draws the boundary in the case of software, the GPL leaves the line-drawing, for now, to the pronouncements of its advocates.

5.2 Open Source License Proliferation

Non-copyleft open source licenses eliminate the uncertainty about the extent to which a licensed work can be combined with another work, because they do not require that derivative works be licensed on the same terms as the original work. But the sheer number of such licenses currently in use, and the likelihood that any single compilation of open source software may be distributed under multiple different licenses, multiplies the uncertainty that any one of these licenses contains.

The open source "movement" seems to take a "bazaar" approach not only to software development, but also to the development of software licenses. The Open Source Initiative (OSI), which currently approves some 72 of the many open source software licenses in circulation, has formed an advisory committee to address the challenge of open source "license proliferation."[20] Creative Commons alone offers six different licenses.[21] For each license there

---

16. *See* Lothar Determann, *Dangerous Liaisons—Software Combinations as Derivative Works? Distribution, Installation, and Execution of Linked Programs under Copyright Law, Commercial Licenses, and the GPL*, 21 BERKELEY TECH. L.J. 1421, 1459–60 (2006).

17. *See id.*

18. Linus Torvalds, *Re: GPL Only Modules*, Dec. 17, 2006, http://lkml.org/lkml/2006/12/17/79.

19. FSF Europe, *Transcript of Richard Stallman at the 4th international GPLv3 conference; 23rd August 2006*, http://www.fsfeurope.org/projects/gplv3/bangalore-rms-transcript.

20. OSI License Proliferation Project, http://opensource.org/proliferation/.

21. Creative Commons, About: License Your Work, http://creativecommons.org/about/license/.

is a "Commons Deed," which attempts to describe the license in simple terms, and a statement of "Legal Code," which is the actual license, replete with disclaimers, definitions, and detailed provisions. The idea of expressing the license itself in simple, readable terms seems not to have been considered, or if considered, to have been abandoned.

All the Creative Commons licenses require attribution, which in simple terms means that "[y]ou must attribute the work in the manner specified by the author or licensor (but not in any way that suggests that they endorse you or your use of the work)." You can also license the work on a "non-commercial," "no-derivatives," or "share-alike" basis, or combinations of the foregoing. So you can license the work on an attribution/noncommercial basis, an attribution/no-derivatives basis, or an attribution/share-alike basis. Or you can license the work on an attribution/noncommercial/share-alike basis or an attribution/noncommercial/no-derivatives basis. Creative Commons offers a Web-based interface to help users figure out which of these licenses they want to adopt, which is helpful, considering the array of alternatives.

The slogan of Creative Commons is "no friction, no legal doubt, no middleman."[22] As Niva Elkin-Koren observes, however,

> Creative Commons' strategy presupposes that minimizing external information costs is critical for enhancing access to creative works. It seeks to reduce these costs by offering a licensing platform. Yet, the lack of standardization in the licenses supported by this licensing scheme further increases the cost of determining the duties and privileges related to any specific work. This could add force to the chilling effect of copyrights.[23]

Such considerations have all the more force considering that the Creative Commons licenses take their place alongside numerous other open source licenses. For the developer of digital content who wants to use stock footage, clip art, production music, or other digital works, nothing matches public domain status, and failing that, proprietary "buyout" media in which the user purchases the right to use the work in any production may actually be preferable to a Creative Commons license, with the legal uncertainty it carries and

---

22. Niva Elkin-Koren, *Intellectual Property and Public Values: What Contracts Cannot Do: The Limits of Private Ordering in Facilitating a Creative Commons*, 74 FORDHAM L. REV. 375, 385 (2005).

23. *Id.* at 410.

the risk it presents that inputs will have to be changed after production if the intended use of the work changes, as it often does.

5.3 Process and Usability

One difference between public intellectual property and commercial law and the legislative license is in the relevant constituencies. Whether influenced by principles or by process, free and open source software tends to be *developer-focused* rather than *user-focused*—and so, too, are free and open source licenses. Raymond states that the "first lesson" of effective open sourcedevelopment is that "[e]very good work of software starts by scratching a developer's personal itch."[24] If the non-developer user has an itch, getting it scratched is purely coincidental. Stallman states that free software follows common-sense morality while "placing the users first," but the "users" to whom Stallman refers are users who are *also* developers. The freedomof "users" to access and modify source code and to distribute modified versions of code is a freedom that can be enjoyed only by a certain kind of user—namely, the user-developer. Stallman's vision is thus also developer-focused.

One of the main reasons that software is as important and prevalent as it is today is precisely that most users are not, and do not have to be, developers at all, any more than the vast majority of people who drive cars need to have more than a vague idea what goes on under the hood. SourceForge.net, "the world's largest Open Source software development web site," hosts (as of this writing) about 1.9 million registered users.[25] Of course, not all developers are registered on SourceForge, just as not all registered users of SourceForge are developers. But we can see that the number of active open source programmers is very small in relation to the total number of computer users. According to the consulting firm Gartner, Inc., "[t]he number of installed PCs worldwide has surpassed 1 billion units. . . ."[26] Nearly 1.5 billion of the world's 6.6 billion people, including 633 million in North America and Europe alone,

---

24. Raymond, *Cathedral*, at 23.

25. SourceForge.net, http://alexandria.wiki.sourceforge.net/What+is+SourceForge.net%3F.

26. Gartner, Inc., Press Release, Gartner Says More than 1 Billion PCs In Use Worldwide and Headed to 2 Billion Units by 2014, June 23, 2008, http://www.gartner.com/it/page.jsp?id=703807.

use the Internet.[27] Considering only those 633 million, the number of registered users of SourceForge.net represents about three-tenths of 1 percent of total Internet users. The other 99.7 percent of Internet users in North America and Europe do not contribute to SourceForge.net and, in all probability, most of them do not read or write source code.

Proprietary software, in contrast to FOSS, focuses almost entirely on the 99.7 percent. Of course, the EULA's constituency is not the general user either. But for non-developer users, software "freedom" is not a matter of freedom to study or change source code, but rather freedom to use software in ways they want to use it. Except in the case of development tools, proprietary software is tailored and marketed to people who are not developers, and in all cases, ease of use is a central consideration. This is a natural consequence of proprietary distribution. Other things being equal, in the commercial marketplace, products that are easier to use will displace products that are harder to use. The market drives usability. With FOSS, in contrast, usability is often wanting.

Raymond himself has recognized the problem of open source usability. In a 1998 essay, he points out that, although the "hackers" who write open source software "can be very good at designing interfaces for other hackers, they tend to be poor at modeling the thought processes of the other 95% of the population well enough to write interfaces that J. Random End-User and his Aunt Tillie will pay to buy."[28] The only problem with this analysis is that, as shown above, the suggestion that hackers are 5 percent of the population wildly overstates their numbers.

In a 2004 essay (which he refers to as a "rant"),[29] Raymond recounts his experience attempting to configure an open source program known as CUPS, the Common Unix Printing System. Raymond calls it "a textbook lesson in why nontechnical people run screaming from Unix."[30] He might have said, "from open source software." Despite the efforts of CUPS's developers to create an "accessible" system, "the best intentions and effort have led to a system which despite its superficial pseudo-friendliness is so undiscoverable that it might as well have been written in ancient Sanskrit."[31]

---

27. Internet World Stats, as of June 30, 2008, http://www.internetworldstats.com/stats.htm.

28. Raymond, *Revenge*, at 218–19.

29. Eric S. Raymond, *The Luxury of Ignorance: An Open-Source Horror Story*, http://www.catb.org/~esr/writings/cups-horror.html [hereinafter Raymond, *Rant*].

30. *Id.*

31. *Id.*

Raymond suggests that open source developers should create a user interface for Aunt Tillie, "the archetypal non-technical user."[32] In the program he tried to use, "Aunt Tillie is already getting the idea that this software was written by geeks without clue."[33] Moreover, Raymond continues, "This kind of fecklessness is endemic in open-source land. And it's what's keeping Microsoft in business—because by Goddess, they may write crappy insecure overpriced shoddy software, but on this one issue"—user interface design—"their half-assed semi-competent best is an order of magnitude better than we usually manage."[34] He concludes, "We talk about world domination, but we'll neither have it nor deserve it until we learn to do better than this. A lot better."[35]

In a follow-up post, Raymond remarks that "the volume of community reaction that thundered into my mailbox far surpassed what I had been expecting," and most of it appears to have agreed with him.[36] He quotes one person as saying,

> If Aunt Tillie can't run your software, scolding her for being a brainless luser [. . .] buys you exactly nothing. Nothing but a 0% market share. Aunt Tillie is *right*, you are *wrong*. She votes with her feet. [. . .] Thanks for being a voice, and one with the street cred not to be dismissed as a (sneer) newbie.[37]

Raymond also notes that the problems are not just with any one piece of software:

> The CUPS mess is not a failure of one development team, or of one distribution integrator. In fact, it makes a better example because the CUPS guys and the Fedora guys are both well above the median in both general technical chops, design smarts, and attention to usability. The fact that this mess is an example of our best in action, rather than our worst, just highlights how appallingly low our standards have been.[38]

---

32. *Id.*
33. *Id.*
34. *Id.*
35. *Id.*
36. Eric S. Raymond, *The Luxury of Ignorance: Part Deux,* http://www.catb.org/~esr/writings/luxury-part-deux.html.
37. *Id.*
38. *Id.*

Another open source programmer writes,

> There's a reason why the 'Linux Revolution' hasn't put so much as a small dent in Microsoft, and I'm able to sum it up in a few words:
> Simplicity.
> Attitude.
> Documentation.[39]

At least two of these three words are user oriented.

The most successful open source projects—Linux and the Apache Web server—are aimed primarily at technical users. Linux has had its greatest success in the server market, in which the users are information technology professionals, and it remains largely a nonevent on the desktop. Citing blunders in user interface design, Raymond remarks, "This kind of crap is exactly why Linux has had such trouble gaining traction among nontechnical users. . . ."[40] Apache is the Web server software for more than 82 million Web sites, including more than 33 million active sites, giving Apache 50 percent of the market.[41] But most Web users are unaware that Apache exists.

Surprisingly, however, for all its candor, Raymond's usability rant seems not to consider that open source software's lack of usability for "Aunt Tillie" might be a direct and predictable consequence of a development process in which, as he points out, the guiding inspiration is a "developer's personal itch." If no developer's personal itch extends to improving usability, then usability can be expected to suffer under such a model. And this development process, in turn, is intimately connected with the open source license.

Raymond describes design steps that open source developers would take if they were "half-smart" about user interface issues "like, say, Windows programmers," or "really smart like, say, Mac programmers."[42] But there is a reason other than smarts that Windows is at least partially better attuned to usability, and that Mac OS, which is as proprietary as it gets, is the most usable. The reason is that the proprietary focus requires an emphasis on the mass user. The disregard, if not disdain, that GPL moralists and many open

39. Joseph Betz, *An Email to Eric Raymond, Regarding My Adventures in LiveCD Linux -or- Why Bill Gates Is Still Rich*, July 19, 2006, http://www.newhorizonssucks.net/LiveCD.html.

40. Raymond, *Rant.*

41. Netcraft March 2008 Web Server Survey, http://news.netcraft.com/ archives/2008/03/26/ march_2008_web_server_survey.html.

42. Raymond, *Rant.*

source pragmatists have for the mass user suggests that, at least for its most intense advocates, FOSS is indeed the hacker's revenge—not only in the sense intended by Raymond's essay that so states,[43] but also as a counterstrike against mass software, by a group that regards itself as a technical elite.

One of the revolutionary effects of the personal computer was that it brought computing to users who were *not* also programmers. In the early days of the PC, each user—even in a business setting—controlled his or her own machine. PC networks were nonexistent or rudimentary, and often there was no information technology department to exert control over the desktop. Users who were technically inclined could write their own programs, but most users relied on commercial off-the-shelf programs, such as Visicalc or later, Lotus 1-2-3, that they could use as they wished. People who had not considered themselves technical could discover new uses for PCs and could experiment with those uses simply by acquiring relatively low-cost software packages and running the software themselves.

As networks became more robust and network communication became more important, the information technology establishment reasserted itself, and in some organizations it asserted itself for the first time. In the name of security and protection against viruses, IT departments restricted the ability of PC users to install software and even to configure their own machines. Lacking administrative privileges, general users no longer had a direct relationship with their computers. Rather, their relationship was intermediated by an IT priesthood that knew best, even when it lacked a basis to appreciate the actual business objectives for which the PCs were obtained in the first place. Likewise, for all the rhetoric about freedom, FOSS is very much about the primacy of the programmer.

Robert L. Glass points out that FOSS projects are also hierarchical, with key decisions being made by "product gurus"—including Linus himself.[44] Although users have the freedom, in principle, to make any changes they desire and to distribute those changes, such freedom is constrained, in practice, by the problem of "forking."[45] When users propose changes in products such as Linux, "[t]he change moves up the hierarchy to the product guru, who then makes a decision as to the whether the change is worthy of

---

43. *See* Raymond, *Revenge,* at 207.

44. Robert L. Glass, *Standing in Front of the Open Source Steamroller, in* PERSPECTIVES ON FREE AND OPEN SOURCE SOFTWARE 87 (Joseph Feller, Brian Fitzgerald, Scott A. Hissam, & Karim R. Lakhani, eds., 2005).

45. *See id.* at 88.

inclusion in the product."[46] If the guru rejects the change and the user wants to distribute a version that contains it anyway, the user has "*forked* the product,"[47] and future users and contributors will have to choose between the two (or more) forks in the product's path.

As Glass explains, forking is uncommon, "with good reason."[48] It can produce "loss of commonality" if multiple versions persist, and as the product progresses through new versions, the changes and modifications in one fork will either be left out of the other fork or added at substantial cost in labor and potential errors.[49] Because of these problems, "the notion of the average user feeling free to change the open source product is a highly mixed blessing, and one unlikely to be frequently exercised."[50] When forking does occur, it can create additional dilemmas for the general user who must choose, often with inadequate information, between the fork's competing tines.

5.4 Usability and Subsidy

Why does FOSS licensing, despite its public-spirited reputation, tend to serve a constituency of developers and developer-users better than general users? One place to look for an answer is in how the costs of FOSS development are borne, by whom, and why. For proprietary software, the answer to such questions is relatively easy. The user bears the costs (and provides the profits) by paying for the product. The proprietary software provider must offer a product for which users will pay. This does not mean that the software will always be the best that might be offered. The provider may try to make up through marketing what it fails to provide in quality, and as suggested in Part 1, information asymmetry may reduce quality. But the basic distribution model is one in which the user pays for what the user gets.

In contrast, with FOSS, the user does not pay directly for the right to use the software. Because FOSS is licensed royalty-free, the cost of developing it cannot be recovered from royalties. The user may pay for a copy, or for services related to the software, or for a machine on which the software runs, or the user may not pay anything at all. The link between the software and

46. *Id.*

47. *Id.*

48. *Id.*

49. *Id.*

50. *Id.*

the user's payment, if any, is attenuated. One way or another, the cost of development is subsidized by something other than a direct payment.

In discussing the economics of open source software, Josh Lerner and Jean Tirole remark that "[t]he decision to contribute without pay to freely available software may seem mysterious to economists."[51] They propose to solve the mystery by pointing to several benefits enjoyed by the "unpaid programmer" who works on an open source project. These benefits include

- improved performance in "paid work,"
- "intrinsic pleasure if choosing a 'cool' open source [project] is more fun than a routine task set by an employer,"
- "future job offers" and other long-term benefits, and
- "ego gratification from peer recognition."[52]

These comments assume that the programmer is "unpaid," at least for the open source development work. In the case of Linux, this is often not the case. Robert Young co-founded Red Hat Software, Inc., one of the leading commercial vendors of Linux distributions. Young observes that, although "the 'lone hacker' is a valuable and important part of the development process, such programmers account for a minority of the code that make [sic] up the Linux OS."[53] Rather, "much of the code in the Linux OS is built by professional software developers at major software, engineering, and research organizations."[54] In fact, he notes, "the talent behind Open Source is by and large the same talent that is behind conventional software."[55] Focusing on embedded Linux, one researcher estimates that "about 90% of the effort . . . is made by programmers at work. . . ."[56]

More broadly, studies show that the majority of the work on open source projects in fact is done by programmers as paid employees. "Many large firms

---

51. Josh Lerner & Jean Tirole, *The Economics of Technology Sharing: Open Source and Beyond,* 19 Journal of Economic Perspectives 99, 102 (2005).

52. *Id.*

53. Robert Young, *Giving It Away: How Red Hat Software Stumbled Across a New Economic Model and Helped Improve an Industry, in* Open Sources: Voices from the Open Source Revolution 122 (Chris DiBona, Sam Ockman, & Mark Stone eds., 1999).

54. *Id.*

55. *Id.*

56. James Bessen, *Open Source Software: Free Provision of Complex Public Goods, in* The Economics of Open Source Software Development 58 (Jürgen Bitzer & Philipp J.H. Schröder eds., 2006).

such as IBM, HP, Computer Associates, and Novell have dedicated substantial resources to (F/OSS) development."[57] According to a study by Karim Lakhani and Robert Wolf, 55 percent of contributors to open source software "contributed code during their work time."[58] Notably, only "38 percent of the sample indicated supervisor awareness (explicit or tacit consent)," and a full "17 percent indicated shirking their official job while working on the project."[59] Such findings suggest that the majority of the programming effort in open source is—intentionally or unwittingly—employer subsidized.

Employer-Directed OSS Development

In the case of employer-directed OSS development, the firm invests in open source development to achieve its business objectives. But the motivation for contributing to software that others can freely use is sometimes unclear. It may also seem surprising that firms can operate successful businesses based on the sale of free software. Young, the Red Hat co-founder, candidly suggests that selling copies of Linux is something like selling water. He points out that "[d]rinking water can be had in most industrial countries simply by turning on the nearest tap," and asks, "so why does Evian sell millions of dollars of French tap water into those markets?"[60] The answer, he says, "boils down to a largely irrational fear that the water coming from your tap is not to be trusted."[61] For the same reason, "many people prefer to purchase 'Official' Red Hat Linux in a box for $50 when they could download it for free or buy unofficial CD-ROM copies of Red Hat for as little as $2."[62]

Although water in a fancy bottle may sell well, the business model that leads to the most private investment in open source software is one in which the software is used to promote the sale of non-free complements. Firms may "participate in F/OSS because the availability of free software increases

---

57. *Id.*

58. Karim R. Lakhani & Robert G. Wolf, *Why Hackers Do What They Do: Understanding Motivation and Effort in Free/Open Source Software Projects, in* PERSPECTIVES ON FREE AND OPEN SOURCE SOFTWARE 9 (Joseph Feller, Brian Fitzgerald, Scott A. Hissam, & Karim R. Lakhani eds., 2005).

59. *Id.* at 9–10.

60. *Id.* at 116.

61. *Id.*

62. *Id.* at 116–17.

sales of complementary hardware or services."[63] Lerner and Tirole explain, "A for-profit firm that seeks to provide services and products that are complementary to the open source product, but are not supplied efficiently by the open source community, can be referred to as 'living symbiotically.'"[64] If no one bought IBM machines that run Linux or IBM services related to Linux, IBM would be unlikely to spend anything on Linux development. IBM's unbundling of hardware and software helped create the software industry in the 1970s, and in a sense, for IBM, Linux facilitates a kind of rebundling.[65]

In *The Wealth of Networks,* Yochai Benkler states that, in 2003, Linux-related services provided more than $2 billion in IBM revenues, which was more than twice the revenues that year from IBM's transfer and licensing of patent rights.[66] It was also twice the amount IBM said it had invested in Linux development.[67] According to Benkler, "IBM has combined both supply-side and demand-side strategies to adopt a nonproprietary business model that has generated more than $2 billion yearly of business for the firm. Its strategy is, if not symbiotic, certainly complementary to free software."[68]

The characterization of IBM's business model as "nonproprietary" is a bit surprising. The IBM hardware and services that generate the billions of dollars in revenue are most assuredly proprietary. The Linux business model of IBM and other firms with similar products and services is also proprietary. The model is based on selling these proprietary complements to free software. Josh Lerner and Jean Tirole have suggested that, when companies such as IBM and Hewlett-Packard release code as open source, the "strategy is to give away the razor (the released code) to sell more razor

---

63. James Bessen, *Open Source Software: Free Provision of Complex Public Goods, in* THE ECONOMICS OF OPEN SOURCE SOFTWARE DEVELOPMENT 59 (Jürgen Bitzer & Philipp J.H. Schröder eds., 2006).

64. Josh Lerner & Jean Tirole, *The Economics of Technology Sharing: Open Source and Beyond,* 19 JOURNAL OF ECONOMIC PERSPECTIVES 99, 105 (2005).

65. *Cf.* Gregory S. Crawford & Joseph Cullen, *Bundling, Product Choice, and Efficiency: Should Cable Television Networks Be Offered à la Carte?,* 19 INFORMATION ECONOMICS AND POLICY 379, 380 (2007) ("[b]undling is a common feature in many imperfectly competitive product markets," and firms in "information industries," among others, "frequently offer products in bundles").

66. YOCHAI BENKLER, THE WEALTH OF NETWORKS: HOW SOCIAL PRODUCTION TRANSFORMS MARKETS AND FREEDOM 46–47 (2007).

67. *Id.* at 46.

68. *Id.* at 46–47.

blades (the related consulting services that IBM and Hewlett Packard hope to provide)."[69]

Proprietary software addresses the potential public goods character of software in its "raw" state by using the law, and often DRM, to make software products excludable. These measures prevent the free user copying that would make software effectively nonrivalrous. In contrast, the IBM Linux strategy accepts the public goods character of the software, but ties it to proprietary goods and services. Such a "tying arrangement" provides a public good in conjunction with the paid-for consumption of a private good. Although the economics of open source software has some attributes of the "razor-and-blades" strategy mentioned by Lerner and Tirole, free parking at a shopping mall may provide a better analogy. Tying in this context does not mean that one *must* buy two items together. Rather, it means that one is paid for and one is free, but the two are likely to be used together.[70]

One result of this business strategy is that it provides IBM and others in its position with an incentive to make contributions that lead to the evolution of the software in ways that complement, rather than substituting for, proprietary services. Shopping malls offer free parking when most of the people who park are likely to be shoppers. Downtown stores are more likely to charge for parking or at least to require validation, despite the additional enforcement costs. Likewise, from IBM's point of view, the optimal level and nature of the contribution to Linux depends on how sales of IBM hardware and services will be affected. In deciding how much to invest in Linux development, and in deciding which development objectives to pursue in its effort, IBM naturally focuses on contributions that will maximize the value of IBM hardware, IBM services, or both, when Linux is used with them.

These choices are not necessarily the same ones that IBM could be expected to make if it were providing a separate proprietary operating system rather than contributing to Linux. Someone building a pay parking garage will place it where the demand for parking, in general, is high. Someone building parking for a shopping mall will place it at the mall. The latter will meet the needs of shoppers at the mall but will not meet the parking needs of city dwellers. Just as an individual FOSS developer may not have an incentive to make open source software easy to use without the services

---

69. Josh Lerner & Jean Tirole, *The Economics of Technology Sharing: Open Source and Beyond,* 19 JOURNAL OF ECONOMIC PERSPECTIVES 99, 106 (2005).

70. *See* Tyler Cowen, *Public Goods and Externalities: Old and New Perspectives, in* PUBLIC GOODS & MARKET FAILURES: A CRITICAL EXAMINATION 1, 10 (1988).

such a developer can provide for a fee, IBM may not have an incentive to make Linux easy to use without IBM consulting services. We find that, in fact, IBM's primary contributions to Linux have been in areas other than usability and user interfaces.

It may or may not be efficient for the mall owner to provide free parking. As a general proposition, it is more efficient when people pay directly for something than when they pay indirectly for it, because subsidies undermine the price system. According to Harold Demsetz, "if the cost of policing the benefits derived from the use of [public] goods is low, there is an excellent reason for excluding those who do not pay from using these goods"—namely, that the exclusion permits the market to "estimate accurately the value of diverting resources from other uses to the production of the public good."[71] Demsetz explains,

> Only where scarcity is absent is it *a priori* reasonable to charge a zero price. Superabundance is the only true *a priori* case for a zero-priced public good. All other goods are such that their provision forces us into resource allocation problems. To solve these problems efficiently, we need information which is obtained by excluding nonpurchasers, *provided that the additional information is worth more than the exchange and police costs necessitated.* In cases where the costs are greater, a zero price can be reconciled with efficiency requirements.[72]

Such an analysis suggests that free parking at a suburban mall may make sense if the cost of charging for parking and enforcing the charge would exceed the cost of providing slightly more parking to accommodate the relatively few people who park without shopping. But the availability of free parking also attracts shoppers. In this respect, the razor-and-blades analogy is also informative. As Joachim Henkel and Eric von Hippel explain, the manufacturer of a "platform" product often "will want to sell the platform—the razor, the ink-jet printer, or the videogame player—at a low margin or a loss, and then price the add-ons at a much higher margin."[73] The reduced price of the "platform" makes the system as a whole more attractive. This strategy

---

71. Harold Demsetz, *The Exchange and Enforcement of Property Rights, in* PUBLIC GOODS & MARKET FAILURES: A CRITICAL EXAMINATION 127, 137 (Tyler Cowen ed. 1988).

72. *Id.* at 138 (emphasis added).

73. Joachim Henkel & Eric von Hippel, *Welfare Implications of User Innovation*, 30 JOURNAL OF TECHNOLOGY TRANSFER 73, 84 (2005).

may not work as well "if users can develop free add-ons for the same platform,"[74] and it works best if, because of intellectual property rights or technical restrictions, the platform can only be used with that manufacturer's add-ons. But "the overall effect depends on details. . . ."[75] For example, "the availability of user-developed add-ons may indirectly increase demand for commercial add-ons for which no free substitute exists. . . ."[76]

By contributing to Linux development, IBM encourages the use of a free "razor" or "platform product" that increases the demand for proprietary complements (including "blade" servers) that IBM offers. IBM is not the only company that offers them. Linux requires a computer, but not necessarily an IBM server, and IBM servers can run other operating systems. Likewise, Linux often requires services, and IBM's investment in Linux development presumably advances its ability to provide Linux services, but Linux and IBM services are not inextricably linked. Nevertheless, IBM's services are highly differentiated, giving it an ability to recover Linux development costs through higher pricing of related services. To a lesser extent, the same is true of its hardware.

The proprietary complements approach used with Linux may also enable IBM and other firms in its position to capture more consumer surplus and convert it to producer profit. IBM's sale of Linux servers or Linux services is the sale of a system, which consists of the proprietary server or proprietary service together with the free Linux software. As Mark Glick and Duncan Cameron point out, a pair of shoes is also a "system," with two components.[77] If consumers were willing to mix left and right shoes from different manufacturers, we would have "open systems competition" in shoes.[78] Instead, people by shoes in pairs, so we have "'proprietary' systems competition."[79] If we assume that the market price for a pair of shoes is $100, and if left and right shoes are equally costly to make, then in open systems competition the market price for a single shoe would be $50. In the pairs or "proprietary systems" that are actually sold, each shoe could be priced separately, but the

---

74. *Id.*

75. *Id.*

76. *Id.*

77. Mark A. Glick & Duncan J. Cameron, *When Do Proprietary Aftermarkets Benefit Consumers?*, 67 ANTITRUST L.J. 357, 360–61 (1999).

78. *Id.* at 361.

79. *Id.*

individual prices of the components would be insignificant, because the market price for the pair would still be $100. For example, if a manufacturer sold shoes in pairs, but priced them separately, and charged $75 for the left shoe, competition would drive the price of that manufacturer's right shoe to $25. "Thus, in this example $100 is the 'baseline competitive' price for a system composed of two components that would, under open systems competition, sell for $50 each."[80]

In the case of shoes, most consumers purchase left and right shoes in equal proportions. When consumers purchase "variable proportions" of the elements of the system, however, the situation changes. "In such a situation, where components are used in variable proportions, it is no longer true that the quantities used of the components are unaffected by the individual prices of the components."[81] This situation often arises with inkjet printers and ink cartridges, or with razors and blades, where razors often tend to be underpriced and blades tend to be overpriced and different consumers purchase different quantities of blades.

The first effect of variable proportions is that "consumers who use relatively more of the aftermarket product"—for example, blades—"pay more for use of the system as a whole"—for example, a razor and blades—"under proprietary systems competition, while less intensive users pay relatively less for the system."[82] To see why this is so, suppose that the open systems competitive baseline prices are $25 for a razor and $5 for a package of blades. If each of two men buys one razor and five packages of blades, then the price of the system will be $50, the total purchase will be $100, and the pricing of individual components is irrelevant. But now suppose that one man, who likes to use fresh blades, buys one razor and seven packages of blades, whereas another man, who does not change blades as often, buys one razor and only three packages of blades. At the open systems prices, the first man would pay $60, and the second man would pay $40. But suppose also that the two razors and ten packages of blades are priced differently from the open systems baseline. A razor sells not for $25 but for $5. Each package of blades, in turn, sells not for $5 but for $9. Two razors and ten packages of blades will still sell for a total of $100, but the amount each man pays will be different from the open systems baseline.

---

80. *Id.*

81. *Id.* at 362.

82. *Id.*

At the open systems prices, if razors sold for $25 and blades for $5 per package, the first man would pay $60—$25 for the razor and $35 for his seven packages of blades—and the second man would pay $40—$25 for the razor and $15 for his three packages of blades. But under the new pricing, the first man pays $68—$5 for the razor and $63 for his seven packages of blades—and the second man pays only $32—$5 for the razor and $27 for his three packages of blades. The effect is that the consumer of larger portions of the proprietary "aftermarket" product pays more than he would under baseline pricing of separate components.

The second effect of variable proportions identified by Glick and Cameron is that "consumers will be encouraged to purchase more of the initial product, but then will use it less intensively because of the overpriced aftermarket component."[83] In the razor example, both men will be more likely to buy a new razor before it wears out than they would be if the price of the razor was closer to its baseline price—although both may use fewer blades than they would at the lower price for blades.

Suppose that IBM spends $1 billion on contributions to Linux, $1 billion on providing Linux-related services, and $1 billion on manufacturing and selling Linux server hardware. Suppose also that IBM earns $3 billion in revenue from Linux-related services and $3 billion in revenue from Linux server hardware. IBM's costs are $3 billion, and its revenues are $6 billion. But the benefits of IBM's contributions to Linux are available to users for free. IBM sells only the services and the hardware. Therefore, IBM must recover the cost of the contributions to Linux, and earn any profit on them, from its services and hardware revenues.

If IBM could sell Linux, and did so separately from the services and the hardware, we could safely assume, even without knowing the exact "open systems competitive price" for each element, that the price of the software would not be zero. It therefore also appears likely that the prices of the services and hardware—like the prices of razor blades when razors are sold below their open systems competitive price—are higher than they would be with separate pricing of software. In this example, to earn a 100 percent return on its total investment while suffering a 100 percent loss on its software investment, IBM must earn a 200 percent return on its services and hardware investments. Because the rights in contributions to Linux cannot be sold, IBM's competitors for services and hardware also must earn

---

83. *Id.*

an increased return on services and hardware if they invest in contributions to Linux.

It follows that heavier users of IBM's services and hardware will pay more for IBM's contributions to Linux than will lighter users of IBM's services and hardware. As Judge Easterbrook observed in *ProCD,* the proprietary EULA facilitates price discrimination, but we now find that FOSS licensing, including the GPL, can also have that effect. And as pointed out in Part 1 regarding *ProCD,* one of the possible effects of price discrimination is not, as Judge Easterbrook suggested, to increase consumer surplus, but rather to capture it for the producer. In the words of Glick and Cameron, "Enhanced 'second-degree economic price discrimination' profits flow from proprietary systems competition partly because there is greater extraction of consumer surplus from high users. That is, high users end up paying more for use of the system than they would under open systems competition baseline prices."[84] Here, the free provision of Linux to IBM services and hardware customers enables IBM to extract more consumer surplus from such customers, while contributing to and receiving the benefits of free Linux development.

There is, in other words, a sense in which Linux—provided, as it is, free of any license fee—is "free beer." But it is free beer that you pay for when you buy the kielbasa. You can have the beer without the kielbasa, but if you drink the beer, you are likely to get hungry. And when you do, you will pay more for the kielbasa than you otherwise would, because its price must cover the beer's cost. Ultimately, those who buy more kielbasa will pay a higher unit price than those who buy less kielbasa but drink the same amount of beer. In contrast, with proprietary software, the beer and kielbasa are sold à la carte—you pay for what you get.

There is nothing inherently wrong with price discrimination. In fact, price discrimination in some circumstances increases efficiency. But because the level and nature of the contribution to the open source software is determined by how it affects the company's ability to price the complements, rather than being determined more directly by how much users are willing to pay for the software, it seems more likely to result in an investment in software that is not necessarily optimal either in quantity or in quality. And when companies intentionally subsidize open source development to promote the sale of complementary products and services, they are not providing something for free, but shifting the cost of the open source

84. *Id.* at 365.

software from users that consume none or relatively little of the complementary products and services to users that consume larger amounts. The more people there are who use only the free component, the greater the extent of the subsidy.

Perhaps the most usable open source software, with the broadest appeal outside the technical community, is the Firefox Web browser. In 1998, Netscape released the source code for the Netscape browser through the Mozilla project. In 2003, the organization became the Mozilla Foundation, and in 2004, it released Firefox, which ultimately derives from the Netscape code. Firefox is thus the descendant of a proprietary software product (which in turn was the descendant, ultimately, of public domain software). Today the Mozilla Corporation, a for-profit subsidiary of the Mozilla Foundation, is responsible for "productizing and distributing" Firefox and other Mozilla software, such as the Thunderbird e-mail client.[85]

Primary funding for Mozilla comes from another proprietary company, Google. "In return for setting Google as the default search engine on Firefox, Google pays Mozilla a substantial sum—in 2006 the total amounted to around $57 million, or 85% of the company's total revenue," and the deal has been extended at least through 2011.[86] In 2007, Google's payment to Mozilla reportedly rose to $75 million.[87] This payment allows Mozilla to hire paid employees to develop and maintain Firefox much like a commercial product, without having to rely on volunteers. Because the Google revenue that provides the primary support for Firefox is based on use by general Web users, Mozilla has strong economic incentives to provide a usable product. The usability of Firefox, in contrast to the lack of usability of many other open source software programs, thus underscores the importance of how open source development is subsidized in determining the nature of the software it will produce.

The Mozilla trademark policy provides that "[t]hose taking full advantage of the open-source nature of Mozilla's products and making significant functional changes may not redistribute the fruits of their labor under any

---

85. *See* Mozilla Foundation Reorganization, http://www.mozilla.org/reorganization/.

86. Jason Kincaid, *Mozilla Extends Lucrative Deal with Google for 3 Years*, TECH CRUNCH, Aug. 28, 2008, http://www.techcrunch.com/2008/08/28/mozilla-extends-lucrative-deal-with-google-for-3-years/.

87. Stephen Shankland, *Mozilla Chairman Unfazed by Google Chrome*, CNET NEWS, Nov. 19, 2008, http://news.cnet.com/8301-1001_3-10102627-92.html.

Mozilla trademark."[88] Indeed, according to the policy, a modified version of Firefox cannot even be described as "based on Mozilla Firefox." Thus, while the source code is available, in principle, to create modified versions of the software, Mozilla Corporation exercises strict control over what actually goes into anything called Firefox.

Unauthorized Contributions

The discussion so far has focused on corporate efforts by IBM and others. Another kind of employer-subsidized open source development is inadvertent, as far as the firm is concerned. Given that 17 percent of respondents in the survey cited above admitted that they were "shirking their official jobs," and others indicated only "tacit consent" by their supervisors, it would appear that a substantial portion of the development effort on F/OSS projects is performed by programmers "at work without the knowledge of their supervisors."[89] Moreover, even if the programmer's immediate supervisor gives explicit or tacit consent, this fact provides no assurance that the supervisor is authorized by the employer to do so. In such cases, the focus again is likely to be on the programmer's own interests. And the adverse effect on efficiency is clear. If a sizable portion of development work is by employees who are not doing their official jobs, the effect is presumably to raise the cost, and indirectly the price, of the other products and services offered by the employers to subsidize open source development.

There is also potentially a significant question about ownership of rights in such software. Many employers in technology fields require that employees enter into agreements pursuant to which work products created at work are owned by the employer, even if they are created without the employer's knowledge. Accordingly, there could be significant questions about the right of employees to contribute such work to open source projects. Despite this fact, many FOSS licenses, including the GPL, do not require that the contributor warrant his or her right to contribute the work in question.

---

88. Mozilla Trademark Policy, v. 1.0.1, http://www.mozilla.org/foundation/trademarks/policy.html.

89. Karim R. Lakhani & Robert G. Wolf, *Why Hackers Do What They Do: Understanding Motivation and Effort in Free/Open Source Software Projects, in* PERSPECTIVES ON FREE AND OPEN SOURCE SOFTWARE 9–10 (Joseph Feller, Brian Fitzgerald, Scott A. Hissam, & Karim R. Lakhani eds., 2005).

Accordingly, a recipient of the work receive a work that contains material owned by a contributor's employer, but the recipient also may have no recourse against the person who provided the material. That there have not been significant numbers of claims making such allegations may reflect the fact that employers do not know about the activity, but there is still at least a potential question of efficiency.

User Innovation

Henkel and von Hippel include open source software in the category of "user innovation."[90] They do not define "user," although they use the term interchangeably with "end user,"[91] suggesting that it does not include, for example, IBM or its employees who contribute to open source development as part of their work for IBM. At most, innovation by actual end users accounts for only a portion—and probably a minority—of open source development. And it is performed by the very small minority of end users who have the technical wherewithal to develop software.

Henkel and von Hippel also note that user innovation is "concentrated among the 'lead users' in a user population"—users "at the leading edge of important trends," who "anticipate obtaining relatively high benefits from obtaining a solution to their needs. . . ."[92] But again, the focus is on the interests and needs of the innovating users. In contrast to manufacturers, "users tend to develop innovations that only they or a few may want, and that creates a high consumer surplus for themselves."[93] As a result, "product innovations developed by users will tend to fill small niches of high need left open by commercial sellers. . . ."[94]

Henkel and von Hippel regard this result as positive for social welfare, because it means that "user innovation *complements* manufacturer innovation."[95] But it is not clear that the analysis holds for open source. Although it is true that open source developers often focus on "obtaining a

---

90. Joachim Henkel & Eric von Hippel, *Welfare Implications of User Innovation*, 30 Journal of Technology Transfer 73, 76 (2005).

91. *See id.* at 75, 78, 82.

92. *Id.* at 75.

93. *Id.* at 73.

94. *Id.* at 78.

95. *Id.* at 73.

solution to their needs"—or, in Eric Raymond's phrase, on "scratching a developer's personal itch"—leading open source products such as Linux and Apache are not confined to filling "small niches of high need." On the contrary, Linux is an operating system and Apache is a Web server: these are the opposite of "niche" products. Moreover, if "high need" means that substitutes are not readily available, Linux and Apache do not meet high need, because substitutes are available. Arguably they are not even "innovative." Linux attempts to be more stable and secure than Windows, but it is derived from Unix, and significant effort has been devoted to replicating functionality that Unix already offers or to achieving compatibility with Windows.

The goal is not to fill a narrow niche but to replace software that is otherwise available with a nonproprietary alternative. In doing so, however, open source developers respond to incentives that are different from the ones that drive proprietary development. The incentives may be provided by employers, such as IBM, that use open source software as a free complement to proprietary products and services and recover the cost by shifting it to higher users of those products and services—a pleasant outcome for users who do not consume the proprietary items, but an outcome that can be expected to shape the contributions so as to make the proprietary items more valuable and necessary. Or the incentives may be more personal, involving either career-related benefits or ideological satisfaction—which may or may not result in software that actually meets the needs or desires of the 99.7 percent of users who consume software without having the ability or the interest to change it.

Open Source-Proprietary Hybrids

The open source licensing model that perhaps best links developer incentives to user needs is one that combines open source software with a proprietary component. Many open source providers "have tweaked their business models to include some kind of additional value only available as part of a subscription."[96] More specifically, the model involves "an 'open core' freely available with 'exclusive' or proprietary features only available when you pay."[97] There is evidence that many chief technology officers, who

---

96. Dave Rosenberg, *Open Source Becomes Paid Software in 2009*, CNET News, Dec. 24, 2008, http://news.cnet.com/8301-13846_3-10128801-62.html?part=r.

97. *Id.*

represent sophisticated users, are "happy to pay for proprietary extensions to open-source software" in return for desired features.[98]

This approach is anathema to copyleft advocates, but it seems most likely to channel the development of the open source product in the direction of meeting the needs not just of contributing developers, but also of the larger set of all users. Open source-proprietary hybrids—which are incompatible with a copyleft licensing model—take advantage of the process benefits of open source, including the bug reduction that comes with more "eyeballs" on the code. Because users pay directly for the proprietary component, however, and not indirectly for the software through separate services, such hybrids also increase the likelihood that the software provider will scratch not only the developer's itch, but also the user's. This result depends on either dedicating the open source component to the public domain or licensing it under permissive terms that are not constrained by the copyleft condition. And the open source-proprietary hybrid provider can offer an even more efficient alternative by selling copies of the proprietary version or licensing them under a minimal EULA.

98. Matt Asay, *CTOs Vote for Open Source, But Buy Proprietary Software*, CNET News, Nov. 12, 2008, http://news.cnet.com/8301-13505_3-10094883-16.html?tag=mncol;txt.

SIX

The GPL, the Public Domain, and the Web

IN *WEAVING THE WEB,* THE STORY OF his invention of the World Wide Web at CERN, Tim Berners-Lee describes how the Web technology came to be dedicated to the public domain. In the year preceding a March 1993 meeting of the Internet Engineering Task Force (IETF) in Columbus, Ohio, Berners-Lee "had been trying to get CERN to release the intellectual property rights to the Web code under the General Public License (GPL) so that others could use it."[1] The University of Minnesota had introduced an Internet search tool and protocol—then better known than the Web—called Gopher.[2] In early 1993, the University announced that it would require a license to use Gopher and would charge an annual fee for commercial users.[3] In response, the industry "dropped gopher like a hot potato."[4]

At the March 1993 IETF meeting, Berners-Lee "was accosted in the corridors" by people wanting to know if CERN would do with the Web what the University of Minnesota had done with Gopher.[5] Berners-Lee "listened carefully to people's concerns and to what they said they would or would not find acceptable."[6] The problem with the GPL was that, "while it allowed things to be distributed and used freely, there were strings attached, such that any modifications also had to be released under the same GPL."[7] He recalls, "In the fallout of the gopher debacle, there were already rumors that large companies like IBM would not allow the Web on the premises if there

1. TIM BERNERS-LEE, WEAVING THE WEB: THE ORIGINAL DESIGN AND ULTIMATE DESTINY OF THE WORLD WIDE WEB 73 (2000).

2. *Id.*

3. *Id.* at 72.

4. *Id.* at 73.

5. *Id.*

6. *Id.*

7. *Id.*

was any kind of licensing issue, because that would be too constraining. And that included the GPL."[8] On his return from Columbus, Berners-Lee "swiftly switched" his request "from getting a GPL to having the Web technology put in the general public domain, with no strings attached."[9] The request was granted, "allow[ing] anybody to use the Web protocol and code free of charge, to create a server or a browser, to give it away or sell it, without any royalty or other constraint."[10]

The argument for using "copyleft" licensing, rather than dedicating works to the public domain or using permissive open source licensing, is that works that are in the public domain or that are permissively licensed are vulnerable to proprietary capture, which reduces user freedom and permits proprietary firms to exploit the work of volunteers. But the case of the Web itself suggests that the picture is more complex. Although the Web technologies have been the subject of efforts to "embrace and extend," with proprietary extensions, the key Web technologies have remained remarkably free despite minimal use of copyleft in licensing them. Moreover, it seems likely that the Web never would have become anything remotely resembling the economic or cultural phenomenon it is today if the copyleft restrictions of the GPL had controlled its birth and early development. Indeed, it is entirely possible that proprietary technology would have been *more* influential, rather than less so, if the Web software had been licensed under the GPL.

6.1 Proprietary Capture: The X Window "Paradigm"

According to Stallman, the problem with public domain software and software licensed under "simple permissive licenses" is that, although the software is free, "anyone can make a proprietary modified version of it."[11] Stallman states that the "paradigmatic example of this problem" is the client/server windowing system for UNIX and Linux known as X Window.[12] Developed in

8. *Id.* It was only in later years that IBM embraced Linux.

9. *Id.* at 73–74.

10. *Id.* at 74.

11. Stallman, *Selected Essays,* at 22.

12. *Id.*

the 1980s at MIT, the X Window System was "released as free software with a permissive license" and was "soon adopted by various computer companies."[13] But these companies "added X to their proprietary Unix systems, in binary form only, and covered by the same nondisclosure agreement," which meant that "[t]hese copies of X were no more free software than Unix was."[14]

The X Window System has been described as "one of the most successful consortium-developed, open standards–based technologies ever."[15] According to Stallman, however, the same approach that led to X's widespread adoption is the source of the "problem." He asserts that the goal of X's developers "was just popularity—ego, essentially."[16] He states, "They wanted a big professional success. They wanted to feel, 'Ah, lots of people are using our software.' And that was true. Lots of people were using their software but didn't have freedom."[17] In other words, the permissive licensing that encouraged use of X Window meant that some people were using proprietary modified versions of X Window, which they could not further modify.

All creative works draw, to some extent, on preexisting ideas and expressions that are in the public domain. Because these ideas and expressions are in the public domain, one person's use of them does not limit another's. The public domain is the ultimate domain of "nonexcludability." Likewise, if one software provider develops a proprietary modified version of public domain or permissively licensed software, there is nothing to stop another software provider from developing another modified version—either proprietary or free—of the same public domain or permissively licensed software.

Why does this option not provide an adequate check on the risk Stallman perceives? Stallman asserts,

> Non-copylefted software is vulnerable from all directions; it lets anyone make a non-free version dominant, if he will invest sufficient resources to add significantly important features using proprietary code. Users who choose software based on technical characteristics, rather than

---

13. *Id.*

14. *Id.*

15. Finnbarr P. Murphy, *Whither the X Window System?*, Aug. 1999, http://www.usenix.org/publications/ login/standards/29.xwindow.html.

16. Stallman, *Selected Essays*, at 171.

17. *Id.*

> on freedom, could easily be lured to the non-free version for short-term convenience.[18]

This explanation is intriguing, because it seems to acknowledge that the creator of the proprietary modified version, through an investment of "sufficient resources," may "add significantly important features" that will make the modified version technically more attractive. From Stallman's ideological point of view, free is always better. But if proprietary treatment of software, and the investment of resources that it elicits, results in a technically superior product that users choose, even though they have to pay for it, it is not clear why that is not a good thing. Indeed, Stallman seems to be describing precisely the process by which proprietary treatment of software can be expected to yield desirable innovation.

In the case of the X Window System, the development of proprietary modified versions does not appear to have blocked the development or the availability of free versions. The X.Org Foundation continues to maintain an open source implementation of X Window, the X.Org Server, which is used in the GNOME and KDE desktops for Linux. It is not at all clear that the existence of a proprietary path has impaired anyone's freedom. Those who use proprietary versions of the software do not have the "freedom" with respect to such versions that the GPL gives free software users. But the existence of the proprietary versions gives them another form of freedom, which is the freedom to choose between proprietary and free versions of the software. And if the choice is constrained by the choice of hardware, then the user also has the freedom to choose between hardware that requires a proprietary version and hardware that can run a free version.

There is also a sense that the contributions of free software developers are being unfairly exploited by proprietary software providers for their own profit. As one post on the Web, commenting on Microsoft's creation of a proprietary version of Kerberos security software, puts it, "Once again, it was piracy of public software. Stolen in order to increase Bill Gates' personal fortune. But it was legal theft. The MIT license covering Kerberos provided no protection against that sort of thing."[19] The idea is that proprietary

18. Richard M. Stallman, *The X Window System Trap*, 1999, updated March 12, 2008, http://www.gnu.org/philosophy/x.html.

19. Joe Barr, *Why I Love the GPL*, Linux.com, Jan. 29, 2005, http://www.linux.com/feature/42001.

software providers should not be able to profit from the work of free software developers. But Stallman has separately asserted that there is nothing wrong with selling copies of free software or with selling related services. It is not clear why, if it is legitimate to sell copies of software one has not developed, or to sell services relating to software one has not developed, it is not legitimate to license a proprietary modified version of software, when one has in fact contributed, by modifying it, and when one's only exclusive rights are in one's own modifications.

6.2 Proprietary Capture and GPLv3

As the GPL has evolved, FSF has intensified its efforts to prevent uses of GPL-licensed software that it deems inconsistent with the basic principles of software freedom. According to FSF, one of the recent "threats" to free software that GPLv3 is designed to address is "Tivoization."[20] The term refers to the TiVo DVR distributed by TiVo, Inc. Like many consumer devices, the TiVo DVR is a computer with an operating system, and that operating system happens to be a modified version of Linux. TiVo complies with GPLv2 by making the source code for the modifications available on its Web site and on disc. But the TiVo DVR also checks for a digital signature in the software. If a user further modifies TiVo's GPL-licensed software, the user-modified version will lack the appropriate digital signature and will not run.

FSF says that "Tivoization is a dangerous attempt to curtail users' freedom."[21] The freedom to modify the source code used in the TiVo is, at most, of academic interest if the modified source cannot be run on the machine for which it is designed. If users could run modified software on the TiVo, however, they might defeat usage tracking and control features. This ability conceivably could affect TiVo's ability to charge for its services and its ability to make and fulfill DRM commitments to content providers. Similarly, running modified code on other devices could have other effects that the device manufacturers might not want.

Section 6 of GPLv3 provides that, for a "User Product"—which is defined as a "consumer product" or "anything designed or sold for incorporation into

---

20. Brett Smith, *A Quick Guide to GPLv3,* http://www.fsf.org/licensing/licenses/quick-guide-gplv3.html.

21. *Id.*

a dwelling"—the licensee that "conveys" a modified version of GPL-licensed software must provide "Installation Information." Such information includes "any methods, procedures, authorization keys, or other information required to install and execute modified versions of a covered work in that User Product from a modified version of its Corresponding Source."

The anti-Tivoization provisions of GPLv3 could lead device manufacturers to permit users to run modified code on the devices, but it seems far more likely that, to the extent they are applied, they will simply lead device manufacturers to use proprietary code. TiVo, Inc., apparently considers the risks of GPLv3 potentially serious enough to preclude the use of software licensed under it. In its Form 10-K Annual Report for 2006, filed April 16, 2007, TiVo stated, under "risk factors," "If the currently proposed version of GPLv3 is widely adopted, we may be unable to incorporate future enhancements to the GNU/Linux operating system into our software, which could adversely affect our business." In other words, if proprietary requirements cannot be met by free software, then device manufacturers will not use it.

6.3 CERN Web Software and Mosaic

In considering whether copyleft increases software freedom or reduces the use of free software, the paradigm case may not be, as Stallman suggests, the X Window System, but rather the much more significant case of the World Wide Web. Referring to the World Wide Web as "W3," CERN issued a public declaration on April 30, 1993, in which it stated that the following CERN software was "put into the public domain":

> W3 basic ("line mode") client
> W3 basic server
> W3 library of common code[22]

James Gillies and Robert Cailliau, the latter a collaborator of Berners-Lee at CERN, conclude in their history of the early Web, "If the [Web] software hadn't been in the public domain, there would have been no Mosaic and the

22. CERN European Organization for Nuclear Research, Statement Concerning CERN W3 Software Release into Public Domain, April 30, 2003, at 2, http://tenyears-www.web.cern.ch/tenyears-www/.

Web might well have languished in the backwaters of academia."[23] This assertion, if correct, suggests that licensing the Web software under the GPL would have made the Internet a very different place today.

Mosaic is the graphical web browser that led to Netscape and Internet Explorer. The original Web browser developed by Tim Berners-Lee was text based. Marc Andreesen, Eric Bina, and others began developing Mosaic in December 1992 at the National Center for Supercomputing Applications (NCSA) at the University of Illinois at Urbana-Champaign. NCSA released version 1.0 of Mosaic on April 23, 1993, one week before CERN dedicated the Web software to the public domain. On April 4, 1994, Andreesen and Jim Clark of Silicon Graphics formed Mosaic Communications Corporation, later known as Netscape Communications Corporation. On October 13, 1994, the company released its first browser, Mosaic Netscape 0.9. Spyglass, Inc., a company formed in 1990 to commercialize NCSA technologies, licensed its own version of Mosaic to Microsoft in 1995, and Microsoft used that version to create Internet Explorer, which it first released in August 1995.

Section 2 of the 1991 version of the GPL grants permission to "modify your copy or copies of the Program or any portion of it, thus forming a work *based on* the Program, and copy and distribute such modifications or work . . . ,"[24] but only if you meet the conditions of the license. These conditions include the requirement that you "cause any work that you distribute or publish, that *in whole or in part contains or is derived from* the Program or any part thereof, to be licensed as a whole at no charge to all third parties under the terms of this License."[25] If NCSA Mosaic "in whole or in part contain[ed] or [was] derived from" any of the CERN Web software, then GPLv2 would have required that any distribution of NCSA Mosaic or any of its derivatives occur under the GPL, with NCSA Mosaic and any such derivative being licensed "as a whole at no charge to all third parties."

The Web code placed in the public domain by CERN included the "libwww" code library. Berners-Lee explained in May 1993 that this code library "forms the basis of many of the browsers" and "deals with the HTTP protocol handling . . . , as well as parsing of the hypertext format (HTML),

---

23. James Gillies & Robert Cailliau, How the Web Was Born: The Story of the World Wide Web 270 (2000).

24. (Emphasis added.)

25. (Emphasis added.)

and negotiation of other available formats."[26] The Mosaic browser developed at NCSA included libwww.[27] NCSA Mosaic thus "in whole or in part contain[ed]" libwww, and if libwww had been licensed under the GPL, then NCSA Mosaic and its derivatives "as a whole" could have been distributed only royalty-free under the GPL. More broadly, NCSA Mosaic, although graphical, was "based on" the CERN Web browser and on protocols, such as HTTP, embodied in the CERN Web software. Even if CERN's libwww had not been included in NCSA Mosaic, it seems likely that licensing of the CERN Web software under the GPL would have precluded distribution of Mosaic or its derivatives under any other license.

6.4 Effects of a GPL-Licensed Mosaic

NCSA distributed Mosaic under a proprietary license, albeit one that permitted free noncommercial use. But NCSA began work on Mosaic before CERN dedicated the Web software to the public domain. As a result, it is possible that, if CERN had licensed the Web software under the GPL, NCSA would have chosen to distribute Mosaic under the GPL rather than not distributing it at all. It seems doubtful, however, that Netscape and Microsoft would have made the investments they did in Web browsers or the Web itself if they had been required to license the resulting software—and all software deriving from it—royalty-free to the entire world.

Netscape and Microsoft would have had considerable difficulty developing Web browsers that were so unrelated to NCSA Mosaic as to be beyond the GPL's reach. Netscape obtained authorization from NCSA to use some Mosaic code (but not the Mosaic trademark). Microsoft obtained a license from Spyglass to use its version of Mosaic in Internet Explorer. Both the Netscape browser and the Microsoft browser were based, directly or indirectly, on NCSA Mosaic, which in turn was based on the CERN software.

Even if it would have been possible for Netscape and Microsoft to build Web browsers that were not derivatives of a GPL-licensed Mosaic, it is not clear that either company would have been prepared to take the

26. Tim Berners-Lee & Robert Caillau, *May World-Wide Web News*, May 1993, at http://www.w3.org/News/ 9305.html#z18.

27. José Kahan, *Why Libwww?*, Aug. 5, 1999, http://www.w3.org/Library/Activity.html.

commercial risk. At the time, there was even less legal authority on the meaning of the GPL than there is today. Guessing wrong on the GPL's impact could have wiped out the entire investment. Netscape co-founders Marc Andreesen and Jim Clark quite possibly would have turned to other entrepreneurial pursuits, as Clark soon did anyway.[28] And without the challenge posed by Netscape, Microsoft might never have turned to the Web.

The Web without the Netscape or Microsoft browsers would not be the Web we know—if it existed at all. In his 1999 book *The New New Thing*, Michael Lewis writes that "[t]he companies born on the Internet," like "Yahoo, Excite, @Home, eBay, and so on . . . derived, one way or another, from Netscape. . . ."[29] Of course, many of the companies born on the Internet in the 1990s have since died, but the Web has survived and flourished. Netscape provided key technologies and a business model that, although it led to some excesses, brought unprecedented investment and attention to the Web.

For example, one of the key drivers of the growth of the Web has been the development of e-commerce. "[E]-commerce has triggered the development of a whole new branch of the software industry, which not only provides software to install and run a Web shop, but also systems for click stream analysis, data mining . . . , and customer relationship management (CRM). . . ."[30] E-commerce, in turn, critically depends on reliable security. It was Netscape, as a proprietary company, that developed the secure sockets layer (SSL) technology on which e-commerce is still based, and it was Netscape that offered the first SSL-enabled Web server.[31]

Netscape also introduced many "Netscape extensions" to HTML and, in December 1995, released JavaScript, which remains a widely used client-side scripting language. Although the Netscape extensions were a mixed blessing in inter-browser compatibility, they gave Web authors greater control over the appearance of their Web pages. JavaScript enabled Web authors to provide more interactive Web sites.

Would such developments have occurred without Netscape? Perhaps, but as Stallman himself acknowledges, proprietary developers may be more

---

28. *See* Michael Lewis, The New New Thing: A Silicon Valley Story 40 (1999).

29. *Id.* at 39.

30. Gottfried Vossen & Stephan Hagemann, Unleashing Web 2.0: From Concepts to Creativity 26 (2007).

31. The Netcraft Secure Server Survey, http://news.netcraft.com/SSL-Survey/.

likely to "invest sufficient resources to add significantly important features using proprietary code."[32] Netscape's initial venture capital funding, its landmark IPO on August 9, 1995, and its early profitable period thereafter gave it considerable resources to invest. Open source developers were free to develop their own browsers based on the CERN Web software, and a number of other browsers existed, but Netscape, and later Microsoft, accounted for all but a very small part of the browser market.

For a GPL-licensed Web browser to have led to the same rapid growth of the Web in all its facets, the free software movement also would have had to have produced the plug-ins on which the Web's functionality depends. These include programs such as Adobe Reader, Adobe Flash, and media players, including Windows Media Player and Quicktime, among others. Although many FOSS plug-ins now exist, proprietary products such as those just mentioned continue to dominate, presumably because they continue to offer more attractive features to users.

The potential negative effects of incorporating free software into proprietary software also do not appear to have been significant, at least over the long term. Netscape did not "lock up" either its standards or its code. Netscape extensions to HTML were used in other browsers. In January 1998, Netscape released the source code of its flagship browser and started the Mozilla open source project, which today maintains the Firefox open source browser. Netscape took this action after it was clear that Microsoft was winning the "browser wars," in which Internet Explorer eventually became the dominant browser. But there would have been no browser wars had Microsoft not also decided to "embrace and extend" the Web, and Microsoft did so because of Netscape. For a time, Microsoft's browser was dominant, but this was more a consequence than a cause of Microsoft's Windows monopoly, and browser dominance did not enable Microsoft to gain dominance over the Web. Moreover, the Firefox open source browser in recent years has gained market share at Microsoft's expense.

The success of the Apache Web server, which is licensed under a non-copyleft open source license, further indicates that, at least in the case of the Web, permissive licensing does not necessarily result in proprietary capture. The Apache project is not only one of the most successful open source projects but also one of the oldest. The first public release of the Apache

32. Richard M. Stallman, *The X Window System Trap*, 1999, updated March 12, 2008, http://www.gnu.org/philosophy/x.html.

HTTP server occurred in April 1995.[33] The original Apache License, which notes that the software "was originally based on public domain software written at [NCSA]," permits use and redistribution, with or without modification, as long as conditions relating to notice, attribution, and disclaimers are met.

Companies can and do create proprietary modifications of Apache, which the license permits them to distribute—but without calling the modified version "Apache."[34] Despite this practice, the open source version of Apache retains its leading market share. In some cases, modifications that were included in otherwise proprietary versions have found their way back into the open source version. Proprietary modification is naturally limited, in part because "once the distribution is modified, any future updates to Apache have to be 'melded' into the custom distribution, which creates an ongoing customer-support burden."[35]

6.5 A More Proprietary Network?

Until the rise of Netscape, Microsoft's vision of the "information superhighway" was entirely focused on the proprietary Microsoft Network. Microsoft introduced MSN on August 24, 1995, as a proprietary online service, along the lines of America Online and CompuServe before it. Microsoft controlled not only the client interface, which was built into Windows 95, but also the content. It was not until the end of 1996 that MSN subscribers were able to use MSN to access the Web, through an interface based on Internet Explorer.

Microsoft's quick turn from a proprietary MSN to the Web was a defensive move. It was a move Microsoft took not because it preferred the relatively open world of the Web but because Netscape had already opened that world to users. Microsoft could not beat the Web, so it had no choice but to join. But what if NCSA Mosaic—and all its derivatives—could not have been commercialized? Perhaps the concept of for-profit open source software distribution would have emerged earlier than it eventually did with Red Hat and

---

33. Apache HTTP Server Project, http://httpd.apache.org/ABOUT_APACHE.html.

34. Vincent Ryan, *Patching Apache*, NewsFactor.com, May 21, 2003, http://www.newsfactor.com/story.xhtml?story_id= 21560&page=1.

35. *Id.*

other commercial Linux distributors. It is also possible, however, that Microsoft would have invested more heavily in MSN, and the millions of people who in the event used the Netscape browser might instead have become MSN subscribers. The information superhighway could have been the often-feared toll road, rather than the Internet as we know it.

Of course, we will never know what would have happened if Tim Berners-Lee had succeeded in persuading CERN to license the Web software under the GPL, before he changed his mind and settled on dedication to the public domain. But the story illustrates a potential effect of the GPL that is not present with dedication to the public domain or most forms of permissive open source licensing. Copyleft can advance software freedom, as Stallman defines it, for the software that gets developed and distributed under the GPL. But copyleft may also discourage the use of such software. A GPL-licensed Mosaic might have gone nowhere, and much that followed might have been more proprietary rather than less so.

In a true "commons," there would be no strings attached. What is there in the public domain to be feared? The dedication of the Web software to the public domain did not result in its author, Sir Tim Berners-Lee, OM, being denied credit. Even without FOSS license terms, the "hacker ethos" would surely rain down condemnation on a developer who tried to take credit for someone else's work. And with large-scale projects such as Linux and Firefox, as we have seen, trademark law probably plays a larger role in quality control than does anything in the license terms.

For software, it is unlikely that public domain works will be effectively locked up through private modification over any extended time period. The core Web software and protocols have remained free, while also permitting a broad range of proprietary strategies that have made possible the Web's global adoption. In principle, any attempt to capture a public domain technology requires either separate market power, such as that of a monopolist, in which case the problem is the monopoly, or a proprietary contribution that in and of itself adds so much value that competitors, who have equal access to the public domain, cannot match it. Moreover, in technology, proprietary extensions to public domain works, or other standard components that are liberally licensed, can have the opposite effect of demonstrating the value of the public domain or liberally licensed components and encouraging their emergence or survival as a standard.

When IBM introduced the IBM Personal Computer in 1981, it followed a relatively open approach. This was necessitated in significant part by IBM's decision to enter the PC market as quickly as possible, which meant deviating from IBM's standard practice of developing all major components in-house. IBM outsourced not only the development of a number of key machine components, such as disk drives, but also both the microprocessor—to Intel—and the operating system—to Microsoft. Bill Gates, in turn, negotiated the right to license the operating system to other computer manufacturers, and Intel could sell them its chips. In addition, IBM liberally licensed the IBM PC bus technologies. Such actions gave rise to the industry of "IBM-compatible" personal computers, including Compaq and many others. The IBM PC became a de facto standard, but at the cost of allowing "clones."

In 1987, IBM introduced a new PC bus architecture known as the micro channel architecture, or MCA. IBM sought to regain its leadership in the PC industry by making MCA a new dominant and more proprietary standard. But competing PC manufacturers began referring to the PC bus as the industry standard architecture, or ISA. They also introduced an expanded industry standard architecture, known as EISA. All these architectures have long since become obsolete, but the key result in the late 1980s was that IBM was unable to achieve adoption of MCA, while ISA and various successors, which were more broadly accessible to manufacturers, prevailed. ISA was not in the public domain, but it was relatively open technology, and the marketplace itself thwarted IBM's effort to replace ISA with MCA.

If GPL distribution may deprive us of some of the benefits of proprietary investment, and if proprietary capture is not, over the long term, a serious problem with dedication to the public domain or permissive open source licensing, then it seems likely that the GPL may—in the name of user freedom—actually reduce user choice.

Conclusion
Going Forward

EVER SINCE THE LATE 1960s, when IBM adopted a "copyright-licensing strategy" for "asset protection" in the soon-to-emerge software industry, most legal users have gained access to software through licenses, rather than as owners of copies. When the personal computer software industry took flight in the 1980s, not only the software but also the license became a mass-market phenomenon. The "legislative license" met with initial skepticism in the courts, but for the most part, that skepticism seems to be gone. Courts in the twenty-first century have shown an inclination to enforce virtually any license a software provider creates, as long as the user clicks "agree."

The trend toward legislation by license is spreading beyond software. As more works are being provided in digital form, content providers are using license agreements to define what users can and cannot do. The practice is beginning to extend even into the realm of printed books. Elizabeth Winston reports that "the Maryland State Bar Association does not sell its Maryland Lawyers Manual, an annual directory of lawyers and judges, to its members, but rather licenses it to them."[1] Members receive the book shrinkwrapped, with license terms that take effect when the reader breaks the seal, and these terms prohibit reselling or lending the book or giving it away, the first sale doctrine notwithstanding.[2]

At least as applied to software, however, the legislative license has not offered benefits commensurate with its costs. The analysis above suggests that the information asymmetry between proprietary software providers and users regarding the meaning and legal effect of software license terms predictably produces licenses that are, from the user point of view, "lemons." As long as the EULA is a custom legal regime in its own right, this asymmetry

1. Elizabeth I. Winston, *Why Sell When You Can License? Contracting around Statutory Protection of Intellectual Property,* 14 GEO. MASON L. REV. 93, 94 (2006).

2. *Id.*

is inevitable, and the results will persist. This is not to say that proprietary software has not brought many benefits to computer users. Proprietary software is especially good at introducing new features, but these features often emerge before they are ready for prime time. Proprietary software is less well known for providing reliability. Flexibility of use terms is also not its strong suit. As the use of EULA-like arrangements expands, these effects will grow.

Free and open software has given the world an alternative to proprietary software, and it has benefitted even those users who are unable or unwilling to pay license fees for software products. But a number of FOSS licenses do so through legislative licenses that are in some ways even more ambitious than the typical EULA. And although FOSS licenses fulfill the agendas of the developers who create them, their developer focus is often accompanied by less-than-optimal software usability. Moreover, license terms that prevent software providers from charging license fees, while permitting them to charge for services or even for copies, mean that the cost of developing the software will be subsidized through some form of payment that is permitted by the license. Such subsidies will often be less efficient than charging directly for use of the software itself.

This conclusion arises without even considering that, according to one of the studies mentioned above, more than one in six open source developers said they contributed at work while "shirking their official job," and others said they spent work hours on open source projects with only "tacit consent" by their supervisors. Even taking into account that allowing employees some latitude may make them happier and therefore more productive, we can see that nontrivial amounts of open source development are being subsidized by unwitting employers and, indirectly, by their customers. This is inefficient and also unfair to those who bear the cost of someone else's benefits.

Even when employers intentionally subsidize open source development, the effect is to shift the cost of software development away from its most direct beneficiaries, which is not always the path to the outcome that best meets user needs. For example, IBM subsidizes its large contributions to Linux development with revenues from its even larger Linux consulting business. In doing so, it engages in a form of price discrimination by effectively charging heavier users of the consulting services a higher price for the combined activities. There is nothing improper about doing so. But when the connection between the cost and benefits of development is attenuated, the responsiveness of development to users is also likely to be diminished.

Copyleft, as implemented in the GPL, is a third enclosure movement—it erects a fence around the commons to keep private contributions in—and in limiting distribution to a single model, it can inhibit desirable proprietary investments. The Web itself demonstrates that dedication to the public domain, or permissive open source licensing that resembles it, is more likely to elicit the combination of voluntary contributions and for-profit activities necessary to sustain an undertaking of worldwide proportions. Copyleft aims to draw innovation into the commons, but in many cases its effect will be to force innovation into more proprietary channels by making the commons too confining.

If proprietary software licenses lead to underproduction of flexibility and reliability, and free and open source software licenses lead to underproduction of usability while in some forms deterring investment, then what is the answer? One obvious conclusion is that the world is probably better off with both proprietary and nonproprietary software than it would be with only one model. The competition between the two models may actually lead to improvements in both that do not arise from their internal dynamics. For example, the asserted greater reliability of FOSS may provide an impetus for proprietary products to become more reliable, and FOSS advocates such as Raymond have explicitly spoken to the urgency of achieving greater usability to compete with proprietary software.

But at base, both models rely too much on legislation by license. Proprietary software providers, not satisfied with the legal framework the Copyright Act offers for distributing software by selling copies, have enacted their own set of rules and restrictions. The Free Software Foundation, rather than dispensing with the licensing approach, has created its own alternative intellectual property regime, through an anti-EULA—the GPL. This book has suggested that the proliferation of legislative licensing undermines the efficiency of both models and threatens to take the digital economy in the wrong direction.

Whereas software "tools" are almost always distributed by license, you can go to the hardware store and buy actual tools with no documentation of the sales contract other than a receipt. Once you own a hammer, the manufacturer and seller exercise no further control over your use of it. You acquire a property right in the hammer that is defined by the public law. If you use the hammer to smash your neighbor's windows, you also incur a liability defined by the public law. So the absence of control by the hammer provider does not mean your rights to the hammer are undefined or that your use of the hammer is unregulated. But the rights and regulations are those enacted by the public legislature or established by the common law (primarily, in this example, the common law of torts).

You can also go to the bookstore and buy a paperback novel with no documentation of the sales contract other than a receipt. Books are different from hammers in the sense that copying a book is somewhat easier than copying a hammer. So we need copyright law, which defines a somewhat more elaborate set of property rights for "works of authorship" than we have for hammers. But you acquire a property right in the printed copy of the book that is defined, and limited, by the public law, and your liability for improper actions, such as copying the book without permission, is also defined by the public law.

From hammer to book to software, there are differences, although they are largely a matter of degree. You can copy a hammer, but doing so is very difficult without a manufacturing facility, and the copy will resemble the original only within the manufacturing tolerances. You can copy a printed book more readily and cheaply, but there are still costs, and unless you have sophisticated printing equipment, the fidelity of the copy will be imperfect. If you are a software provider, or a user of software that is not protected by DRM technology, you can copy the software easily and cheaply, and the copies will be exact. In all three cases, the producer has fixed costs and variable costs, and the ratio of fixed costs to variable costs increases as you move from hammer to book to software.

But it does not follow that, whereas the sales of the hammer and the book are documented with a simple receipt, it is desirable from a social point of view to document the software transaction in a long, complex, privately written document that ordinarily means nothing to one of the two parties and that defines a custom legal regime governing not only the transaction itself but also the user's rights with respect to the product. The conditions for achieving "optimal terms" do not exist, even when the market is otherwise highly competitive, and the software itself may suffer as a result. In addition, as Merrill and Smith's analysis of the *numerus clausus* principle suggests, the customization of property rights imposes significant costs on third parties that are not reflected in the original price.

Imagine what the world would be like if the lengthy proprietary EULAs governed the tools you buy at a hardware store. When you went to the store to buy a hammer, your choice among products would not be a choice merely between their attributes as hammers. In fact, you would not be able to buy a hammer. You could only license it, and you would have only such rights to use it as the license conferred. If you ever ran afoul of the license, you could be forced to give the hammer back. For example, the EULA might permit only one named user of the hammer. It might also restrict the use of the hammer to projects involving your own personal residence, so that if you were to use the hammer on the job at a construction site, you would be in breach.

The hammer could be an old-fashioned ball peen design, long since in the public domain, but the EULA would say that you could not make a ball peen hammer of your own based on the same design, whether or not it was in the public domain. The EULA would surely prohibit lending the hammer to a next-door neighbor—after all, such a practice would reduce the sales, or rather the licensing, of "original" hammers. And the EULA would provide that the manufacturer had no liability if, while you were swinging the hammer, the head happened to fall off and break a window. In some future technological environment, the hammer provider might even embed a miniature radio transmitter and receiver in the hammer handle so that the provider could make sure you were complying with the license.

The point is not that this scenario is likely to happen. The point, rather, is that it is not. And for good reason—it makes no sense. If the buyer of a hammer were presented with a EULA containing thousands of words and written at a level not likely to be understood by a person with less than a post-graduate education, then we could safely assume that most hammer buyers would not read it. And so the various custom conditions would compete not for your business, but to outdo each other in how they managed to restrict the user and "protect" the hammer provider. The process would not yield efficient terms, but rather terms that would be systematically biased against the user. To the extent that the quality of hammers reflected the quality of the terms, it would also be lower. No one would seriously propose adopting such a distribution model for hammers.

Now assume that, thanks in significant part to the contributions of several large hammer manufacturers, boxes of nails came to be provided free of charge. But imagine that they were provided under another kind of license. This license is also very difficult to decipher. If you succeed, you see that it says you can use as many nails as you want. If you build, say, birdhouses with the nails, however, even though you bought the wood for the birdhouses and crafted them yourself, you cannot sell the birdhouses. Rather, you must either use them only in your own backyard or give them away, because they contain the free nails. Perhaps you will now give away birdhouses, while supporting yourself by some other means. But if you have any thought of selling your birdhouses, you will simply avoid using the free nails to build your birdhouses. As long as "proprietary" nails are available, this is not too much of a problem. Obviously, though, if only the free nails were available, birdhouse construction—and construction of many other items from wood—would experience a sharp decline. If your primary goal is to promote all forms of construction, you would do better to give the nails away with no strings attached.

Software intended for the commons need not be locked into the commons, with the likely effect of restricting proprietary investment or locking it out altogether. One who builds on works in the public domain has no need to decide in advance how the works will be used or what the possibilities of the works will be. The full range of options for distributing the works is open. Proprietary capture of public domain works has not proved to be the intractable long-term problem copyleft predicts, except possibly in cases of monopoly, where the problem is not the vulnerability of the public domain, but the monopoly itself.

Going forward, we may never be able to distribute software and other digital works as simply as hammers and nails, but we should find a way—perhaps through a truth-in-licensing act or modest Copyright Act revisions of the kind mentioned in Chapter 3—that allows the rules governing the transaction and their use to be clear, concise, and within a limited set of readily understandable alternatives, set forth in a minimal EULA or simply in the public law. When the box says "includes 3 installs," people can make an informed comparison with another box that says "includes 1 install." Competition over this term can and will occur. When the box says "student and home edition—noncommercial use only," there is more of a question of interpretation—what is "noncommercial"? But even so, there is at least some basis to compare. When the terms are thousands of words long and require a post-graduate education to understand, then there is no basis to compare and no reason to expect anything but a bad result.

If it is true that we are moving toward an information economy, this fact is an argument not for enforcing ever-more-complex license terms that cast their lines into everything we do. Rather, it should prompt us to find a way to deliver tangible information products to end users so that buying a software product has results that are just as predictable and just as well understood as the results of buying a hammer or a book.

Acknowledgments

I AM INDEBTED TO Matt Gallaway of Oxford University Press for making this book happen. From start to finish, he has patiently and skillfully guided me through the process, helping me in countless ways. In addition, David Barg, Alan Blinder, Evan Cox, Jameson Doig, Simon Frankel, and Yosh Mantinband have provided many helpful comments and suggestions. Thanks also to Mark Jacobsen and my other friends at Promontory Interfinancial Network.

Of course, none of these people has any responsibility for any errors that remain. The views that I have expressed are mine alone. Promontory, for which I serve as general counsel, provides technology-based services to financial institutions, but it is not a software publisher and does not take sides in the software licensing debate.

As a lawyer, I have represented both software licensors and software licensees—although not, I should emphasize, in the same transaction—and I have not written this book as an advocate for any particular set of interests in the licensing debate. I have simply tried to take a close look at the software license and describe what I see. If my observations are mistaken, they are at least mistaken in good faith. And if the book makes people rethink the assumption that complex legislative software licenses are desirable or inevitable, it will have served its purpose.

Finally, my family deserves a very special thanks—not only for tolerating my absences to work on the book, but also for giving me the motivation to see it through.

Table of Cases

Index